The
Liberal Arts
in a Time
of Crisis

THE LIBERAL ARTS IN A TIME OF CRISIS

Edited by

Barbara Ann Scott

with the assistance of
Richard P. Sloan

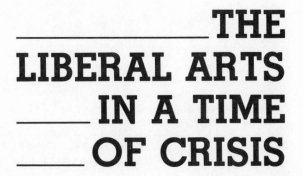

New York
Westport, Connecticut
London

Copyright Acknowledgment

"Ideology and the Politics of Higher Education," by Michael Engel, *The Journal of Higher Education*, Vol. 55, No. 1 (January/February 1984) is reprinted by permission. © 1984 by the Ohio State University Press. All rights reserved.

Library of Congress Cataloging-in-Publication Data

The liberal arts in a time of crisis / [edited] by Barbara Ann Scott.
     p.   cm.
   Includes bibliographical references.
   ISBN 0-275-93295-8 (alk. paper)
   1. Education, Higher—United States. 2. Education, Humanistic—United States. 3. Education, Higher—United States—Curricula.
  4. Education, Higher—United States—Aims and objectives.
  I. Scott, Barbara Ann.
  LA227.3.L48   1991
  378.73—dc20   89-48666

British Library Cataloguing in Publication Data is available.

Library of Congress Catalog Card Number: 89-48666
ISBN: 0-275-93295-8

First published in 1991

Praeger Publishers, One Madison Avenue, New York, NY 10010
An imprint of Greenwood Publishing Group, Inc.

Printed in the United States of America

The paper used in this book complies with the
Permanent Paper Standard issued by the National
Information Standards Organization (Z39.48-1984).

10 9 8 7 6 5 4 3 2 1

For a new renaissance of liberal learning

Contents

Acknowledgments

I would like to express my gratitude to Richard P. Sloan, my colleague and friend, for his expert editorial assistance during the early stages of the manuscript's production.

Our collaboration began in 1980 and 1981 when we shared the responsibilities for conceiving, planning, and cochairing an intercollegiate conference on *The Liberal Arts in a Time of Crisis*. To both enterprises he gave much energy, skill, and devotion.

The conference, prompted by our joint dismay over the curricular and pedagogical trends in higher education, drew hundreds of educators from the northeastern states to the State University of New York College at New Paltz in January 1981. The two-day agenda featured a large and stimulating variety of panels and workshops with many nationally prominent speakers from such fields as education, journalism, science, industry, and politics. Collectively, they generated an important and timely dialogue on the meaning and value of liberal education.

This book, initially inspired by the conference proceedings, represents an effort to extend the dialogue to an even larger audience. Many of the chapters are based upon presentations made by conference participants. The exceptions are those by Huel D. Perkins, Jean Bethke Elshtain, Stanley Aronowitz, and Henry A. Giroux, which were solicited subsequent to the time of the conference in order to enhance the book's thematic coherence.

I am grateful for the professional advice, cooperation, and encouragement given me by the book's various contributors as well as by my colleagues and friends, John J. Neumaier, Sally Luther, Howard "Stretch" Johnson, and the late Kenneth T. Skelton.

Barbara Ann Scott

Introduction

American higher education today is afflicted with a crisis of purpose as
important, perhaps, as the budgetary crisis that has been making headlines. Now, more than ever, criteria of efficiency and expediency dic-
tate the content of the curriculum and threaten to suffocate any bona
fide intellectual culture. Under directives from academic policy planners the new curricular focus is two-fold: reemphasizing the practical
and mass marketing the "higher learning."

During the century-long development of the academic system, pressure
from public and private philanthropy was periodically applied to systema-
tize and standardize the curriculum to suit the needs and criteria of
collegiate benefactors. A prominent trend was the increasingly practical
focus of the curriculum: the introduction and enlargement of applied
scientific disciplines, technical and engineering programs, and training
for the professions and business administration. The result was the gradual erosion of the theoretically oriented liberal arts tradition, the
bedrock of the higher learning.

Historically, curricular practicality presupposed and fostered the
specialization and departmentalization of academic disciplines. This
trend is currently intensifying. Esoteric and often incommunicable spe-
cialties have multiplied. Increasingly, they have become locked into a
labyrinth of isolated and mutually antagonistic departments. The tragic
result has been a narrowing of the intellectual horizons of academic personnel and the loss of a holistic approach to knowledge. Scholars take
refuge in their professional enclaves and busy themselves with bureaucratic research. As teachers, their mission seems, more than ever, to be
confined to mechanically disseminating bits of information and training
persons with marketable skills.

Perhaps one can understand how, in the contemporary academic climate, the traditional ethos of professionalism has combined with new in-
securities to foster defensive postures in the faculty. The result has
been the pursuit of a narrow parochialism and a compulsive pragmatism.
As Ernest Becker once wryly observed: "Each professor tries to win students' allegiance to his discipline; each discipline joins in the great
scramble for converts; claims that it is a true science and contorts itself to prove it. Fad is king."(1)

This sorry situation is camouflaged, however, by a great deal of hypocrisy. Verbal allegiance and respect paid to the traditional ideal of
an interdisciplinary general education is backed by too little substance.
The continuation or restoration of distribution requirements and a token
number of survey courses at the introductory level constitute the dubious
basis of a general education for most undergraduates. The graduate, pro-

fessional, and business schools have, for the most part, already abandoned any such pretensions.

As the liberal arts have lost ground, technocratic, utilitarian, and
vocational interests have come to prevail.   In the social sciences, for
example, the curricular trend is toward more applied studies, devoted to
such enterprises as behavioral engineering and the production of administratively useful knowledge or of personnel for the "helping professions."

Leading centers of academic policy planning, moreover, have fostered
and legitimated these developments.   Recent master plans and policy studies from the Carnegie and Ford Foundations, for example, the Committee
for Economic Development, and other leading planning organizations are
explicit in their emphasis on so-called "manpower development."   Again
and again the call is for "new types of curricula," especially those having "more practical and vocational value," combined with improved vocational guidance to ensure that students, in the words of the Carnegie
Commission on Higher Education, "develop more realistic job expectations."(2)

In tandem with such curricular goals, academic policy planners propose to encourage wider diversity, specialization, and stratification of
post-secondary institutions, ranging from vocational schools, agricultural and technical institutes, and public community colleges to elite private four-year colleges, universities, and professional schools.   The new
institutional tier system, they expect, will be based upon more efficient
tracking and channeling mechanisms in order to "meet the nation's varied
manpower needs."(3)

Another facet of the curricular reorganization now under way is the
standardization of its content and its mechanical and passive absorption
by masses of students.   In recent years, this has been rapidly facilitated by automation and the "upgrading of teaching technologies,"(4) especially in the form of televised and computerized instruction.   Such
curricular developments have evidently come to represent the new technocratic ideal of scholastic efficiency.

American higher education's crisis of purpose has still another di-
mension.   Commensurate with the suffocation of intellectual culture, a
widespread anti-intellectualism has come to prevail on the nation's campuses.   In part, it has been stimulated by the emphasis on practical and
vocational studies; in part, by the decline in standards of excellence
and scholarship; in part, by the proliferation of courses more designed
to distract, titillate, or entertain, than educate.   In this regard,
pragmatic realism on the part of professional staffs coincides with the
ill-conceived demand for "relevance" on the part of students.

To be sure, few academic administrators or policy makers would see
it that way.   From their point of view, the new emphasis upon practical
and vocational curricula simply represents a rational response to the
current crisis of American labor: namely, the overproduction of overeducated workers. Academic "crisis management" has, in other words, forced
the reorganization of curricular priorities to meet the new needs set by

government and industry. The "new practicality," they argue, does not constitute a crisis of the curriculum.(5)   Rather, it is simply a matter of fiscal and administrative necessity. Besides, it can be amply and artfully justified by evidence of consumer (i.e., student) demand.

We shall argue the contrary. The attempt by academic administrators to resolve the intertwined crises of finance, governance, and surplus labor has provoked a profound crisis in the content of the curriculum and the purposes higher education is supposed to serve.

The new practicality, in comfortable alliance with the pragmatic professionalism of faculties and administrative staffs, constitutes a powerful centrifugal force that has dissociated intellectual activity from the pursuit of reason and from its true center in the liberal arts curriculum. The result has been the trivializing of the academic enterprise and the intellectual impoverishment of much of the academic community.

The decade of the 1990s has given fresh urgency, we believe, to a reexamination of the mission of higher education. Is it, we must ask ourselves, primarily to develop "useful" knowledge and train people with marketable skills? Or is it to nurture critically aware and intellectually able citizens? Must educators acquiesce to the market orientation of so many of today's students? Or is it possible to convince them of the relevance of the liberal arts and sciences?

This book is an effort to address these questions and articulate, ultimately, a defense of liberal learning. It is divided into three sections. Part I explores the politics and ideology underscoring the development of curricular policies and pedagogical trends in colleges and universities today. Included in it are chapters by Emil Oestereicher, Michael Engel, Jean Bethke Elshtain, Alfred McClung Lee, Stanley Aronowitz and Barbara Ann Scott. In Part II Leon Botstein, Henry A. Giroux, Huel D. Perkins, Elizabeth Briant Lee, Rosette Liberman, Henri Peyre, Gilbert J. Sloan and Ronald Colman provide some guidelines for recapturing and revitalizing higher learning in America. In a concluding "Coda," several of the contributors (Stanley Aronowitz, Henri A. Giroux, Michael Engel, Jean Bethke Elshtain, and Alfred McClung Lee) make a collective rejoinder to the currently popular conservative crusade for literacy, by examining its shortcomings and offering instead some transcendant visions and transformative strategies.

Barbara Ann Scott, with Richard P. Sloan

Part I
Curricular Policy, Pedagogy, and Politics— A Critical Reappraisal

Introduction to Part I

The chapters in this section offer a critical reappraisal of the persistent crisis of higher learning in the United States. Emil Oestereicher lays the groundwork for more contemporary manifestations of the crisis by revealing the historical contradictions associated with the emergence of the educated citizen within the bourgeois society and culture of the seventeenth to nineteenth centuries. The next two papers by Barbara Ann Scott and Michael Engel, respectively, examine the politics behind recent curricular policy planning and the ways such policies have been ideologically defended. Jean Bethke Elshtain then turns to the issue of classroom pedagogy and its relation to the general deterioration of intellectual discipline and scholarship, which Alfred McClung Lee, in a related chapter, finds manifested in "the dread of innovation" among college faculty. Finally, Stanley Aronowitz and Barbara Ann Scott each continue the examination of the literacy crisis by analyzing the shortcomings of recent reform movements and recommending some needed alternatives.

In examining the historical origins of what we consider a traditional liberal arts education, Emil Oestereicher discusses the relationship between the demands of citizenship for emerging commercial classes in the seventeenth century and the study of history, politics, economics, and philosophy. "The very concept of rational public debate," Oestereicher argues, "requires that its participants have access to education and information." The liberal arts curriculum, accordingly, arose in conjunction with the decline of feudalism and the rise of the democratic state.

But there is more to the development than this. What accounts, Oestereicher asks, for the intense need to place ourselves in the universe? It is the birth of the modern self, the development of the now-familiar tendency to see ourselves as independent agents, clearly separated from social definitions. "The concepts of history, culture, nation, and citizenship," Oestereicher contends, "became a substitute for rootedness in a traditional community."

Thus, the liberal arts arose as a by-product of the evolution of the person as an individual and the requirements of citizenship. Regrettably, the decline of the liberal arts, in Oestereicher's judgment, is related to these very same events. The emergence of the individual failed to replace the traditional community; the growing "public sphere" was almost always restricted to those with property, thus disenfranchising the great majority. By the time the rights of citizenship filtered down to those with fewer resources--that is, as the size of the public sphere increased--they had been weakened by the increasing concentration of power and means of production. Citizenship had become "deprived of all authentic political and cultural content." The ideal of a liberally educated person, Oestereicher concludes, is "in danger of oblivion."

Barbara Ann Scott, in the first of two chapters in this section, examines the "new practicality" evident not only in contemporary higher education planning but also in the minds of today's students and teachers. She sees in this attitude a crisis of purpose afflicting education, from the community colleges to doctoral-granting institutions. Is education to be sought for the general benefit it confers upon one's life and for the understanding of nature and society it ideally provides? Or does it function merely to fulfill the utilitarian goals of industry and government? Are colleges and universities, in other words, merely "service stations" along the road to economic success? Recent statements by educational policymakers and by students alike indicate that the latter alternative is currently the more popular one, and Scott marshalls some distressing evidence in support of this contention.

At the community colleges today one-half of all students are enrolled in "career education" programs--the heir to vocational training. Moreover, much federal support for two-year colleges is specifically earmarked for these career education programs and is unavailable for programs which prepare students for further study. Even the prestigious Carnegie Commission on Higher Education has stated that community colleges serve primarily an occupational function. In such career-oriented curricula, the fate of a liberal education is obvious. It is irrelevant to the world of work.

But this "new practicality" can also be seen at the four-year colleges and universities. There is today an increasing emphasis on making the curriculum more responsive to the needs of industry and government. Scott underscores what is already wellknown: namely, that college students participate in a desperate scramble either to get into professional schools or to secure a good job. In pursuit of these goals, they have developed a new attitude of pragmatism. Their pragmatism, moreover, is both shared and compounded by educational planners who, in the name of cost-efficiency, seek to eliminate from the curriculum the under-subscribed and, therefore, less marketable programs. As a result, the traditional liberal arts curriculum, which is seen to have little "cash-value," is severely threatened.

Critically evaluating the application of orthodox economics to higher education policy, Michael Engel argues that in the uncertain economic climate of today, policy planners, eager to maximize gains and minimize losses, will invariably apply cost/benefit analysis to various curricular programs. From a market model perspective, liberal arts programs are the

least directly related to immediate success in the job market.   College
administrators, therefore, consider it a wise investment to concentrate
on those areas of the curriculum which will yield the greatest return and
withdraw from those which are irrelevant or unprofitable.   Such a calculus, Engel contends, places the liberal arts at an extreme disadvantage.

Moreover, rigorous adherence to the market model endangers not only
liberal arts curricula but also public higher education, for in a free
market system, government should not be involved.   Rather than attack
this market ideology, public education officials have, in Engel's view,
sought to work within it by altering curricula, waging battles over tuition increases, and seeking to make education more cost-effective by increasing faculty responsibilities and class size.

Eventually, Engel believes, this strategy will fail as resources diminish and public higher education will be forced to choose between defending itself and its traditional liberal arts curriculum and becoming
coopted by industry, as exemplified by the Dover Project in Massachusetts.

Ultimately, the solution lies, not in attempts at compromise with
the market ideology, but rather in a direct challenge to it.   Such a
challenge would involve, first of all, stripping away the "objectivity"
of the model.   Secondly, it would require examining the nature of work
itself, not merely what is needed by the job market today.   "While voca-
cational training gives the individual a let-up in the job market for the
time being," Engel argues, "the humanities and social sciences—ideally—
expose the context of values and institutions that determine what kind of
work is going to be available and what it will be like.   This ultimately
broadens the individual's choice, in enabling him or her to adjust to or
attempt to change the situation, and to be fully aware of the alternatives.   Such a purpose is consistent with the responsibilities of a public college or university and with the long-run interests of the stu-
students."

In conclusion, Engel states that public higher education is a mutual
responsibility of government and citizens in a democratic society.   It is
a right, not merely a privilege, of a citizen to receive an education adequate for effective participation in public decisionmaking.   Liberal
arts constitute such an education.

Invoking medical metaphors, Jean Bethke Elshtain directs a critique
at what she calls the "therapeutic classroom," in which professors function more as therapists administering to their students' emotional needs
for security, warmth, and social support as a precondition for learning.

Proponents of this presumptive "radical" pedagogy, Elshtain argues,
do their students (and themselves) a disservice by diluting any meaningful intellectual content in favor of of establishing "good vibes" in the
classroom.   Although claiming to have renounced the authoritarianism of
the traditional classroom, these psychopedagogues, to Elshtain, actually

promote a covertly coercive and elitist pedagogy that denies students "the respect and dignity of being subjects" who act and think and instead objectifies them as "patients" in need of an emotional "cure."

Ironically, these presumptive radicals share the cause of the promoters of practical and vocational curricula, by their instrumental approach to the classroom, by their insistence on instant results, and by their search for subject matter that is useful, experiential, relevant, and uptodate. Such an approach, Elshtain contends, "conduces toward and legitimates a profoundly anti-intellectual and crude instrumentalism" and is, therefore, implicitly reactionary, rather than radical.

Rejecting the usual dichotomy of the traditional, "authoritarian" classroom, on the one hand, and the radical or "therapeutic" classroom, on the other, Elshtain offers an alternative which unites the strengths of both models. Specifically, it is one which borrows from the traditional model in its insistence that teachers need to convey authority without being authoritarian and in its defense of intellectual rigor and high performance standards. It draws upon radical and feminist pedagogy by incorporating a concern with students' lives and experiences as a vehicle for illuminating the broader and more abstract issues of the subject matter. This "reflexive scrutiny," however, need not degenerate into a radical subjectivity. Although excellence and equality are often presented as mutually exclusive, Elshtain insists they "must go hand in hand."

In a chapter companion to Jean Elshtain's, Alfred McClung Lee explains how the stifling of intellect and innovation in higher education has come about by the bureaucratic routines and implicit codes of conduct which govern the activities of many academic professionals. To ensure their survival chances in a plutocratic capitalistic society, Lee argues, "most scientists and artists accept the notion that they must first of all be assimilated professionals, people who know their place and role in the existing power structure and who will work contentedly within it." As a result they will be likely to make "careerist compromises" with their intellectual integrity. Fearing thought, which is potentially subversive to established order, academicians frequently resort to techniques of obfuscation rather than illumination, routinization rather than innovation.

Such techniques include devotion to overwrought and pretentious methodologies, "apologies for the status quo, and abstract theory of an intolerant and sectarian sort." As a consequence of these practices, the advancement of science and the pursuit of humane learning have been reduced to a squabble among warring factions, each isolated from the others by great conceptual distances.

Stanley Aronowitz' ambitious chapter examines the current crisis of the liberal arts, not only from the perspective of those who must suffer from it but, ironically, from those who believe it is in their best interest to stimulate it. Those who most suffer are, of course, those whose access to higher education has historically been the most limited: the working class, women, and minorities. It is the defenders of the market place ideology who promote the crisis, by encouraging institutions of higher education, primarily the four-year liberal arts colleges and the community colleges, to conform to the demands of the market place and eliminate or at least drastically cut back on the liberal arts curriculum in favor of more technically oriented programs.

Higher education in the United States today is at an impasse. Although colleges and universities are experiencing dramatic reductions in financial support from state and private agencies, the demand, nonetheless, for a college education has never been higher. This increased demand is a function of a change in the meaning of a college degree. We have become what Randall Collins calls a "credentialized society," and the college degree is such a credential. Rather than represent an acknowledgment of academic accomplishment, it now represents more of a social credential, unrelated to competence. It has, for the working class, replaced the journeyman's card for entry into the labor force.

The increased demand for educational credentials together with the influx of students into higher education (spurred by the open admissions policies of the 1970s) have, in turn, stimulated the increasing bureaucratization and stratification of the academic system. In the topmost tier of a three-tier system are the elite private colleges and large state universities. At the bottom are the community colleges, and in the middle are the four-year liberal arts colleges. With the influx of working adults, women, and minorities, the mission of the lower tiers has been perceptibly modified: reduce liberal arts programs and increase technical training. At the upper level, the liberal arts have been preserved, at least to some extent, in the interest of providing "breadth" for students who major in technical/professional disciplines. Thus, "the crisis of American higher education consists not only in its budget difficulties . . . but also in the contradiction between its traditional mission of providing the cadre for . . . industrial and service production and the new demand that it become a multi-layered mass technological training institute."

Aronowitz argues that the current trends in the academic system, however, are contrary not only to the interests of credential-seeking students and technocratically-oriented faculty but also, paradoxically, to academic, corporate, and political elites whose aim, presumably, is to preserve their social power and their ability to administer a society facing grave economic and political challenges.

According to Aronowitz, the struggle to preserve the curricula of the traditional liberal arts is important not simply because they embody Western bourgeois culture but, more fundamentally, because they are also the precondition for developing critical thinking and literacy:

> To the extent that the academic system is confined (and con-
> fines itself) to producing technical knowledge . . . society
> itself is deprived of social and cultural knowledge of which
> power is, in part, constituted. Thus, the formation of a cri-
> tical cadre able to span a wide area of political, cultural,
> and social knowledge is an absolutely essential condition for
> crisis management.

In this way, the defense of liberal education may not only be in the intrinsic self-interest of students and faculty--empowering them with the
tools of intellectual and social emancipation--but, paradoxically, also
in the system's interest.

In a companion piece to her earlier discussion of the rise of the
"new practicality" in the college curriculum, Barbara Ann Scott examines
the parallel decline in performance standards of both students and faculty. The presumptive quest for "scholastic efficiency" (in Thorstein
Veblen's words) has, Scott argues, "transformed professors into 'professional entrepreneurs,' students into credential hustlers, and the curriculum into a wasteland of trivia and pseudoscientific pretense."

One side of the deterioration of standards is represented by those
narrowly specialized, pragmatic professors whose intellectual integrity
has been sacrificed to the expedient pursuit of the R & D dollar, the resort to research gimmickry, and the accumulation of merely quantitative
measurements of their academic worth (i.e., aggregate enrollments and
published output).

Another (and more familiar) side of the decline in standards is manifested in the new cognitive illiteracy among many of today's college
students that, Scott argues, is "as pervasive as it is perverse." Demanding "relevant" course offerings and expedient routes to the academic
degree, "many students reveal themselves pathetically as mere credit junkies on vocational highs."

In neither case, however, is the decline of literacy and liberal
learning attributable to voluntarism, as the conventional wisdom suggests. Both students and faculty are subject to a variety of external
pressures, constraints, and inducements (financial and otherwise) that
condition their choices for the expedient, the experiential, or the entrepreneurial.

Scott goes on to criticize those faculty who, in the name of a radical pedagogy, promote a "benign permissiveness" in the classroom, de-
flate expectations, and inflate grades. Such an approach has often
backfired, degenerating into a mere laissez-faire approach to learning.
She instead insists that "intellectual discipline is necessary to the
development of incisive critique and, ultimately, radical thought and
practice." Authentic radicals--such as Veblen, Aronowitz, C. Wright
Mills, Ernest Becker and Christopher Lasch--have, to their great credit,

consistently understood this.   Such a quest for "critical literacy" demands exacting criteria of scholarship and a breadth and depth of knowledge found in the bedrock of the liberal arts and sciences curriculum.

In a concluding section, Scott critically examines the dimensions of
the "literacy crusade" being mounted by mainstream policy research organizations and by disgruntled academics such as Allan Bloom and E. D.
Hirsch.   She contends that concerns for literacy emanating from both the
conservative and liberal wings of the academic establishment have serious shortcomings.   Among them are: (1) the ignoring or trivializing of
the connection between "the rising tide of mediocrity" (in the words of
the National Commission on Excellence in Education) and the technicization of the academic curriculum;   (2) the misplaced emphasis upon the extrinsic rewards of a college education (e.g., the supposedly high-paying
jobs in high-technology industries and government);   and (3) an instrumental approach that blocks the achievement of critical literacy.

Scott urges radical educators to be vigilant in defending and extending the liberal arts and sciences curriculum and promoting high academic standards.   It is important to remember, she argues, that "the
broad tradition of bourgeois culture and liberal learning has often
yielded, unintentionally or otherwise, a radical payoff: namely, the
liberation of critical thought and democratic action."

1 The Depoliticization of the Liberal Arts
EMIL OESTEREICHER

Liberal arts education has traditionally been identified with the classical ideal of cultivation. For several centuries now, the cultivated individual has been expected to have a good appreciation and understanding of the sciences, the humanities and the arts. Although some academic purists have argued that the ideal of the cultivated individual has had or even should have very little to do with everyday political, social, and psychological concerns, my intention in this chapter is to show how this very argument has contributed to the emergence and to the subsequent decline of the liberal arts.

The emergence of the liberal arts, or the arts befitting a free man is closely interwoven with the gradual rise of the commercial classes to a position of political, economic, and cultural dominance. The revolutions of the seventeenth and eighteenth centuries promoted Greek culture and Roman law and politics in an effort to counteract the political and cultural elitism of aristocratic Europe. The task of establishing a civil society, based upon private property and a universal legal system, necessarily required the recovery of the classical ideal of citizenry and a corresponding notion of the "public sphere." The "public," as opposed to the "private" sphere, is the terrain upon which legally free and equal individuals engage in rational debate concerning public issues and governmental decisions. The very concept of rational public debate requires that its participants have access to education and information. Thus, at least on the level of ideology, a democratic theory of culture replaced the aristocratic notion of two cultures, one for the elites and one for the masses. To acquire the arts befitting a free man became considered one of the rights and obligations of citizenship.

The ideals of Greece and Rome, the notions of republicanism, democracy, constitutionalism, citizenship and neoclassicism in the arts also fulfilled the important political function of providing heroic images for

the members of the rising commercial classes.   The construction of these
ideals was especially important because heroism, integrity,   and altruism
typically had   been considered   aristocratic virtues,   and had never been
predominantly associated   with the bourgeoisie.   In fact, life in modern
civil society   necessarily involved an   attitude of flexibility, calculation, and a capacity for rational compromise.

Thus, for example,   it is not   surprising that in England during the
eighteenth century Shakespeare's   tragedies were often   performed with an
altered, happy ending.   For with the decline of heroic values, associated
with the fall of the great   feudal families during and after the Wars of
the Roses (1455–85), what had still appeared as a tragic loss to a large
enough public during the sixteenth century could no longer   exert similar
force by the eighteenth.   The progressive individualism,   the optimism,
and the almost infinite   adaptability of the Robinson Crusoes already had
captured the imagination of the public,   and the tragic inability and un-
willingness of Shakespeare's great   characters to compromise their values
or to adapt   to new forms of life with   new types of virtues   appeared as
anachronistic.   The psychic rigidity of the tragic hero, the courage with
which he confronts fate,   acquires an aura   of tragicomedy in the work of
Cervantes.   The tragic life of Don Quixote in the world peopled by Sancho
Panzas signifies   the   transformation of tragedy   into farce.   In such a
disenchanted world,   prose replaces   poetry and   individualism   replaces
great individuals.

In a sense,   one may argue that   classical education   in the liberal
arts and the idea of a   "well rounded invididual"   have functioned to re-
concile a fundamental contradiction between the heroic and supposedly altruistic image of the citizen, and the self-centered egotism of the average entrepreneur.

This contradiction has, of course, remained a central concern of
modern social and political philosophy fluctuating between the heroic republicanism of Oliver Cromwell,   John Milton,   Jean Jacques Rousseau, and
the Jacobins and the supposedly enlightened egotism of the utilitarians.
The theory of the harmony of interests and the philosophical anthropology of utilitarianism   already represent a   recognition that   modern civil
society is not the product of an altruistic citizenry, but rather that of
competing individuals.   The discrepancy   between the ideal and the real,
and the rejection of the theory of the harmony of interests, led Hegel to
attribute universal interest   to the state.   The state is to mediate the
conflicts of civil society   in view of the   common good.   It is exactly
this theory of the state and civil society that Karl Marx was reacting a-
gainst in his earliest published works. The reason why Jacobin and Bona-
partist theories of the state are less than convincing is due to the fact
that they contradict   the nature of civil society.   And if neoclassicism
and all forms of "state" art   seem to be pretentious and inauthentic,   it
is because the citizen aspect of life is almost always intertwined with
the egocentric individualism of everyday existence in bourgeois society.
This is why a truly positive hero in the novel has always remained uncon-

vincing. Heroic aspirations such as those of Julien Sorel in Stendhal's *The Red and the Black* or those of Dorothea in George Eliot's *Middlemarch* necessarily collide with the prosaic and selfish character of everyday life.

Despite the discrepancy between civic duty and individual self-interest, the liberal arts remained tied to a democratic theory of culture and citizenship. For men such as Thomas Paine, Thomas Jefferson, Benjamin Franklin, Jean Jacques Rousseau, Maximilien Robespierre, and Immanuel Kant, reason was not only a universal human capacity but the political obligation of citizenship. Cultivation was considered to be the duty of all free men, whether merchants, farmers, or mechanics.

This democratic theory of culture necessarily involved a radical rejection of the patronage system, wherein the most creative elements of society are paid employees of a privileged aristocracy, and thus remain in a state of dependency.

Thus far, the major political and social factors that accounted for the emergence of the Western ideal of classical cultivation have been been discussed. But these political and social factors alone could not convincingly explain the profound personal attachment a British gentleman, a German burgher, or a French bourgeois would often develop to what he considered to be his cultural or civilizational heritage. And in many cases this attachment was much too authentic to be explained strictly in terms of the enhancement of one's prestige and lifestyle. There must have been something more than competition with the aristocracy for a cultural hegemony to have emerged that produced the intense need on the part of the individual to place himself in a meaningful cosmos, to seek clues in the past that would help him explain his present and hopefully predict his future. It was, furthermore, only in modern Europe that the understanding of the individual's biography became problematic. As long as the self remained the product of clear social definitions, as in traditional societies, self experience remained virtually inseparable from the experience of society, nature, and the divine.

In modern civil society, however, traditional social restrictions are removed from competition and accumulation, and the individual becomes responsible for his own destiny. Once life is defined as an individual responsibility and one's self is no longer given by tradition and reaffirmed by myth and ritual, life is experienced as an historical progression. The entrepreneur is what he makes of himself; he is an independent agent experiencing progress in his life.

Biography becomes history, experienced as irreversible development. In the absence of traditional controls, the individual has to develop self-control. This, however, is contingent upon control over the conditions of one's everyday life. Thus, there is a need to render these conditions predictable, to reduce their elements to quantifiable entities so they can be subsumed under universal laws. The laws of the external world, of nature, and of society, defined in terms of mechanics and market mechanisms, are altogether removed from the emotive "inner self."

It was probably to connect the emotive inner self with a meaningful cosmos in an increasingly secularized world that history more and more came to be seen as something closely tied to one's personal identity. The concepts of history, culture, nation, and citizenship became a substitute for rootedness in a traditional community.

While the search for reason in nature and in the market yielded quantifiable information and empirical generalization, reason in history was seen to be unfolding in terms of unique cultural values and institutions. The capacity of the human mind to impose rational order upon experience and the general progress of history in the direction of reason and freedom were seen to be universal. One could, for the first time, look upon one's life from a "world-historical" perspective and define the purpose of life in terms of an historical or civilizational mission. History thus became the foundation of a liberal arts education. Through history one could develop an empathy with and an understanding of the values realized in the greatest achievements of Western civilization.

Nevertheless, the rationalism, the historicism and the humanism of the Enlightenment could never fully compensate for the loss of a traditional community. In his everyday life, the individual experienced himself as someone apart from the ideal community exactly because the community remained an ideal yet to be actualized. The frustration of the experience of longing for something that one could not have probably contributed to the romantic irrationalist and existentialist assault upon rationalism and universalism during the nineteenth and twentieth centuries.

Thus, the decline of the liberal arts ideal is rooted in the very contradictions of a bourgeois society and culture that had produced it to begin with. The ideals of liberty, fraternity, and equality, universal human rights, civic duty, cultural and political democracy never became applicable to the overwhelming majority of humanity, and often directly contradicted the exigencies of the market and capital accumulation.

The democratic humanist ideal of the cultured citizen with his fully integrated critical intellectual faculties could not prevent the growing fragmentation and specialization of knowledge that was taking place under the impact of an ever-increasing and elaborate capitalist division of labor.

Furthermore, these ideals were closely tied to the notion of the "public sphere," but even in seventeenth century Holland or in eighteenth century England political participation was restricted to those with property, and the "poor"--that is to say the overwhelming majority of the population without property--were excluded from most of the rights of citizenship. The gradual extension of the rights of citizenship coincided with the reduction of the public sphere, the concentration of the means of production in fewer and fewer hands, and the growth of state power in all spheres of life. Thus, citizenship was gradually deprived of all authentic political and cultural content. With the disintegration of the public sphere, and with the depoliticization of the concept of citizenship, the liberal arts themselves became depoliticized, and more and more seemed to have little, if any, relevance to contemporary life.

What seems to be happening to the ideal of the liberal arts in the United States today is comparable to certain trends in Europe and especially in Germany after the defeat of the republican revolutions of 1848. Until 1848, a very significant proportion of the best of the German intelligentsia hoped that the cultural ideals of Greece and Rome, of the late medieval German city-states, and of the Enlightment could provide the political and cultural framework for a unified German republic. But by 1848 it became clear that the unification of Germany would be accomplished not through a bourgeois democratic revolution but rather by means of an imposition by the Prussian military state. The imposition of a military and a state bureaucracy, rapid industrialization, the monopolization and cartelization of the economy, and the rise of a commercial popular culture, all stood as obstacles to the further development of liberal ideas. The democratic theory of culture was given up altogether. The notion of the citizen, never firmly rooted in the German experience, was largely forgotten. One was not a citizen, but rather a subject of the German state.

The aristocratic theory of two cultures was restored, but in a much more degraded form. For in aristocratic Europe, besides high culture that was accessible only to a small elite, there existed highly elaborate traditional folk cultures that enriched the life of the overwhelming majority of the people who were peasants. The rapid growth of large-scale production and, with that, the destruction of traditional peasant communities, also resulted in the replacement of traditional folk cultures by a commercial popular culture. The liberal arts were more and more restricted to the universities. Thus, it was no longer the citizen but rather the university professor who became the upholder of what came to be known as civilizational values. And since the German professor was considered, and most often considered himself to be, a servant of the state, he tended to refrain from political criticism. In fact, political concerns were no longer considered to be within the domain of intellectuals. The criticism of contemporary life was restricted to a critique of the vulgarity of mass culture, and the supposedly dehumanizing character of the modern industrial city.

Thus culture—or rather, *kultur*—became detached from everyday political concerns, and politics was no longer considered to be a likely or desirable activity for the cultivated man. This fostered the familiar image of the professor as a total idiot when it comes to any sort of practical matter. Under these circumstances an alliance emerged between the leaders of *kultur*, the leaders of capital, and the leaders of the state. The population was exhorted to obey their wise leaders, engage in the consumption of commercial *kitsch*, and memorize meaningless Greek and Latin phrases in the *Gymnasium*. The vacuum left by an absence of the public sphere was filled by armies of born-again mystics, vegetarians, sun worshippers, racist romantics, technical experts, and dutiful public servants, all dreaming of the warmth of a *gemeinschaft*. The lack of political experience made individuals especially vulnerable to the promise of miraculous cures. It was exactly this schizophrenic separation of culture and politics that brought classical music to concentration camps during World War II and moved the philosopher Martin Heidegger to consider the "inner truth" and "greatness" of the National Socialist movement in helping the "encounter between global technology and modern man."

The ideal of the liberal arts and modern culture, in general, is rooted in politics in the classical sense of the word. The original upholders of a democratic theory of culture rejected the Aristotelian distinction between contemplative and practical wisdom. For the notion of education was tied to the vision of a public sphere, to the concept of the citizen whose civic duty was to practice his wisdom in everyday life. Unfortunately, this theory has always remained an ideal in contradiction with the real. Nevertheless, as long as this ideal has been strong, it has tended to have a positive democratizing effect upon reality. It may have been an important contributing factor in preventing the emergence of fascism in many bourgeois democracies during the Great Depression. Today, with the depoliticization of citizenship, this ideal is in danger of oblivion. A reversal of this trend necessitates the repoliticization of the liberal arts and of citizenship, a task that certainly involves much more than a well-intended rehashing of curricula by academic committees.

2 Promoting the "New Practicality": Curricular Policies for the 1990s

BARBARA ANN SCOTT

Thorstein Veblen and Robert Maynard Hutchins, a generation apart, each wrote a book titled, *The Higher Learning in America*. The common denominator of both volumes was an indictment of the utilitarian corruption of the college curriculum and an impassioned defense of the pursuit of learning for its own sake. The vocational training vogue, in particular, Hutchins contemptuously labelled a "service station approach" that was threatening to turn the traditional liberal arts colleges into mere "trade schools." To Veblen, universities had become something akin to modern department stores, "competitors for traffic in merchantable instruction."(1)

Apparently, the dilemma was a familiar one two thousand years ago, for Aristotle was moved to ask, "Should the useful in life . . . or should the higher knowledge be the aim of our training?"(2) Today, there is fresh urgency to the issue that so troubled these passionate prophets of recent and ancient times. With the vocational vogue now gathering momentum on college campuses, the general education that Hutchins championed at the University of Chicago is more and more losing its allure. As one observer noted: "Young people are inclined to think that in a bad job market, majoring in accounting, electrical engineering, or hospital administration makes more sense than majoring in philosophy, literature, or the classics."(3)

A front-page story in *The New York Times* summed up the "new practicality" with the headline, *STUDENTS FLOCK TO JOB-RELATED COURSES*. Noting the "nationwide trend" of booming enrollments(4) in such fields as business administration, accounting, engineering, agriculture, and mining, a *Times* report explained: "In a quest for better job credentials, students are deserting the humanities and many of the social sciences for academic programs that they consider more practical."(5) Among those students stalwart enough to resist the general stampede and remain in liberal arts degree programs, many are nonetheless "seeking vocationally oriented minors to go with their less marketable majors."(6)

The new practicality among college students is also, it seems, fostering a new parochialism.   The American Council on Education reports that today only 3 percent of undergraduates are enrolled in any programs dealing with international affairs, other nation-states or cultures.   Enrollments in foreign language courses have declined drastically over the past two decades.   In the late 1960s, language courses attracted more than 15 percent of undergraduate students.   Two decades later, this share had dropped to less than 9 percent.   Meanwhile, language requirements for college admissions "have been abandoned by all but 10 percent of our 3,200 academic institutions."(7)

These trends, however, are not only a matter of student attitudes and choice.   The new practicality is also gaining new promoters among policy planners and new practitioners among academic administrators. Carl Kaysen, the vice-chairman of the prestigious Sloan Commission on Government and Higher Education, unambiguously listed as one of the major functions of higher education "the application of knowledge to the solution of practical problems in the wider society."(8)   Not long ago, the President's Task Force on Higher Education bluntly criticized a "tendency to concentrate on liberal arts" in many of the public colleges across the nation.   As a corrective, this blue-ribbon panel declared: "Occupational training must become more acceptable in the minds of students, their parents and potential employers."(9)   This was also the explicit goal of former U.S. Commissioner of Education Sidney P. Marland, Jr., when he enthusiastically explained the federal government's commitment to career education as an effort to "gear all education to the world of work."(10)

Just how much the new practicality has inspired the thinking of academic policy planners is quite clear from the Carnegie Commission on Higher Education's plans for overhauling the college curriculum.   Criticizing the present "pace and organization" of the learning experience as unnecessarily rigid, which has "limited the flexibility of colleges in undertaking reforms," the commission stressed the need for making college education more "adaptable" and "advantageous" to individual students and, at the same time, "more useful" to society.(11)

Among the commission's many practical proposals were to speed up the instructional process and shorten the time in formal education.   In this way, a B.A. degree could be had in three years, a Ph.D. in four.   Also, it recommended expanding educational credentials so that a degree or certificate would be given to students "at least every two years and in some cases every year."   Finally, higher education should be focussed more toward work.   At the top of the commission's agenda in this regard was the expansion of vocational education both inside and outside the formal college, the facilitating of work-study arrangements with public and private employers, and the encouragement of "stop-outs" and precollegiate military service and work experience, for which academic credit might be given.(12)

In its policy report on higher education, the Committee for Economic Development (CED) announced a similar set of curricular goals and similar enthusiasm for curricular efficiency as had the Carnegie Commission. Hailing the possibilities of "non-traditional education," especially under the stimulus of government philanthropic initiatives, the CED called upon college executives to "explore the possibilities of new modes of instruction, new types of curricula, new educational timetables and alternative methods of degree granting in order to provide wider diversity of educational opportunities and the greatest possible effectiveness in the use of resources."(13)

Although the new curricular practicality has many dimensions, academic policy planners clearly have at the top of their curricular agenda the promotion of career education.

CAREER EDUCATION: VOCATIONALISM BY ANOTHER NAME

The latest fad in educational circles, from junior high through college, career education was first conceived and promoted by Sidney P. Marland, Jr., in 1971 when he was the U.S. commissioner of education.(14) It soon became a cornerstone of federal education policies under the Nixon administration and has been generously funded in the years since. When first begun almost two decades ago, $850 million was authorized over a three-year period for career education at the post-secondary level alone—a generous sum in those days. Despite the budget-cutting fervor of the Reagan administration in its first two years in office, spending increases were authorized for career education of close to $100 million over the $701.4 million appropriated during the final year of the Carter presidency.(15) In the succeeding five fiscal years, again despite substantial cuts in other education programs, spending for career education was held constant at an approximate annual average of $754 million. All told, during the eight years of the Reagan administration, the federal government subsidized career education by more than $6 billion.(16)

The career education movement is, to be sure, more than a by-product of federal philanthropic largesse. Since its eventual beneficiaries are, by and large, private employers, it is hardly surprising that corporate and foundation interests feel a strong commitment to its success and a willingness to contribute generously to its support. Most private philanthropic support of vocational curricula has, first and foremost, gone to the private sector. The American Banking Association, for example, has initiated and financially underwritten a banking program at Texas Southern University; a substantial grant from the Ford Foundation went to establish a graduate school of business at the Atlantic University Center1(17) and a consortium of high-tech companies contributed $6 million to the University of Minnesota to set up facilities for micro-electronics, automation, and software design.(18) Recently, American University found itself at the center of a storm of controversy when it accepted a grant of $5 million from multimillionaire arms merchant Adnan Khashoggi to underwrite construction of a sports and convention center. In addition to having the center named after him, Khashoggi was rewarded for his generosity with a seat on the university's board of trustees. Having first earned international notoriety as a key go-between in the "Iran-Contragate" scandal, Khashoggi is, at this writing, under federal indictment for allegedly helping Ferdinand and Imelda Marcos "loot the Phillipines."(19)

No single private institution demonstrates the corporation-college connection more conspicuously than the Massachusetts Institute of Technology (MIT), whose campus is "dotted with buildings donated by Exxon, Campbell Soup, Texas Instruments" as well as by industrialists Alfred P. Sloan and George Eastman. MIT's ties to Exxon, in particular, were cemented not long ago with an $8 million grant to finance combustion research, while the W. R. Grace Company contributed $8.5 million for commercial applications of microbiology research, two of the largest single corporate contracts.(20) In the decade from 1978 to 1988, corporate-financed research there more than quadrupled, outstripped only by the robust investment of the Department of Defense (DOD) in military-related research, which in 1987 totaled $408 million, making MIT the number one academic beneficiary of DOD largesse.(21)

Corporations are only too happy to have a strong federal commitment to and sponsorship of programs such as career education, even if most of the funds to to vocational training at the public colleges. The advantages to private business and industry are two-fold: first, the provision of a supply of technically skilled labor and, second, the provision of private occupational training at public expense. Moreover, the colleges that have instituted such vocational training programs appear to be amply accommodating to the needs of area employers. One spokesman from an interest group 'representing the community colleges may not have been exaggerating when he said that when "corporate managers . . . announce a need for skilled workers . . . college administrators trip over each other in their haste to organize a new technical curriculum."(22)

Evidence of such academic and corporate cooperation (in alliance, of course, with government) can clearly be inferred from recent statistics showing that of the more than 9 million students attending community, technical, or junior colleges, two-thirds are enrolled in vocational programs, the most popular being electronics, nursing, data processing, secretarial, business, and law enforcement.(23) Of course, the vocational vogue at the college level is largely a function of the extensive groundwork laid in the junior and senior high schools. According to the U.S. Department of Education, as early as 1975 (four years after the federal program began) career education was firmly entrenched in 5,000 of the nation's 17,000 school districts.(24)

Other centers of career education with more direct and immediate ties to business and industry are the proprietary schools and colleges run by such corporations as I.T.T., Bell & Howell, R. J. Reynolds Indus-

tries, R.C.A., Holiday Inns, and the Xerox Corporation.   At least eighteen corporations and industry associations have been authorized to grant
academic credentials, ranging from associate of arts degrees to doctorates.(25) One of the oldest, General Motors Institute (GMI), founded in
1919, was the first fully accredited college in the United States owned
and operated by an industrial corporation, and offering GM employee-stu-
dents four majors (in industrial administration, and mechanical, electrical, or industrial engineering. "During their years at GMI," a journa-
list observed, "most students seem to absorb GM's relentlessly optimistic
corporate ethic."(26)   In 1982, GM's official proprietorship came to an
end, when GMI became incorporated as an independent, non-profit college.(27)

A 1985 report of the Carnegie Foundation for the Advancement of
Teaching, Corporate Classrooms: The Learning Business, found that cor-
porate-run education has become a booming $60-billion-a-year enterprise,
"similar to the cost of the nation's four-year colleges and universities,
both public and private," and approaching "the total enrollment of those
same institutions—about eight million students."(28) One recent innovation has been the establishment of satellite universities through the
corporate exercise of cooperative philanthropy. The first was the National Technological University created in 1985 by I.B.M., the Westing-
house Corporation, the Digital Equipment Company, and other firms that
use "satellites to broadcast courses to corporate classrooms around the
country and abroad."(29)

The patterns of cooperative planning and promotion are as conspicuous as the patterns of cooperative philanthropy undergirding the career
education movement. They have helped to coordinate the new vocationalism
administratively, give it nationwide momentum, and orchestrate public
consensus behind it. Fortune magazine explained the necessity for such
interinstitutional cooperation by noting that the new programs "obviously
cannot be carried on by educators, alone; they require the active collaboration of the business community, which stands to benefit from their
success."(30) One of the leading quasi-governmental planning bodies, the
National Commission on the Financing of Post-Secondary Education, called
upon the nation's colleges and universities to increase their efforts to
secure accurate data on local "work force requirements." Recognizing the
need to improve communication and cooperation between corporations and
the campus, the commission strongly recommended that all post-secondary
institutions "develop a greater capacity for expanding and contracting
their professional and occupational training programs according to continuing measures of demand."(31)

COOPERATIVE EDUCATION AND THE CORPORATE ETHOS

In the past two decades, a movement to rationalize the corporation-
college connection, along the lines recommended by the National Commis-

sion, gathered momentum and secured federal sanction under the title, *cooperative education*. This, quite simply, is career education pushed to a closer and cosier connection with business and industry. Cooperative education operationalizes the proposals of the Carnegie Commission, the CED, and other planning bodies for "work-study" and "stop-out" arrangements with public and private employers for which academic credit is given for work experience. The Carnegie Commission in its policy report, *Less Time, More Options*, was particularly explicit in urging the expansion of innovative forms of education

> outside the formal college, in apprenticeship programs, proprietary schools, in-service training in industry and in military programs; appropriate educational credit should be given for the training received, and participants should be eligible for federal and state assistance available to students in formal colleges.(32)

The State University of New York (SUNY) has long championed the cause of cooperative education at its sixty-four campuses. Its 1972 Master Plan, for example, caught the spirit and substance of the Carnegie policy report by specifying that new cooperative arrangements be made with the state's "industrial plants, government agencies, professional offices, hospitals, clinics, laboratories, courthouses, modern farms, and even shopping centers."(33) Statewide, the cooperative education movement has been fueled by the enthusiastic support of SUNY's recent chancellors. In March 1975, then-Chancellor Ernest L. Boyer candidly outlined the State University's hopes and plans for a new "University-Industry Task Force: The University wants very much to help management and labor become more productive and, at this time of unprecedented unemployment, we have a special obligation to retrain individuals in new career fields." One of the first accomplishments of the new task force was to sign a major agreement between SUNY and the state's largest corporation, the New York Telephone Company, aimed at "relating the resources of the University much more closely to the world of work." Under the precedent-setting agreement--intended as a model for cooperative education programs in the state--several of the SUNY colleges were to offer vocational training and retraining courses to the telephone company's 85,000 employees. Upon conclusion of the historic accord, telephone company President William M. Ellinghaus enthusiastically remarked, "This is one of those happy instances where everyone benefits. The University extends its services more widely. Our business gains better trained, more expert personnel which, in turn, benefits the public."(34)

Clifton Wharton, Jr., who succeeded Boyer as SUNY chancellor, issued a call for an upgraded "knowledge extension service, whereby the university's research, scholarly and professional resources are made available to industry, commerce, city and state government."(35) He declared that this was in keeping with SUNY's third mission, public service, encapsulated in the university's motto: *To Learn—To Search—To Serve*.

By the mid-1980s, it has been calculated, at least half of   the nation's two- and four-year colleges had contractual arrangements for cooperative education programs with employers—whether corporations, government agencies, or professional associations. According to *The Chronicle
of Higher Education*,

> Under the typical contract, the college provides the education
> or training, which is often tailored to the specific needs of
> the employer, as well as the faculty members who teach the
> courses.   The company usually, but not always, recruits the
> employees for the program and provides classroom facilities
> and some administrative assistance.(36)

A few such contracts are for liberal arts courses, but most, understandably, are for business education or technical training.

Pace University, for example, set up a special Office of Corporate
Education Services (OCES) in 1981 with some fifty different programs of-
offered "off the shelf" on corporate sites.   The director of the OCES
candidly explained Pace's motive: "We are in the business of serving the
corporate community primarily for new markets"—in order to offset, in
short, declining numbers of traditional-age students with corporate-com-
mandeered workers. "Colleges and universities [after all]," he went on,
are in the educational contracting business primarily to make money."(37)
In Orange County, California, the community college system has joined
with 400 nearby firms, many of them top Pentagon contractors, to form the
"Technology Exchange Center."   Chancellors of the eight colleges in the
system sit on a board of directors with corporate chief executive officers "to anticipate job openings and plan training programs to fill them.
Students use space and equipment at the industry sites and companies get
pre-trained employees at low cost."(38)

The new practicality of college administrators and their corporate
counterparts is being reinforced by a multimedia blitz directed to present and future educational consumers.   Over the past decade and a half,
the public has been inundated with newspaper reports, feature articles in
magazines, television specials, and paperback bestsellers, with such provocative titles as *The Case Against College* and *The Over-Educated American*,(39) that have as their common denominator a defense of the new
practicality. If one must go to college (and it is not clear that one
must), at least make it "career education," these media seem to say. The
unmistakable message, according to Jerome Karabel, is that "vocational
training is a 'no nonsense' approach which, unlike vaguely directed liberal arts programs, pays off in dollars." In view of the currents of anti-intellectualism in American culture, "this pseudo-populist appeal,"
Karabel adds, "is quite powerful indeed."(40)

In an article titled, "Learning How to Earn," *Parade* magazine ac-
cented how many easily accessible community colleges are retooling their

curricula more and more to career education.   While addressing the question, "College Who Needs It?", *Time* magazine gave its editorial approval to a mid-western college which now offers degrees in automobile body repair and mechanics. Shortly after the federal government announced plans to underwrite career education, *The Wall Street Journal*, in an editorial praising the new federal initiatives, expressed the hope that a career orientation would give students a greater sense of purpose and reduce the numbers "drifting aimlessly into college," which had heretofore denied "needed skills and talents to the economy."(41) Probably the most potent effort to push the new practicality with the general public was a CBS television special bearing the provocative title (reminiscent of *Time* magazine's), "Higher Education, Who Needs It?"   The program's audience was given the distinct impression, according to Jerome Karabel, that "the shortest road to the bread line is by way of the college gate." Sardonically, Karabel summarized the program's not-so-hidden message:

> Myths . . . [CBS claims] have caused students to flock to liberal arts programs leading to the B.A.   The central myth is that college is the 'only stepping stone to high-status careers.' Instead, the show informs us, jobs and money are really located elsewhere.

> With Ph.D.'s portrayed as parking lot attendants, and a tough-talking Ford executive informing us that at least 80,000 openings are available for automotive mechanics at this very moment, more career education is obviously needed.(42)

The Reagan administration's flamboyant secretary of education, William J. Bennett, offered a version of the "College, Who Needs It?" argument. Commenting more from the perspective of an educational elitist critical of academic mismanagement and deteriorating performance standards, Bennett made headlines by telling the press that if some day his infant son were to ask him for $50,000 to start his own business in lieu of tuition for an Ivy League education, he might "think that was a good idea."   Bennett proposed the $50,000 option, he remarked, to challenge the assumption that "wonderful things must come to pass when you get a degree."(43)

THE NEW "PRACTICAL" LIBERAL ARTS

The popularizers of the new practicality in the mass media and its promoters on college campuses have helped to stimulate still another trend: namely, the gradual infusion of a "practical" focus into traditional liberal arts courses and curricula. This change has resulted from the self-conscious efforts at fiscal crisis management on the part of college administrators in order to salvage liberal arts programs and re-

verse the decline in student interest and enrollments. One small liberal
arts college in Illinois, for example, recently "superimposed a Business
Preparation Program on top of its liberal arts curriculum" that, the college's administration reported with pride, may be "combined with any
major field of study."   The program calls for a nineteen-hour sequence
of required courses with such titles as: "Career Planning and Human Development," "Case Studies in Business," "Career Entry Seminar," and
Business and Society."   Students must also take courses in computer pro-
gramming, accounting, and marketing. A college brochure explains the rationale behind the new program: "We . . . have a strong belief in the
liberal arts background as a sound beginning for a flexible business career. We are aware, however, that it takes more than a degree to land a
job."(44)

Throughout the academic system, such efforts to refurbish the liberal arts with the new practicality have been picking up momentum.   Music
majors at Oregon's Willamette University may now "combine their liberal
arts preparation with training in music therapy."   Penn State's French
Department, according to *The New York Times*, has developed a program with
the College of Business Administration.   In addition, Eastern Michigan
University trains managers for cultural institutions, while Baruch College in New York has "a similar program to give history majors the business expertise to run historical societies."(45)   Economics departments
throughout the country are adding special programs, minors, and major
"tracks" in accounting and business administration to supplement their
more theoretically-focused traditional curricula.   The field of mathematics has experienced a similar transformation from "pure" science to "applied," largely fueled by the boom in computer technology.

But the biggest boom of all seems to be in the rising demand for
business courses.   "Such courses have become so popular," a *New York
Times* report notes, "that they are even being offered at the most prestigious liberal arts schools."   In 1985 Wesleyan University introduced the
first accounting course in its 153-year history, while at Amherst financial accounting reappeared in the curriculum after a twenty-year absence.
"Dickinson College in Pennsylvania, rated among the top ten liberal arts
colleges by *U.S. News and World Report*, established a policy and management studies major in 1981 . . . At Bryn Mawr, people with business and
administrative experience . . . are brought in to teach seminars.   At
Oberlin, its first 'executive-in-residence,' a vice-president of Equitable Life, taught a two-week business management course for credit."(46)
Such curricular trends have, of course, presupposed and fostered both the
rapid expansion of career counseling and placement services, and the similar expansion of corporate recruiting on campus.

In the early 1980s an influential policy study, *Global Stakes: The
Future of High Technology in America*, made headlines when it argued for a
$1 billion "crash program . . . of integrating the humanities with tech-
nology education," financed jointly by the federal and state governments
and private industry. The $1 billion in start-up funds was to be used to

"buy equipment, finance scholarships and research in math, engineering, and computer sciences." Calling it a "modern Morrill Act" (after the legislation which created the federal land grant colleges), the report's authors sought to make high technology central to the college curriculum, even at the tradition-bound liberal arts colleges, in order to "balance the goals of employment and enlightenment."(47)

Encroachments upon the liberal arts seem destined to spread. This prospect is all the more certain in view of the continuing growth and prosperity of the community colleges--the institutional vanguard of the new vocationalism.

COMMUNITY COLLEGES: ACADEMIC "SERVICE STATIONS"

Of all the institutions in the academic tier system, the public community colleges have become the prime laboratories for vocationalizing the academic curriculum and fulfilling higher education's "public service" mission. As a result, they have achieved the dubious distinction of being "service stations" of the academic world.(48)   It is not at all surprising that the policy planning literature implicitly views them that way.

The Carnegie Commission, for example, in its well-known policy report on *The Open Door Colleges*, argued for occupational education being given "the fullest support and status within the community colleges." Moreover, the Commission called for "coordinated efforts" at the federal, state, and local levels to "stimulate the expansion of occupational education in community colleges and to make it responsive to changing manpower requirements." A collateral function of the community college, in the Commission's view, is the provision of "continuing education" for adults and a second chance, so to speak, for four-year college drop-outs. Inasmuch as the "average adult may have to shift his/[her] occupation three or four times" in a lifetime, the easily-accessible, programmatically-updated community colleges offer the best insurance "against educational and occupational obsolescence."(49)

The Commission is quite emphatic about the need to specialize the community college curriculum and, in so doing, to differentiate its content more conspicuously from that of the four-year liberal arts colleges and universities. These colleges, according to the Commission, have a unique role to play and "should be actively discouraged by state planning and financing policies from converting to four-year institutions." The main reason the Commission offers for, in effect, permanently consigning the community colleges to a lowly two-year status is that otherwise "they might place less emphasis on occupational programs and leave an unmet need in the local community.(50)

The American Association of Community and Junior Colleges (AACJC), the leading interest group representing the two-year colleges, has also sought to save local colleges from suffering "unmet needs" through its

advice to its member colleges. In a policy report enthusiastically promoting career education, the AACJC argued: "Career education as a concept can be the vehicle through which community and junior colleges undertake a fundamental reformation of their curricula to make them more
responsive to emerging needs and less dependent upon their tradition as
the lower division of the four-year institutions."(51)

The AACJC has been a consistent champion of practical education ever
since its founding in 1920, so it came as no surprise when it further
urged its member colleges to "consider the development of occupational
education programs linked to business, industry, labor, and government a
high priority."(52)   To facilitate their cooperation in meeting this objective, AACJC staff researchers periodically prepare brochures and book-
length reports advising member colleges on how best to "sell" the new
practical curricula.

Just how much of a marketing mentality prevails today among community college administrators was amply evident at a statewide deans' conference held in Poughkeepsie, New York. Two local community college administrators who were participant-observers at the conference reported
(with considerable dismay) that the overwhelming consensus was in favor
of popularizing the new practicality whenever and wherever possible. One
of the conference speakers stressed repeatedly "the need to vocationalize
liberal education." He insisted that each college professor justify to
each class the "usefulness of his or her course in the job hunt." Another speaker was reported to have claimed that "students have the right
to ask of any course, 'How much is this worth? How much can I get for
this?'" Evidently, he meant "worth" and what one "gets" in a strictly
practical and pecuniary sense.(53)

An important component of the vocationalizing of the community college curriculum--one that is often overlooked--is that the vocational or
career education programs are designed as "terminal" for the students who
elect (or, more accurately, are channeled into) them. What is even more
overlooked is the role that philanthropy has played in generating this
outcome. It is quite clear from recent policy reports that skill-train-
ing at these colleges is not designed to facilitate and encourage access
to "higher skilling" at the higher tiers of the academic system, still
less to a broad-based liberal arts education. On the contrary, provisions of federal vocational legislation--such as the Vocational Education
Act of 1963 and the Higher Education Amendments of 1972--specifically
prohibit the subsidizing of vocational training in baccalaureate degree
programs or in college preparatory (or "transfer") programs at two-year
institutions.(54)

Moreover, the pattern of federal subsidies for curriculum development has been quite lopsided in favor of vocational programs. For example, of the total monies appropriated in one year for community colleges,
$850 million was earmarked for vocational education and less than one-
third as much ($275 million) for academic programs.(55) Such selective
and discriminatory dispensing of public philanthropy documents the gov-

ernment's commitment to filling shortages in semi-skilled technical occupations more than any presumptive commitment to "universal access" at the so-called "open door" colleges. According to historian Steven Zwerdling, such unequal funding, moreover, not only "deepens the division between transfer and terminal education" at these institutions, it also "leads to separate facilities and separate administrations for academic and vocational education and, ironically, may contribute to the low status currently assigned to vocational programs."(56)   The tacit promulgation, in short, of a separate-but-equal policy at the community colleges has been a cornerstone of curricular reform.

ELITE COLLEGES: LAST BASTIONS OF THE LIBERAL ARTS?

In the preceding sections, I called attention to the hegemony of the new practicality in the curricula of the community colleges and its partial infusion into liberal arts courses and degree programs elsewhere in the academic tier system.   But how widespread, we might ask, is the eclipse of the higher learning?   Have the upper tiers of the academic system--in particular, the doctoral-granting research universities, and some of the private four-year colleges--been able to resist the vocational vogue and administrative encroachments upon their pursuit of liberal education?

Judging from recent trends and anticipated policy agendas, there is little cause for optimism.   If anything resembling a general education in the liberal arts remains in present-day higher education, it is increasingly becoming the curricular monopoly of the elite universities, especially in the private sector.   But even within that uppermost tier of the academic system, there are centrifugal tendencies.   The experience of Rhode Island's Brown University may provide an interesting case in point.

One of the charter institutions of the elite Ivy League, Brown received nationwide media attention when, in response to the campus struggles of the 1960s and students' demands for "relevance," it instituted a sweeping reorganization of its undergraduate curriculum.   Brown abolished distribution requirements and most compulsory course sequences in 1969, made numerical or letter grades optional (permitting evaluation instead on a pass/fail basis), and instituted a variety of innovative, interdisciplinary programs, contract majors, and independent study options.   At many institutions, with poorly-motivated students and indifferent faculty, such curricular license would have been a disaster and, in practice, often was.   At Brown, however, with its first-rate faculty and academically ambitious students, the new curriculum proved an intellectually rigorous, stimulating, and challenging experiment.   This was largely attributable, most observers agree, to the success of the so-called "Modes of Thought" courses--a series of seminars which focused upon fundamental concepts and methods of inquiry and took an interdisciplinary approach to the subject matter.

By the mid-1970s, however, as *The New York Times* reported, "the reforms that were hailed as 'the most flexible and progressive undergraduate curriculum to be found in any major American university' [were] struggling for survival against heavy odds."(57)   The Modes of Thought program, in particular, the *Times* noted, seemed to be "on the rocks." in the "desperate scramble" to get into graduate and professional schools or to legitimize the baccalaureate degree to prospective employers, "more and more students [were] insisting on the old-fashioned grades," while only 10 percent of the students took advantage of the various independent and group study opportunities.   The "impassioned spirit" and politicized consciousness of 1969 were being displaced, in short, by new attitudes of pragmatism and pre-professionalism.

A student editorialist explained the shifting definitions of curricular "relevance" at Brown and elsewhere: "For today's career- and success-oriented students . . . the new strain is more down-to-Earth than esoteric, and more likely to help someone earn a buck than discover truth or launch a crusade."(58)   The practical brand of relevance was manifesting itself, he reported, in the popularity of Engineering #26, "Mechanical Technology," a course that had been in the Brown curriculum for twenty years, but that had now taken its place beside that seeming pinnacle of the new practicality, a course in bartending, offered by the Student Employment Office "to train students for jobs."   Both courses evidently were "enjoying unmitigated student interest, and somewhere in the vicinity of 100 would-be bartenders were turned away [that first semester] due to an enrollment limit for that course."(59)

This anecdote may overstate the depths to which curricular "reform" has sunk in the Ivy League.   There are, to be sure, important reservoirs of the old-style relevance as well as academically respectable and rigorous courses in liberal arts disciplines at colleges in both the private and public sectors.   Even more important, there are signs of a revival of interest in general education, with its tell-tale distribution requirements and predictable program sequences.   The pace has been set by Harvard University, which, more than thirty years after the publication of its pioneering "Redbook," *General Education in a Free Society,* approved a revised distribution requirement in five subject areas (literature and the arts, history, social and philosophical analysis, science and mathematics, foreign languages and cultures), with a tightened core of courses from which students choose approximately half of their total degree program.(60)   Other colleges are now following Harvard's lead by reinstating or refurbishing general education programs.   Such efforts won the blessing of many federal and state education officials such as William J. Bennett, secretary of education in the Reagan administration, and leading foundations such as the Carnegie Foundation for the Advancement of Teaching.(61)

There is a second major aspect to the curricular changes taking place among institutions in the upper tier of the academic system.   Its primary inspiration stems from the economics of cost-efficiency and the

politics of management control.   Cost-efficiency in the higher echelons
of higher education has had its most conspicuous curricular consequence
in the paring down of graduate programs and the limiting of access
through such mechanisms as reduced financial aid and fellowships, tougher
admissions criteria, and propaganda about the dismal job market for advanced degree recipients.

Claiming to make "more effective use of resources," leading policy
planning organizations have resolved to consolidate and centralize the
top-most tier.   The Carnegie Commission is quite explicit on the matter:
"State coordinating councils and similar agencies should develop strong
policies . . . for preventing the spread of Ph.D. programs. . . . We also strongly recommend the continuous review of existing degree programs
with a view to eliminating those that are very costly or of low quality
and the concentration of highly specialized degree programs on only one
or two campuses of multi-campus institutions."(62)

In the guise of "sound fiscal management," the Academy for Educational Development recommends:

* Abolishing departments or academic programs that have too
  few students to justify continuation;

* Abolishing language requirements; ultimately abolishing language departments with too few students;

* Eliminating master's degree programs in science and mathematics;

* Requiring the faculty to defend every single academic program now being offered.(63)

State education departments and coordinating agencies have already been
moving swiftly and efficiently to follow the planning commission's directives.

The curricular reorganization of American higher education, prodded
by private and public philanthropy, has had far-reaching consequences.
In a sense, the transformation of the curriculum is but one manifestation
of a larger transformation. Specifically, it has been part of a comprehensive stratification strategy, devised by leading centers of policy
planning, which has served to reinforce the structural inequalities of
prestige and power among institutions and tiers of the academic system.
The expansion of vocational and applied studies at the lowest tiers, together with the concentration in the highest tiers of more theoretical
and rigorous liberal arts programs, compounds the polarization between
top and bottom.   Increasingly, as we have seen, higher learning becomes
the curricular monopoly of the elite colleges and universities, while
"lesser" institutions devote themselves to more standardized, trivial-

ized, and vocationalized programs.

Just as the differential prestige and power of academic institutions affects the life-chances and self-images of their personnel, conversely, the social composition of the institutions reflects and reinforces their location within the tier system. By the same token, the hierarchies of both institutions and personnel reinforce and, in turn, are reinforced by the hierarchy of the curriculum. The overall structural consequence, accordingly, has been a reshaping of the form as well as the content of post-secondary education in America.

3 Ideology and the Politics of Public Higher Education: Responses to Budget Crises and Curricular Reorganization

MICHAEL ENGEL

Public higher education has fallen on hard times in the past two decades. In the name of "new realities" such as declining enrollments and
lack of funds, state and local governments have cut back on financial
support, terminated programs, fired faculty and staff, and raised tuitions. At the same time, many of the same governments have shown an increasing willingness, especially in the northeastern states, to maintain
or increase levels of direct or indirect support for private higher education. Liberal arts programs in the public colleges are evaluated increasingly in terms of their relevance to the needs of private industry.

The response of those involved in public higher education has been
apologetic and defensive. The orthodoxies of the new realities by and
large go unchallenged, and the relationship between government and private higher education goes unquestioned. Public higher education is defended in terms of the "productivity" of curricular offerings. The result is a political strategy that accepts the prevailing policy direction
and in a muddled way attempts to mitigate its impact. The issue becomes
especially crucial in light of the attitudes of the Reagan administration
and now the Bush administration toward federal financial aid to higher
education.

This chapter makes a case against this kind of response and a case
for an alternative basis on which to conduct the struggle for public
higher education with a strong liberal arts component. The ideological
and methodological context within which the alternatives for higher education are currently being discussed is inherently inimical to the survival of the public sector. Quantitative applications of the market model
have dominated the study of public policy in higher education and have by
their very nature limited the debate on alternatives. An effective defense of public higher education requires a different set of values, justifications, and approaches to research that would avoid the self-defeat-

ing position of doing battle using the enemy's rule book and arsenal of weapons.

Empiricist methodology is the mainstay of research in American social science. In its purest form, its goal is the development of a body
of knowledge in the social sciences supposedly untainted by normative
considerations. This is to be accomplished by amassing quantitative data
that can ultimately be used to construct social theory. The data-gather-
ing process is best advanced by reliance on the methods of the physical
sciences, which stress quantitative approaches as the best means of producing research results that are empirically replicable. Then the future
direction of society can hopefully be charted on the basis of the "objective" findings of social science. This philosophy, although increasingly
challenged of late, still generally shapes the daily work of contemporary
social scientists.

The field of political science is no exception to this, nor is the
sub-field of public policy, which examines the nature and impact of government decisions on public issues. As James Anderson points out,

The most useful policy evaluation for policy makers and administrators and policy critics who wish to have a factual basis
for their positions is the systematic evaluation that tries to
determine cause-and-effect relationships and rigorously measures the impact of policy. It is, of course, often impossible
to measure quantitatively the impact of public policies, especially social policies, with any real precision. In this context, then, to 'measure rigorously' is to seek to assess as
carefully and objectively as possible the impact of policy.(1)

This effort at measurement is consistent with the construction and
application of theoretical models that provide a framework for quantitative analysis of public policies. The "market model" lends itself ad-
mirably to this purpose in studying educational policy. The market model
attempts to explain the exchange of goods and services in society as the
result of the interactions among buyers and sellers seeking to maximize
their individual gain under conditions of unrestricted competition.   The
ideological thrust of the market model is that the free market works to
allocate goods and services in a way that "maximizes the utility" of all
involved and, therefore, simultaneously serves individual and societal
interests as well as balancing conflicting demands on resources.   "The
market, if functioning properly, will be an unbiased arbitrator of economic desires, constantly guiding economic activity toward equilibrium."(2)

The dominance of market model/empiricist approaches in education
policy analysis has produced a set of conclusions that, unsurprisingly,
favors the appolication of free market values to higher education policy
and maintains that proper evaluation of policy effectiveness must be in
quantitative terms. These approaches serve to attack public higher edu-

cation, rather than promote it.

Research based on market model/empiricist approaches treats higher education as a form of investment toward the goal of economic growth.

> An investment in education . . . is just as much an investment as a new factory or public bridge. An initial expenditure is undertaken with the hope of generating a higher return of net income in the future. For education, the private costs are the direct tuition and fees associated with schooling, the indirect opportunity costs of not being able to work full time, and the loss of leisure. The higher return is the increase in earning over what that student would have earned if he[/she] had not received the extra education. Implicit in applying investment theory to the individual as well as to the businessman is the assumption that both are attempting to maximize their future incomes . . . in their investment decisions. Thus, they undertake the investment which yields them the highest return.(3)

Education is a form of investment in human capital, and although this is different from investment in physical capital, the differences are considered from this point of view to be "mostly in degree, not in kind. Thus, one theoretical structure is useful in understanding all types of investment behavior."(4)

If higher education is considered an investment, the immediate concern is determining "the relative profitability of education and of its component sectors."(5) Investment in a market economy is justifiable—"rational"—only in terms of maximizing gains from the input of resources. The basic tool for this calculation is cost-benefit analysis: the relation of present costs to future benefits. The returns that benefit those other than the individual making the investment are referred to as "spillovers" or "externalities." Therefore, the rewards of education that spill over into the environment are the basis for a social investment to complement the individual's investment.

The implications of this approach for public policy in higher education are clear: (1) continuing social and individual investment in higher education is justified only in terms of its relative contribution to economic growth as indicated by individual and social rates of return; (2) the role of government is limited to compensating for deficiencies of the market or paying for "externalities" insofar as these are quantifiable; (3) the issue of who should pay for higher education and how much depends on the relative magnitude of social versus individual benefits, also calculated in terms of rate of return; and (4) curriculum revision, especially in the public sector, must proceed in the direction of consumer demand and industrial need. The task of public policy research becomes the measurement of applicable variables.

Numerous attempts have been made to measure the value of investment in education in terms of growth. Theodore Schultz states that "investments in education may explain a large part of the otherwise unexplained economic growth of the United States," and consequently their continuation is justified.(6)   Edward Denison concludes that educational investment compares favorably with other forms of capital investment as a stimulus to economic growth, and therefore, "additional provisions for education will make a significant net contribution to long-term economic growth."(7)

Research on rates of return reaps similarly favorable results with some exceptions.   Estimates of rates of return to the individual for a four-year college education run at around 12 to 14 percent.(8)   One study concludes that "both social and private rates of return are in most countries relatively high and compare favorably with rates of return to investment in physical capital."(9)   But Lee Hansen cautions that a consideration of other statistical factors "would have the effect of reducing the relative rates of return, especially at the higher levels of schooling,"(10) and concludes, along with David Witmer, that "universal higher education . . . will produce some economic benefits but at a high cost."(11)

The ultimate empiricist faith is expressed by Richard Eckaus, who states that if there were sufficient "quantitative knowledge about all the inputs for the various outputs," one could visualize "a grand synthetic program" that "would then specify the optimal amounts of education of various types which should be given, just as it would specify the optimal rate of investment in the different types of physical capital and the best use of natural resources."(12)

The justification of investment in terms of economic growth might have provided political advantages in the relatively prosperous 1960s when most such articles were written. In the economic stagnation of the 1970s and 1980s, the policy implications for public higher education were not so attractive. If growth is no longer an attribute of all sectors of the economy, then higher education must invest in programs consistent with existing "growth sectors," whatever they may be, and disinvest in others. This puts higher education, and liberal arts programs in particular, at the whim of wherever the market happens to be at any one time. Social investment in higher education is then pegged to the ability of institutions to adjust to current economic trends as measured by rates of return. Similarly, the rights and responsibilities of students, faculty, and administrators become defined in terms of enhancing the "marketability" and "productivity" of student "investors."   The concept of economic growth is, therefore, a two-edged sword as far as the survival of public higher education is concerned.

The market model/empiricist approach places the question of government involvement in higher education in a very narrow framework. The extent of that involvement depends upon the measurement of "externalities," for "without it, rational assignments to the costs of education by users as against taxpayers cannot be made."(13)   It is not sufficient, claims Richard Freeman, to merely enumerate the externalities.   "The listing of

possibly valid, possibly mythical benefits rapidly becomes sterile. For
people who believe that such benefits are important . . . it is incumbent
to provide numerical estimates of what they amount to."(14) One such attempt, which ilustrates the impossibility of such a task, is Burton Weisbrod's estimate of the spillover effects of elementary and secondary education in Clayton, Missouri. The estimate is made in terms of financial
benefits; only three pages are devoted to "external non-monetary benefits," measured by voting participation. As Weisbrod himself points out,
"Benefits from education may indeed take many forms, some of which--and
possibly the most important--defy measurement in money terms."(15)

Given the difficulty of measuring social benefits, some economists
pursue empiricist logic to its limits and claim they do not exist.   Milton Friedman believes that the argument for "neighborhood effects" of
higher education is weaker than that for elementary and secondary education.(16)   Even if they do exist, says Robert Hartman, "we do not know
whether subsidies are necessary to support the externalities of higher
education."(17)

Within the limits of the market model, the only alternative rationale for justifying government involvement lies in the "market imperfec-
tion" argument. Under ideal conditions, the free market itself would determine the "equilibrium price" of higher education. In the real world,
however, the market operates under imperfect circumstances: monopolies
on supply or demand, restrictions on the mobility of resources or products, poor consumer information, and so on. To Singer and Feldman, "Only
when market imperfections such as these can be found can a case be made
for government intervention to alter the free choice of individuals.
is in fact present."(18) This point of view would be attractive to those
who feel that unquantified social benefits are a weak basis for advocat-
ing public support of higher education. Government action would consequently be called for to improve the performance of the market by breaking up monopolies of supply (for example, by deregulating higher education) or by providing loans to guarantee equal access to the market.

It should be quite clear that none of this provides any justification for the existence of a network of tax-supported low-tuition public
colleges and universities. By the standard of "externalities" and "market imperfections," such institutions are economically irrational.   They
restrict the market by granting selective subsidies; there is no measurable "objective" basis for their existence; and they indiscriminately
subsidize private investment in higher education without any relation to
the balance of social and individual benefits. The logical conclusion
would seem to be phasing out such institutions in favor of more selective
public policies in higher education. Such action is--for now--limited by
political constraints. But the more such reasoning is accepted, the
weaker those constraints become. Government support for public universities and colleges is indefensible within the limits of the market model.

The financial policies suggested by research in higher education are
the following: (1) higher, perhaps "full-cost" tuitions; (2) loans ra-

ther than grants as a means of aiding individual students, and as a replacement for institutional aid of all kinds; (3) aid to private institutions, channeled through students, to compensate for the oversubsidiza-
tion of public institutions. As D. K. Halstead points out,

> Proponents of higher tuition suggest that since the student
> most directly and fully benefits from an education, determina-
> tion of his[/her] fair share of the cost can best be resolved
> by letting market action in the sale of education set prices on
> a competitive basis. . . .Society, as a secondary beneficiary,
> would be willing to support higher education, they argue, to
> the extent of the unpaid balance.(19)

Moreover, if potential investors are to make rational decisions, they
ought to know the real price.

> The price of college attendance--tuition--should reflect the
> full resource costs to state taxpayers of providing college
> training. If students and their parents are confronted with
> these full cost prices, they will make decisions about whether
> to go to college and about what type and location of college to
> attend in full recognition of the real resource-cost implica-
> tions of their choice. This should lead to a more efficient
> allocation of resources.(20)

The detailed development of fiscal policy proposals consistent with
these general goals has been the responsibility of the Carnegie Commission, the Committee for Economic Development, the Brookings Institution,
the Sloan Commission, and several Department of Education task forces.
Their power and prestige have given legitimacy to the free market approach in financing higher education. Although the private commissions
and institutions neither agree totally with each other nor with all the
tenets of neoclassical economics, they share a clear consensus on basic
policy directions. All recommend narrowing the tuition gap between public and private colleges, channeling government aid through students,
putting greater emphasis on loans, and changing curricula in light of the
changing student and job markets. The last by no means implies the out-
right elimination of liberal arts programs but places an emphasis on economic over intellectual rationales for their continuation. The ideological and empirical justifications for these proposals are also similar in
the various reports: public-private competition as a means of promoting
efficient resource allocation in higher education; student choice and
"self-help" as a major value; and declining enrollments and fiscal stringency as "given" conditions of the environment.(21)

Government studies have taken similar paths. The Second Newman Report, emphasizing the importance of competition and choice, opts for federal policies that would narrow the tuition gap. The National Commission

on the Financing of Post-Secondary Education concluded that the policy most favorable to low-income access to higher education was an increase in both public college tuitions and individual student aid; the least favorable was open enrollment and free tuition for the first two years in public colleges.(22)

These commission reports provide the informational basis for policymaking in higher education. Their *a priori* acceptance of market model ideology and their virtual unanimity on policy directions sets a similar tone for the deliberations among those responsible for determining the future of public higher education.

The most dramatic example of the implementation of such policies was the end of free tuition at the City University of New York in 1976, which was dictated less by financial necessity than it was by the strength of the political forces that viewed free public higher education as an unwarranted luxury, inconsistent with market model concepts. This is evidenced by the continued willingness of the state government of New York to subsidize private higher education through the Tuition Assistance Plan. The "fiscal crisis" merely provided the opportunity to eliminate an anomaly to the prevailing direction of public policy in higher education finance. The relatively feeble protest that ensued indicated the the extent to which even those who were part of the City University community accepted the arguments of market theorists.

The logical next step in state policy on higher education is the "voucher system." In New Jersey, the State Commission on Financing Post-Secondary Education has already suggested a demonstration project, citing the "allocative inefficiency" and "adverse redistributive effects" of public higher education. "The philosophy which provides the foundation of the Commission's financing model is the market concept," it states. "If students with little buying power are subsidized directly by the state . . . institutions will be forced to compete for students."(23) As long as the calculus of social versus individual benefits is accepted as the basis for deciding who pays for higher education, public colleges and universities will continue to face tuition increases and cuts in state appropriations.

Public institutions have responded in various ways to the increasing pressure for coordination of curricular offerings with the job market. Most have attempted to balance a liberal arts core with additional vocational programs. But this option becomes increasingly unworkable as appropriations diminish. Public higher education is then left with two basic choices: defend the liberal arts in terms other than those of the market model or adopt the policies currently being developed in Massachusetts.

The development of public higher education in Massachusetts was both belated and abortive. The expansion, which began in the late 1960s, was cut short during the fiscal crisis of 1975-76. Since then, the three universities, ten state colleges, and fifteen community colleges have undergone a significant decline. In 1979, Governor Edward J. King took office with a commitment to political and economic cooperation--a "social contract"--with the state's expanding high technology industries, trading financial incentives and tax breaks for new jobs.

The state system of public universities and colleges now faces integration into this arrangement. In 1977, the "Commonwealth Center for High Technology/Education" began operations in Dover, Massachusetts. Enthusiastically supported by state college officials in cooperation with the computer industry's "High Technology Council" and specifically with the Digital Equipment Corporation, the "Dover Project" is developing, more or less obscured from public view, a curriculum for the state colleges that will provide a trained labor force for the high technology industries. In the words of the former chairman of the State College Board of Trustees, "It's the first place in the United States where there is a total interaction of the state and business community." This description is not inconsistent with that of Samuel Bowles, co-author of *Schooling in Capitalist America:* "It's an out-and-out bribe . . . a rip-off . . . [to turn] over to private business the development of curriculum."(24)

Up to now, the result has merely been the proliferation of computer science programs. But not until recently have the administrative means existed that would make possible the coordination of the entire state system in line with the "social contract." This occurred in the spring of 1980, when the legislature, by simply amending the annual budget, reorganized the system in line with the governor's preferences, replacing the five separate governing boards with a fifteen member Board of Regents, appointed by the governor, and holding full administrative and financial power over all the campuses. Named as chairman was James Martin, president of the Massachusetts Mutual Insurance Company; the balance of appointees largely represented private higher education and high-technology interests. Within the limits of tight budgets (made tighter by the passage of "Proposition 2½" tax limitation initiative), strong liberal arts programs and high-technology priorities cannot long coexist. Although the Dover Project was dismantled in 1981 and the regents have had some sobering lessons in the politics of education, they have since begun to develop a five-year plan consistent with their financial and ideological orientation.

Therefore, in all the major areas of higher education public policy, the lesson is clear: if the market model and its quantitative applications are accepted as a means of determining where higher education should go, one is inevitably led to the acceptance, as well, of policies that threaten the survival of public higher education and its liberal arts curriculum. Effective opposition to those policies cannot logically be developed within the limits of the market model. The necessity for such opposition becomes more critical in light of the ideology and policies of the Reagan and now the Bush administrations, as well as what appears to be a return of the fiscal crisis on the state and local level.

It is, therefore, disheartening to observe that those committed to

public higher education are so reluctant to challenge the prevailing ideology. The usual political response is to attempt some form of compromise. As of the mid-1970s, the Association of American State Colleges
and Universities was unable to be any more inventive than suggesting
"federal programs which benefit private colleges as well as public colleges" or any more daring than proposing that "federal and state governments should consider very carefully the extent to which public funds
should go into making it possible for students to attend very expensive
institutions."(25)   Since that time a more militant tone has developed,
but the overall reluctance to challenge basic ideological assumptions has
not changed.   The result is self-defeating battles over how much tuition
will increase, what amount of public money should go to private colleges,
and which liberal arts programs should be replaced. This leaves the forces defending public higher education squabbling among themselves.

What is needed is a more thorough articulation of an ideology for
public higher education which challenges the dominant values and approaches and expresses a politically meaningful and attractive alternative to mobilize its constituencies. Little has been done toward that
end, even in the context of radical or "revisionist" theories of education. Such critiques have been limited to elaborations of the elitist
nature of American public education without outlining a democratic alternative.

There are at least four components of such an ideology which require
extensive discussion and elaboration: (1) a critique of market ideology
and empiricist methodology as applied to higher education;   (2) a statement of the relationship between the liberal arts curriculum and the nature of work;   (3) a clear distinction between the "public" and "private"
principles in higher education, from the public sector point of view; and
(4) a concept of public higher education as an expression of mutual responsibility between government and citizens.

The market model is open to criticism on its own methodological
terms. The authors of one study state that "conceptual and analytical
inadequacies stemming from limited theoretical development and refinement
substantive questions [and] also limit considerably their explanatory and
predictive power." They add that the "market-related characteristics" of
higher education do not fit the competitive market model in any case.(26)
A similar objection is raised by Robert Paul Wolff, who states that the
market is a faulty measure of demand for human needs such as higher education.(27)   Beyond such methodological criticism, Russell Thackrey offers the argument that "consumer sovereignty" in an education market
makes rational long-range planning impossible, and is hence inefficient
as a means of determining the allocation of resources.(28)

There is precious little writing along these lines, and what exists
does not go to the heart of the matter. A comprehensive critique of the
market model/empiricist approach must first of all strip it of its "non-
ideological" veneer and its pretensions to "objectivity," with specific
reference to educational policy. The purpose would be to make it clear

that concepts of education are related to social values and ideology. At that point, one can begin to characterize education as something other than a market commodity. This chapter has attempted a beginning in that direction. There is no lack of critiques of the market model and empiricism in the social sciences, and it is not hard to find social philosophies which see human services, in general, as entitlements rather than privileges. There is, however, a curious lack of specific applications to higher education—or for that matter, to education as a whole. Such a body of literature needs to be developed.

The issue of vocationalization of the curriculum goes far beyond the scope of this chapter. It must be pointed out here, however, that an ideology of public higher education must take account of it. Although the argument is frequently made that liberal arts education is the best preparation for employment, rarely is that argument connected to the overall goals of public higher education. Toward this end it would be useful to emphasize the distinction between the transitory needs of the job market and the demands inherent in the nature of work itself within a given socio-economic context. It can be argued that liberal arts education develops the capability to deal with the latter, whether in terms of individual adaptation or collective attempts at change. In other words, while vocational training gives the individual a leg up in the job market for the time being, the humanities and social sciences—ideally—expose the context of values and institutions which determine what kind of work is going to be available and what it will be like. This ultimately broadens the individual's choice, enabling him or her to adjust to or change the situation, and to be fully aware of the alternatives. Such a purpose is consistent with the responsibilities of a public college or university and with the long-term interests of the students. The full development of these ideas would require a separate study—indeed, the point here is that such studies should be pursued toward the goal of a political program for public higher education.

The third component derives from the observation that there has been too great a readiness by all concerned to accept the exclusive claims of private higher education to economic efficiency, personalized treatment of students, high standards, and, above all, diversity of choice.(29) The recent custom of private colleges describing themselves as "independent" implies the opposite for the public sector: "The very presence of private institutions is a forceful reminder that independent nonpolitical education is not an unattainable ideal."(30) Rarely are statements such as this challenged. In fact, the idea that public colleges are somehow less capable of being creative, innovative, and independent seems universally accepted.

Thackrey presents a different perspective by focusing on the issue of responsibility. The "public principle," he argues, is education open to all, supported by progressive taxes, and "obligated both to be responsible to the needs of society, and to be publicly accountable for the use of tax funds. . . .The private university has no 'public responsibility,' except that which it chooses to assume. . . . To describe such an institution as 'independent' is a contradiction in terms.   It is independent of public control, wholly dependent on its single source of funds."(31) From this point of view, the independence of private higher education is really exclusivity. By contrast, the public sector has the potential to draw upon a wide range of people to both contribute to and benefit from the development of knowledge in the public interest, while maintaining a responsibility to society as a whole through its governing institutions.

That potential has been rejected from opposing ideological perspectives within the public higher education community. On the left, the argument is that, given the nature of our political and economic institutions, real accountability and responsibility cannot be achieved unless they are radically transformed. On the right, the argument is that the market ideologists are correct: government can never do an effective job; therefore, the public sector must remain as nothing more than a special favor to lower-income groups or must seek justification within the limits of the market model.

The point of this chapter has been that the conservative argument and its variations are contradictory and self-defeating and cannot be used effectively as a basis for the defense of public higher education. This leaves the question of the extent to which government and citizens are mutually responsible for higher education within the present social context.

Most "revisionist" historians of public education have presented the argument that its development is consistent with the elite interest in dominating the masses. Assuming this perspective is accurate, one is left at a political dead end. If one assumes along with Bowles and Gintis that "the emergence and evolution of [public education] . . . represented an outgrowth of the political and economic conflict arising from development],"(32) one can draw on a tradition of democratic values to formulate a contemporary ideology.

If public higher education is the outgrowth of conflict between adherents and opponents of democratic processes, it is worthwhile to explore the more progressive aspects of its historical development and to relate them to the present. The Morrill Act, for example, may have been open to varying interpretations of its purpose, especially in terms of the issue of vocational versus liberal arts education, but Brubacher and Rudy have a point in stating that it "stood pre-eminently for the principle . . . that every American citizen is entitled to receive some form of higher education."(33) Although Robert Paul Wolff's argument that the covert purpose of the ideal of social service by the university to society is "to rationalize and legitimate the existing policies . . . of American society"(34) made some sense in the context of the Vietnam era, it ignores a nobler history. The "Wisconsin Idea" of a university-government alliance in the public interest, and an extension of the university's services to the people of the state, occured in a far more progressive context. That there is no such context at this point in United

States history does not invalidate the potential for such a role for public higher education.

A prime contemporary example of these traditions in public higher education was the Open Admissions policy at the City University of New York [CUNY], which made all local high school graduates eligible for admission to the network of CUNY community colleges. It was, as Ira Shor points out, "born by popular protest ahead of state implementation. Public policy was almost written in the streets."(35) Open Admissions was neither new nor revolutionary, but in combination with free tuition it was profoundly radical yet squarely within American tradition, taking seriously the right to education as a responsibility of government. It simultaneously took the American Dream at its word and exposed its contradictions, thus deepening the understanding of those involved of what a struggle for public higher education really meant. Open Admissions appealed to a racially and ethnically diverse constituency and united them. It embodied the type of program that would arise out of a concept of public higher education as a social responsibility, posing an explicit challenge to the free market calculus of benefits. For these reasons, it was passionately defended and vehemently opposed; it posed the issues all too clearly.

Public higher education as a mutual responsibility between government and citizens means that the state owes citizens the right to an education adequate for them to be involved in making decisions that affect them, and citizens have the obligation to use what they have learned in a socially responsible manner and to repay the society in some way. This might mean nothing more revolutionary than free tuition repaid by progressive taxes, or it might mean professional education repaid by a period of national service. The specifics have to be worked out politically, but the principle needs to be established now, within the framework of a critique of market ideology, vocationalization, and publicly subsidized private schools and colleges.

Far from requiring the development of an advanced political ideology, the ultimate defense of public higher education lies in an understanding of the history of American education and the adherence to its most progressive and democratic traditions. There is no need to be more modern or empirical or objective than the Workingmen's Party of Philadelphia, which stated its philosophy of education 150 years ago:

The original element of despotism is a monopoly of talent, which consigns the multitude to comparative ignorance, and secures the balance of knowledge on the side of the rich and the rulers. If then the healthy existence of a free government be . . . rooted in the will of the American people, it follows as a necessary consequence, of a government based upon that will, that this monopoly should be broken up, and that the means of equal knowledge, the only security for equal liberty, should be rendered, by legal provision, the common property of all clas-

ses. . . . Until the means of equal instruction shall be equally secured to all, liberty is but an unmeaning word, and equality an empty shadow.(36)

4 The Therapeutic Classroom: A Critique and an Alternative
JEAN BETHKE ELSHTAIN

Are students patients? Are teachers doctors bringing medicine to make the ill well? If these questions startle, or seem ill-placed, it may be because we ("we" being those engaged in the pedagogical enterprise) are so thoroughly immersed in the *therapeutic mentality* that we do not realize the presumptions we bring to bear in the classroom which aim to turn it into the academic analogue of the therapist's couch. The chapter that follows involves a critique of the *therapeutic classroom* described previously,(1) and then articulates an alternative that defines the enduring strengths and excellences of an earlier pedagogical mode without falling into a nostalgic tribute to the (putative) "good old days" when teachers had unquestioned authority and students knew their place. This alternative, though more broadly applicable, will focus most specifically on the pitfalls and possibilities of "feminist pedagogy."

Within the emotional hothouse of the therapeutic classroom, students are encouraged to bring forward their unfinished "emotional business," for in so doing, they will accomplish several things. First, they will become less artificially repressed and this will, presumably, promote learning. Second, they will create a "sense of community" in contrast to the nasty rigidity that pertains to the "authoritarian scholar/lecturer" model of the classroom. It is worth examining this image and the presumptions that underlie it, with a skeptical eye.

The presumption is that students are distressed, isolated, helpless, dominated by feelings of worthlessness, anxiety, and "invalidation," propelled by incompletely expressed and painful "unfinished emotional business" which makes them appear "stupid, tense, rigid, and repetitive."(2) It may seem odd for a teacher--particularly one who claims to represent some sort of radical perspective--to regard pupils in such a demeaning manner. But by construing students as semi-comatose emotional wrecks, the teacher has the nearly irresistible opportunity to act as a therapist, using the classroom as an exercise in group therapy. For the claim is that it is only when students' collective and individual emotional problems are dealt with that something called "learning" can take place. Students preoccupied with their personal lives, shattered by "bad experiences," must be shored up with "good vibes" and positive "validation," and this can only be done by allowing them to "vent" their personal problems. The teacher facilitates all this venting by rejecting the traditional model, in which the teacher is a scholar-lecturer, because that would be labeled "authoritarian." Since no one wishes to be authoritarian, the label puts us off immediately; this negative construal of what teachers have traditionally done is a set-up to push us away from anything that smacks of past practice.

The preferred mode for the therapeutic classroom is one in which various strategems and techniques are deployed to get students busy finishing their emotional business and, simultaneously, to teach them in an atmosphere of warmth and support. Through these strategems the teacher helps students reach the optimum place—where they will feel secure enough to bring forward all the emotional content that is presently crippling them; hence the emphasis on skillful management and "good vibes." The unstated assumption, of course, is that student preferences, were they known, would mesh with those of the kind teacher-therapist who, where emotional business is concerned, clearly knows best. But she or he cannot let the cat out of the bag straight off or students would retreat further into their repressed shells.

Approaching students as *patients* who are sick, rather than *subjects* who act and think, lends itself to a manipulative approach in the classroom. The traditional authoritarian classroom is explicitly condemned as coercive. The alternative put forth by the therapist-pedagogue is called communitarian or egalitarian or democratic because the teacher has repudiated coercion, even her or his own authority. But this produces other results. Manipulation through "good vibes" slides all too easily into a *covertly* coercive model when students are not informed in advance that they are regarded as sick, nor told in advance that the teacher sees the classroom as therapy to cure them. At least when one is being overtly coerced one knows who is doing what to whom; within a manipulative environment, where a teacher has a hidden agenda, students are treated with less dignity and respect, for all the pedagogical cards are not out on the table.

In explicitly repudiating teacher authority, having relabeled it authoritarianism, hence bad, the classroom therapist accepts a more insidious exercise of power. Power that comes masked in the mandate to "feel good" cannot be confronted directly by the student. Coercion, however, can: the student knows who is being a bully. Within a manipulatory framework the student does various exercises for her or his own good, not because they have some intrinsic value but because the teacher, having eschewed authority, nonetheless has the power to insist upon them. To accept this defense of the teacher's power is to countenance the use of manipulative power--more insidious because it is disguised and dishonest.

Defenders of therapeutic pedagogy claim that a noncoercive, nonmanipulatory option is available. But first it is necessary to explain the substance of the learning that is to go on once the noxious weeds of repression and bad feelings have been extirpated.

Part and parcel of psycho-pedagogy and the therapeutic classroom is a notion, often implicit but sometimes explicitly framed, that most traditional learning in authoritarian classrooms was useless, foisting off on abject, passive students irrelevant material aimed at shoring up authoritarian structures or promoting an elitist view of culture. The objections run along two parallel lines: first, that the method (scholar-lecturer) was bad by definition, and, second, that the content of what was being taught was either pointless or ultimately pernicious, having no higher aim than gearing most students for second-class status and lives of limited aspiration and unlimited oppression, or nearly so. This made learning a painful weapon used to club students over the head that, once internalized, became an enemy within doing society's dirty work in the inner recesses of student minds.

Concern with method leads therapeutic pedagogues to an obsessive concentration on classroom strategems and tactics to get students feeling good and unthreatened. A series of demeaning exercises are frequently deployed to this end, including something called "news and goods." This tactic is applied to college-level classrooms, although it was initiated in elementary school classrooms as "show and tell." "News and goods" generally occurs at the beginning of each class period. It consists of sharing something "nice" with the class. The teacher participates by offering up some piece of her or his personal life--perhaps a song. This presumably creates "good feelings" that further buttress classroom "community." A second recommended strategem is the "cocktail mix," a period during which students are asked to write conversational topics on tags which they then pin on their shirts or blouses. Tagged students wander the classroom, seek out someone with an interesting tag, and talk for ten minutes. Then it is time to make new tags in order to facilitate fresh conversations.

Recommendations for proper reaction to traditional curricula are problematic and patronizing to students. It is difficult to find time for learning in the therapeutic classroom because so much time has been spent helping students to deal with bad feelings. The therapeutic teacher's work is never done in this regard. The upshot is that the content of student discourse in the classroom is always suspect, viewed as bearing some hidden emotional freight or import that is surely more vital than the intellectual substance of what the student is saying. This means there is a good chance that substantive questions will be ignored or slighted, while the suspected symptom motivating the utterance is scrutinized by drawing the student out with leading questions that aim to get at the repressed material.

But teacher-therapists must be teaching something and they must fig-

ure out some way to evaluate how students are doing with reference to
what is being taught and, presumably, learned. Widely shared recommendations in this regard include a refusal (on the presumption this is somehow, in itself, a radical gesture) to require the usual papers or examinations. Students are often asked to set their own goals, even to evaluate themselves or one another. But because the teacher must turn in a
grade, a contract system is sometimes favored which enables "anyone to
get an 'A' who chooses to do the necessary quantity of work."(3)   The
stress, clearly, is on method with no reference to content. In this way,
the substance of intellectual work recedes in importance.

Content seeps into the picture but in a diluted form, encapsulated
in the imperative that the substance of what is being taught must be
"relevant right away, if it doesn't relate to immediate social or personal issues, we say, that it is really useless, and we are exploiting the
students by teaching it."(4)   This is a most unfortunate argument.   In
the name of radical teaching and helping students feel better, it thoroughly undermines their capacity to think through difficult subject matter, to absorb themselves for the sheer joy of it in texts by great
thinkers and writers who exemplify a particular mode of excellence. Rather than countering the trend toward the new practicality that, in practice, promotes anti-intellectualism and locks students, particularly
those in public higher education, into second-rate standards under the
presumption that they ought to be gearing themselves for the world "as it
is," therapeutic pedagogues serve this end. (Preparing for 'reality'
roughly translates into employability along the lines of current market
demand.) Though this, surely, is not what teacher-therapists who fancy
themselves 'radical' have in mind, it is precisely what their methods
promote in the end. In conceiving of the classroom in instrumental
terms--with the explicit political aim of turning out a particular product, of constituting students into objects of particular kinds--therapeu-
tic teachers join hands with those they ostensibly oppose. In their theoretical presumptions and their insistence on instant results they, and
celebrants of the new practicality are brothers and sisters under the
skin. Theirs is a position not unlike one attacked by Antonio Gramsci as
implicitly reactionary when he lamented the burgeoning of vocational
schools ("those designed to satisfy immediately produced interests") and
the demise of the traditional, formative, or classical school. The
thrust toward practicality, with its insistence on the immediately usa-
ble, was only apparently democratic; in fact, Gramsci concluded, "It is
designed not merely to preserve social differences but to crystallize
them."(5)

The method and presumptions of therapeutic pedagogy, with its celebration of manipulative techniques and its downgrading of intellectual
content, conduces toward and legitimates a profoundly anti-intellectual
and crude instrumentalism. One might counter with the argument that the
therapeutic teacher has, so to speak, "bigger fish to fry." That is,

she or he is out to smash capitalism or bring down authority or, less
apocalyptically, to promote equality or participatory democracy. To attain these good ends, the argument implicitly runs, one must do what is
necessary. However, the methods deployed do not, it would seem, attain
the ends sought. But more important, these good ends do not justify
means that demean students and push them toward positions and goals of
the teacher but of which students are not fully appraised. This is to
reduce students, human beings, to the status of objects. This is to lock
radicals into a morally obnoxious posture that bodes ill for the future
world to be created in their political and ideological image. As Paolo
Freire warns, the radical should not become the "prisoner of a 'circle of
certainty' within which [she or] he also imprisons reality."(6)

As argued above, the contrast model usually posed--traditional
classrooms versus radical or therapeutic classrooms--is wrong and tends
to wash out other options. There is a better alternative that draws from
the traditional image an insistence that teachers do have something to
offer and must openly acknowledge, not cagily deny, their authority in
the classroom and retains the belief that intellectual rigor and academic
standards are vital and important. We can draw from the therapeutic pedagogues their genuine concern for students (although their techniques and
presumptions are ill-placed), and their insistence that student lives and
experiences not be split entirely from the pedagogical enterprise.

A teacher-led pedagogical enterprise of the sort called for need not
necessarily lead to coercive classroom methods--this link is a contingent, not a necessary one. What animates the insistence that teachers be
teachers and not facilitators, pals, or therapists is a recognition that
learning and experience count for something (crude leveling is one of the
tendencies of our society that radicals and feminists should do all in
their power to oppose) and that we cheat students by pretending we are
all "equals" when they rightfully look to us for what our learning and
experience might offer them. This does not mean every teacher *deserves*
respect; the office, after all, should not be equated with the person in
terms of how students are to formulate their judgments concerning individual teachers. Rather, the argument is that the office itself bears authority intrinsically related to the ends for which that office exists,
and requires holders of that office to carry out, with responsibility and
decency, those ends. That individual teachers so often disappoint students should not surprise us. It should, however, disappoint us. But
this disappointment should lead to a call for better teachers, not to
silly or ill-conceived plans to replace authoritarian teachers with good-
vibe therapists.

The task of the teacher-led classroom is learning. It is not to
feel good, nor to create an instant community, nor to presume some inti-
macy that does not exist and is inappropriate in any case. Ideally, the
classroom is a forum within which attempts at persuasion rather than coercion or manipulation take place. To repudiate learning and the traditional notion of "wisdom" is to capitulate to the structural imperatives

of advanced capitalist society which precisely work to homogenize experience and to eliminate distinction.   Learning and persuasion are the key
elements, then.   Persuasion because it preserves the student's moral autonomy to accept or reject that which is being taught.   Learning because
the life of the mind has intrinsic joys and because the discipline associated with, indeed required by, the genuine pursuit of knowledge is necessary to attain self-respect and to achieve the moral autonomy required
if we are to stand up against repressive powers-that-be.

Before turning to the specific implications of this argument as a
mode for teachers of feminist sensibilities, a few words are in order on
what is all-too-often construed as a necessary fissure between the twin
goods of equality and excellence in education.   That so many have been
seduced into believing these imperatives are at odds with one another may
help to account for the emergence of the therapeutic classroom that, mud-
dle-headedly, aims to promote equality, often confused with levelling, by
rejecting supposedly elitist demands and standards.

Those who have suffered most from the institutionalization of such
presumptions are inner-city underclass children, both white and black.
At one point the prevailing view was that they really could not be expected to learn much, so little could be demanded of them in an academic
sense.   Instead, the emphasis was on taking the edge off some of the
worst effects on behavior and personality of their "culture of poverty."
These demeaning views have been successfully challenged by some inner-
city teachers within the public schools; more often, however, they have
been challenged by forceful and unique teachers (Chicago's Marvella Evans
comes to mind) who have had to go outside the structure to set up classrooms that demanded much of the "disadvantaged" young, including reading
classical texts, and much, as a result, was learned.   The consequence of
such immersion in a classical curriculum, illuminated by examples drawn
from their own lives, has been, by all accounts, an upsurge in pride and
self-respect.

Equality and excellence must go hand-in-mind. To junk excellence in
the name of equality, or what passes for it, is to capitulate to the most
mindless tendencies of our perilous age. This holds doubly true for feminist pedagogy.(7) My focus here will be on how those teaching feminist
theory and politics can incorporate concern with individual students and
their life experiences into a teacher-led enterprise that stresses excellence and close attention to textual exegeses.   The teacher must insist
at the start that a classroom is not, and cannot be, a support group.
Although consciousness may ultimately be raised, consciousness-raising, a
particular sort of highly intense discourse between and among peers, cannot serve as a model for the classroom. Teachers are not peers and one's
fellow students should not have the privileged access into the intimate
details of one's life that are shared among friends.

It is paradoxical that some feminists came to identify systematic
thinking with "male-identification" and rejected attempts to establish
and attain intellectual standards as the basis for coherent theory as un-

acceptable because they somehow were inauthentically "felt." This led
to the bizarre notion, expressed by one of my students some years ago,
that all feminists were under an obligation to like or to agree with all
other feminists, although they might differ starkly from one another.
This is not a coherent stance in the world; moreover, it is a demeaning
imperative that takes up one rule of the "old femininity"--that women
must "make nice"--and raises it to the level of a demand of the new feminism. Susan Sontag is right to insist that "the only intelligence worth
defending is critical, dialectical, skeptical, desimplifying."(8) That
kind of intelligence does not emerge from therapeutic exercises nor from
liking everyone or believing that one cannot distinguish between and
among points of view if they come with the feminist *imprimatur* affixed.

To incorporate a concern with student lives and experiences in a
nondemeaning manner, then, requires that such experiences be taken seriously when they serve to illuminate and to illustrate the broader general
issues and questions being addressed in the classroom. As students bring
previously held, perhaps unreflective positions into classroom discourse
and open them up for scrutiny and debate, they are moving in a manner not
unlike that conceptual dialectic of the Platonic dialogues, from received
opinions and "conventional wisdom" to a rethinking, to what Madeleine
Grumet calls reconceptualization. In Grumet's terms, "reconceptualization means to conceive again, to turn back the conceptual structures that
support our actions in order to reveal the rich and abundant experience
they conceal."(9) This "reflexive scrutiny" need not descend into a radical subjectivity within which experiences are unshared and mutually exclusive. Rather, through the give and take of the teacher-led classroom,
through a complex dialectic between abstract concept and personal experience, between universal and particular, we reclaim the classroom as a forum for decency and excellence even as we reconceive ourselves as reflective human subjects.

One method that Grumet suggests, and that seems particularly apt, is
autobiography--a mode that opens up personal reflections to critical
scrutiny and that links the student, as the *author* of her or his own
tale, with *authority* in the broader sense. (Authority is here construed
as *auctoritas*, the ability to command respect, to gain a respectful hearing. It is distinguished from that authority lodged in an institutional-
ized role.) To be the author of one's story, and to link that story to
those other human stories embedded in great novels, dramatic and compel-
ling social theories, even beautifully abstract geometrical theorems, is
to see oneself, in the best sense, as part of the ongoing adventure of
the human race. It is to begin to shoulder that personal responsibility
inseparable from social concern.

There are many ways to go about attaining decent pedagogical ends.
But to believe that good ends can be achieved through methods and presumptions that are indecent in the sense that they detract from our human
capacities for intellectual reflection, for pursuing knowledge, for plow-
ing through difficult conceptual puzzles, is to pursue a chimera. We, as

teachers, should leave therapy to therapists' offices and take up once again the responsibilities of our calling. In this way we can best serve the well-being of our students.

5 The Dread of Innovation in Universities

ALFRED McCLUNG LEE

Customary sets of ideas and practices are traditional in the European and American social science professions. One or another set dominates the thought and action of a great many of their practitioners. At the same time, each of the social science disciplines is kept alive by the creative refusal of certain individual scientists to adhere to those customs.

"Customary sets of ideas and practices" do not refer to the glittering and hypocritical codes of ethics commonly enacted by professional societies. Those codes sound great. They are meant to appear fine and enobling. They are couched in the moral idealizations of our society. They are the public relations facades for professionals. They are not meant to be taken too seriously by those initiated into a profession's mysteries. Those who try to implement such ethical codes are usually young idealists who annoy the established and who bother even more the older individualists and radicals.

On the contrary, what is meant are the practical modes of actual conduct and rationalization evolved in the operating mores of a profession's exemplars, the theories and procedures on which careers are typically based, the ways to get ahead that every sophisticated practitioner in a given field has somehow come to know. Professional societies do not enact such patterns as rules of conduct, even though their leaders exemplify them in their behavior. The substance of these patterns is passed on from generation to generation by example and by informal and even confidential counsel.(1)

Religious apologists, political and business propagandists, and willing academics have put together the public relations codes of ethics for professionals down through the ages. Practical professional mores, which do not differ basically from one profession to another in our society, have their roots in the modes of operation of ancient tribal, medical, legal, and religious experts. These mores have been nurtured as

well as exemplified down through the ages by their successors. They provide the working pattern for professionalism as it is seen today in the
usual behavior of the vast majority of clergymen, physicians, lawyers,
social scientists, and other specialists.

The situation is such that we can rather accurately apply to the
present European-American academic scenes a statement of Francis Bacon in
his 1605 *Advancement of Learning Divine and Humane*. He asserted,
"Amongst so many great foundations of colleges in Europe [and now, I
would add, in the United States] I find it strange that they are all dedicated to professions, and none left free to arts and sciences at
large."(2) To be sure of their chances to survive in our plutocratic
capitalistic society, most scientists and artists accept the notion that
they must first of all be assimilated professionals, people who know
their place and role in the existing power structure and who will work
contentedly within it. For a social scientist who wishes to be creative,
these terms of operation leave unopened many doors to intellectual exploration and experimentation. They make the social scientist an apologist and a technical tool for those who dominate the status quo.

Many would-be scientists and artists in our society are tempted by
the great adventures and beauties and opportunities for human service to
be found in free-ranging thought of an innovative sort. Those possibilities entice the more idealistic students. Early on, however, they learn
the problems traditionally associated with devotedly engaging in such activities. Teachers advise them that those pursuits lead to an individualistic struggle against vested interests, that daring might cost young
academics chances at beginning jobs, or at the least the security of a
continuing contract after a trial period. At the same time, signs over
other gates to careers tempt social science novices with promises that
they can still be intellectually free and creative even though they have
to make careerist compromises. By the time they have pierced the hypocrisy of those promises, if they ever do, they will be so shaped by their
professional socialization that they will not want or be able to change
course.

As Ralph Waldo Emerson said in his 1841 essay, *Self-Reliance:* "Society is a joint-stock company, in which the members agree, for the better security of his bread to each shareholder, to surrender the liberty
and culture of the eater. . . . It loves not realities and creators, but
names and customs."(3) Or, in words that reflect Bertrand Russell's own
lifelong struggles against the anti-intellectualism of vested privilege,
"Men fear thought as they fear nothing else on earth--more than ruin,
more even than death. Thought is subversive and revolutionary, destructive and terrible; thought is merciless to privilege, established institutions, and comfortable habits; thought is anarchic and lawless, indifferent to authority, careless of the well-tried wisdom of the ages. . . .
Thought is great and swift and free, the light of the world, and the
chief glory of man."(4)

What, then, is this informal set of practices in terms of which pro-

fessionals thrive behind pretentious facades of idealistic ethical codes
and linguistically ornate technology and theory?   Let us look briefly at
the nature of those practices and then examine their relation to their
chief products--overwrought methodology, apologies for the status quo,
and abstract theory of an intolerant and sectarian sort.

Oversimply and too optimistically, Karl Marx and Friedrich Engels in
The Communist Manifesto (1847) claimed that the "bourgeoisie has stripped
of its halo every occupation hitherto honored and looked up to with rev-
erent awe. It has converted the physician, the lawyer, the priest, the
poet, the man of science into its paid wage laborers."   On the contrary,
the halo was just made into a more standardized item of adornment.   And
the professionals mentioned only became "paid wage laborers" in part.   To
the extent that they could, with the aid of professional associations,
they tried to act like members of the bourgeoisie, the class Engels regarded as including "modern capitalists, owners of the means of social
production and employers of wage labor."(5)

Except for job-holding technicians and rare innovative individuals,
professionals adapt to their vocations the huckstering and manipulative
methods common to other contemporary business speople.   Even where they
have salaried connections, as in the case of university professors, they
are often not content to teach and conduct independent research; they
also seek research assignments under contract or grants with which to
swell their incomes by exploiting students and junior colleagues.   Even
the once individualistic enterprise of writing a textbook has in some cases now become a profitable product of an academic sweatshop, written under an entrepreneurial professor's direction by anonymous "collaborators"
paid largely in terms of an alleged gain in "experience."

It should be granted, however, that in order to operate, society
needs great platoons of technicians who can and will fulfill the promise
of their trade, vocation, or profession in a fairly conscientious manner.
They need not be innovative.   In fact, those they serve usually prefer
that they should not be innovative. The chief problem that routine technicians present to their customers, clients, patients, or students is the
possibility that they might distort their services for purposes of self-
interest. In our plutocratic society, that is a very real possiblity,
even a probability.

The informal patterns for conduct traditional in European-American
professional groups are thus characterized by exaggerated self-interest,
by as much exploitation of opportunities for individual or collective
gain as the practitioners assume they can get away with.   In medicine,
this means seeing as many paying patients per hour as possible, splitting
fees with cooperating specialists, and prescribing as many expensive sur-
gical and other procedures as the traffic, insurance carriers, and people's anatomies will bear. In law, the practices include the unwarranted
prolongation of litigation, the unnecessary legal requirement to use lawyers for a wide variety of simple actions and clearances, and special
deals between supposedly opposing attorneys. The manner in which too

many lawyers prey in subtle or crude ways upon the estates of the de-
fenseless deceased and their beneficiaries is an old story. Illustra-
tions have already been given of the chief procedures through which pro-
fessionally assimilated university professors exploit their statuses—
self-serving practices that their ethical codes and association ethics
committees try to excuse or disguise.

When we look into the social behavior of social science practitioners, one of the chief emphases that confronts us is the maintenance not
so much of a discipline as of a thriving body of technicians. The problem becomes how in our society a social science discipline can thrive as
a science, how it can contribute to a more accurate and inclusive por-
trayal of the nature of human society, how it can be made to serve more
comprehensively the needs of people, including oppressed and exploited
people; in other words, how it can become an instrument to make society
more livable.

Attacking that problem depends chiefly upon the services of those
who refuse to adhere to the informal operating mores traditional among
professionals in capitalistic society. It requires social scientists
like Jane Addams, Thorstein Veblen, Mary Ellen Richmond, and W. I. Thomas
who could not wangle the protection of academic tenure in any university.
It requires social scientists like William Graham Sumner, whose tenure
kept his radical attacks on capitalism, on our plutocratic government,
and on imperialism from having him drummed out of the faculty of Yale U-
niversity. It requires social analysts like Karl Marx, Friedrich Engels,
James Connolly (the Irish labor organizer and writer), and Margaret San-
ger (the agitator for birth control), and investigative journalists such
as Agnes Smedley, Lincoln Steffens, George Seldes, and I. F. Stone, who
never held regular academic jobs. The latter group's keen insights may
be too polemically stated to rate as "proper" social science, but they do
not need such a rating. Their influences upon social scientists have
been decisive and constructive.

Let us now look briefly at the three prime products and instruments
of professional practices: methodology, apologetics, and abstractions.
These might also—less elegantly but perhaps more accurately—be labeled
game-playing, brown-nosing, and woolgathering or perhaps cult-building.
In speaking of these careerist recourses of socialized professionals in
the social science fields, it is not intended to belittle the use of
well-indicated and needed research methods and of theories that summarize
accurate social observations. But while methods and theories are essential instruments, methodology and abstractions are usually destructive
masters or mistresses.

To scrutinize pretentious methodology is closely to question its
practitioners about real life situations behind their statistical manipulations, situations that can only be perceived and comprehended firsthand
through participant observation. No one quarrels about the necessity for
the use of tested methods to determine the representativeness of social
observations. Such methods are needed. Too much social science, how-

ever, is based upon complicated manipulations of superficial or careless-
ly derived and assembled data, often elicited by *a priori* questions put
to subjects by untrained interviewers.   So much more has been accomplished by observers trained in objective, participant empathetic perception who try to see and understand people more fully and intimately in
their day-to-day lives and in crisis situations.

Apologetics, or brown-nosing those in power, should need little further illustration beyond what is contained in so many of our textbooks.
Too often students in social science courses are merely told how they can
and should adjust noncontroversially to our existing social "order." Too
little attention is given to destructive influences in society in which
we usually unquestioningly participate. The influences discussed should
include not only those damaging to students and their families but also
to the complicated variety of people who constitute society. If students
were given a realistic picture of how multinational corporations and particularly "defense" manufacturers irresponsibly abandon local communities
and play with international tensions, of how business practices routinely
create and maintain unemployment and generate urban and rural slums, of
the flagrantly class-biased and race-biased character of the administration of justice, of the collusive arrangements between so-called legitimate businesses and the underworld, and of all the rest, they might not
be so bored as they often are with social science classes. They might
even vow to do something to work for a better society when they graduate.
On the other hand, the easiest way to get tenure in an American university is to gain a reputation as a sophisticated expositor of capitalistic
apologetics.

A few words about abstractions or woolgathering and our ideological
sectarianisms: Ever since the days when it was fashionable to debate how
many angels might conveniently dance on the point of a pin, academics
have spun fanciful, clever, and ornate webs of words that only the initiated could really understand and fully appreciate and that they hoped
would attract a cult of those wishing to be the initiated, the insiders.
In many of these webs that became the bases of warring sects, the elitist
theories of Plato and Aristotle were merely restated and elaborated.
When one of sociology's cult-makers, the late Paul F. Lazarsfeld, was introduced, it was often said that there were perhaps only half a dozen or
so other specialists in the whole world who could really understand his
"far out" theories.   As much has also been said about Talcott Parsons'
theories. It would be much more to the point of social science development to be able to demonstrate that either one had actually done a great
deal to improve our knowledge of the workings of human society.   That
would be a difficult case to make.

Abstractions would possibly be a harmless game if they did not so
often give birth to intolerant and conspiratorial sects. However, true
believers in symbolic interactionism, in ethnomethodology, in path analysis, in Marxism, in Freudianism, in sociobiology, in Parsonsian or Mer-
tonian functionalism, and in all the rest cannot but help but remind one

of the confusing variety of Christian and other religious sects or of left- and right-wing political factions. As Ted Goertzel puts it, "Petty feuds between 'quantitative' or 'qualitative' sociologists, or between positivists and dialecticians, may do little more than disguise the substantive emptiness of the work done by those on both sides of the metaphysical barricades."(6)

To far too great an extent, sectarianism becomes an end in itself. The establishment and maintenance of the integrity of a cult becomes a time-consuming and energy-wasting preoccupation. Perhaps the greatest losses to the social science disciplines have resulted from the ridiculous social distances that have developed and been strengthened among sociology, ethnology, cultural anthropology, social philosophy, social work, social history, social geography, political science, economics and related disciplines. The only ideological struggle in a social science that makes sense is one between independent and radically scientific social scientists, on the one hand, and those caught up in conservative or liberal game-playing, brown-nosing, and intolerant woolgathering or cult-building, on the other.

Some people may regard the chief thrust of these remarks to be that one cannot have a viable career in social science and still be a creative scientist. That does not necessarily follow. It is true that a number of creative people have a rough time of it, and that the principal social science associations have yet to support the case of even one creative untenured professor against a seedy and unproductive departmental establishment. In spite of the resulting losses of creative people, the surprising and encouraging thing is that many relatively independent minds make contributions to the advancement of science—in spite of the "system." It is not easy, but it can be done. It requires dedication and astute strategies. It demands a precise grasp of the nature of social roles available and of how they may be used without throttling the user. Sometimes the work of a radical social scientist can best be protected and facilitated by having the security of a secondary or back-up means of earning a living, a hedge against the temptation to conform and against the possibility of losing a job for not conforming.

The best antidote to stuffiness, the best gateway to creativity for a student of society, appears to be active and intimate participant observation in social processes. This might take the form of attempting to apply social science knowledge, of clinical social science, of legal or legislative probing, of reformist activities, or of thoughtful, investigative journalism. It means the involvement of a careful and thoughtful observer in social action situations that throw social relations into starkly realistic relief. Such opportunities are sometimes seized by social workers, trade unionists, lawyers, political activists, governmental officials, and media reporters as well as by those who are labeled social scientists. All of such observers taken together—to the extent that they are insightful—help us to gain a clearer knowledge of social processes. Gloria Steinem, as a feminist movement leader and writer, and

Bella Abzug, as a public speaker and legislator, give us their intimate insights into practical social affairs. Julian Bond and Andrew Young, as brilliant black politicians, bring to their eminent positions insights into the nature of human society obscured from and many times shocking to white Americans but highly valuable as a perspective correction for everyone. Staughton Lynd, as an accomplished social historian frowned upon by establishment historians, retrained himself to become an attorney and now works on behalf of cause organizations, including labor groups. Examples of more strictly social scientific contributors to our knowledge are Pamela A. Roby, Victoria Rader, Frances Fox Piven, and Richard A. Cloward, specialists in poverty and class stratification; Jan M. Fritz, Elizabeth J. Clark, Thomas J. Rice, and the late Irving Goldaber, leaders in developing clinical sociology; Barbara Ann Scott and Paul Von Blum, constructive critics of educational systems and processes; and David G. Gil and Jerold M. Starr, analysts of recent social trends.

Of all these, it might be said, as it was of the late Margaret Mead in an editorial in *Science*, the weekly of the American Association of the Advancement of Science: "Life was her great adventure. . . . Science and the humanities came together at Margaret Mead's hands. . . . She could bury herself in a fishing village of 100 souls and still keep her perspective of a swarming and predatory larger world with equal capacities for goodness and mischief, and dream that it might yet save itself."(7)

It is to be hoped that innovative people will continue to appear and to defy the informal practical mores for professional conduct, the dread of innovation in universities, and remain curious and productive social scientists.

6 Academic Freedom, Literacy, and the Liberal Arts

STANLEY ARONOWITZ

The irony of the current crisis in higher education is that even as successive administrations in the 1970s and 1980s have reduced aid to colleges and universities, the importance of these institutions has grown in all spheres of society. In the 1920s post-secondary education was reserved for two quite disparate groups: those destined to rule America's giant corporations or the state and those belonging to all social classes able to climb into the professions. For the vast majority, working class and middle class alike, higher education was not an option. Most factory jobs could be learned in a few weeks. Skilled trades could be learned by a prolonged apprenticeship, most of which could only be justified on economic or bureaucratic grounds, not on criteria derived from the requirements of the work itself. Shopkeepers acquired business acumen by imbibing tradition, or in more complex enterprises hired a small coterie of experts, mostly attorneys and accountants, to handle such issues as tax matters, bankruptcies, and mergers and consulted bankers and loan companies on investment decisions.

However, as Randall Collins has persuasively argued, we have entered a "credentialized society" in the past thirty years.(1) The degree or certificate may not train labor better to perform paid work; indeed, even in professions such as medicine, engineering, and the law, most knowledge is acquired by performing tasks at the work place. However, credentials have become a rite of passage, a prerequisite for civil service exams, a sign that a certain process of formation has taken place. In Pierre Bourdieu's terms, completion of a prescribed post-secondary course signifies *cultural capital*.(2) The "new class" of professionals and subprofessionals, most of whom are engaged in some form of wage labor, may not enjoy job security in an economy that is characterized by a period of permanent technological revolution, mergers, rapid-fire business starts and almost as rapid failures, and massive regional and global shifts in capital location. These changes have required intellectual as well as manual labor to become increasingly mobile. In both cases, possessing cultural capital in the form of a credential becomes a code of legitimate formation--that is, educational socialization recognized by employers and by the larger society as constituting adequate preparation for occupational status. It tells the employer that the applicant has endured the recognized rituals of initiation into the historically evolved occupations.

The academic system has replaced the old craft and professional traditions that were rooted in local geographic space or occupied a secure place in a status hierarchy. Industrial society obliterated these traditions, creating the problem of how to determine the suitability of a given worker for the job. Recall the journeyman's cards performed this function for the crafts and, contrary to received wisdom, professionals were primarily certified by other professionals until late in the nineteenth century, rather than by schools. Later, state certification was added through exams, most of which were written by those whose professional formation was, for example, through "reading" law, assisting senior physicians, or working for a self-employed professional (usually civil) engineer. As labor became mobile, following the movement of industrial capital, a new mechanism had to be found to assure employers of the technical and, more important, social competence of the prospective employee. The growth of the academic system for credentialing labor corresponds to the rationalization of production and its concomitant bureaucratization. It was the "objective" criterion invented to replace the tradition that certified competence on the basis of impersonal evaluation.(3)

As higher education became cultural capital, we see the passing of the "self-made" person--the autodidact who gained fame and/or riches by entirely individual means. (A partial exception is the entertainment/sports professions, in which the academic system plays a smaller role. However, in recent years musicians, actors, and directors have received more and more training in college departments, which have become primary recruiting grounds for Broadway and Hollywood, and football players are almost completely recruited from the college campus.) Now the term "self-made" connotes a person's ability to rise within a fairly well-established corporate or bureaucratic hierarchy. Since specific credentials are now overproduced (like most commodities), there is no correlation between the degree and obtaining a particular job; the degree, as I have stated, is merely a rite, a prerequisite, a sign of social and occupational formation. Therefore, individual worth is increasingly measured by the place of one's school in the academic hierarchy and his or her place within the school. Since even these prerequisites are no longer sufficient to assure placement, landing a job becomes a sign of worth and presumed individual initiative. Of course, the reproduction of the ideology of status is made necessary, not by the facts of the academically linked labor market, but by that specific trait of American ideology--individualism. In contrast to many Western European countries where students travel through the centralized school system with an exquisite sense of collective fate, American schools are not only localized, but the distinction between the private and the public is built into the status hierarchy. Further, the grading system and the stress on individual achievement reproduces an ideology in which the student experiences his or her difference from all others. The two main points of distinction are presumed intelligence and the value placed upon hard work. In either case, students are encouraged to internalize their own responsibility for success or failure. (The student was bright but fooled around too much; or, despite outrageous school behavior, the student managed to get wonderful grades, proving that no matter what, "the cream always rises to the top.")

Since the content of most work is undergoing constant change, the higher the degree, the less specialized it becomes, regardless of the field. For example, possessing a degree from Harvard, Columbia, or Yale law schools signifies nothing about the quality of the training of a particular candidate, even less the differential acquisition of specific knowledge relating to particular fields of the law. It merely constitutes a basis upon which leading corporations, major public agencies, and important law firms may recruit cadre. A Harvard degree is a *social* credential and has almost nothing to do with technical qualifications. It signifies that the candidate has forged links with established networks and achieved a grade necessary to obtain the degree. Since the corporate mode of industrial organization that dominates all organizations in our society is organized along both bureaucratic and hierarchical lines, the major qualification for a prospective employee is his or her generic understanding of the organization rather than specific knowledge. The lower one descends in the academic hierarchy, the more particular types of technical knowledge are constituted as qualifications, because the work performed is likely to be more specialized.

The academic system performs a second vital function: it reproduces the ideology of opportunity. Here I do not mean to suggest that "ideology" is merely "false consciousness." Credentials are necessary rites of passage to bureaucratic and technical labor; they therefore connote important knowledge for a system in which knowledge is capital. It follows that attaining a degree presupposes possession of this cultural capital. The stress on educational credentials among racial and national minorities and women responds to the labor market. Even those among these groups who were able to "rise" to semi-skilled jobs in the unionized monopoly sector in the 1940s and 1950s have lost their economic niches in the wake of the partial deindustrialization of intermediate technology industries such as auto, steel, and electrical manufacturing. Displaced from industrial labor, many have entered the academic system in order to qualify for jobs in the communications, financial services, corporate administration, professions associated with computers, and other scientifically based technologies. Having arrived on the scene, they discovered

what blacks found when they bought old houses in former Jewish and Eastern European neighborhoods.   During the first rain, the cellar flooded,
the foundation eroded, and the walls and ceiling were termite ridden.

Of course, the discovery that many universities have lost their
groves and ivy to gypsy moths cannot deter the aspiration to post-secondary education. Credentials are the only game in town; especially in circumstances where the work place is defined in terms of the manipulation
of symbols to produce codes and signs rather than things.   In a society
where power and knowledge are ineluctably linked, achieving a degree replaces the high school diploma because it signifies knowledge of how systems work, more than specific technical knowledge for which the student
still requires substantial on-the-job training.(4)

I do not mean to imply that a basic background in mathematics and
physical science is not needed for those aspiring to perform technical
and scientific work.   Nor can the vocabularies of the social sciences and
their logical structures be dispensed with by people wishing to work in
economics, human services, and social research.   I am contending, however, that these types of knowledge are generally available to the dedicated, disciplined autodidact, as much as law and medicine were during
earlier periods of our history. Schools are miniature societies more
than centers of technical and scientific education.   In schools students
learn how to operate within the historically evolved culture with particular modes of organization at different levels of the occupational and
social hierarchies.

It is not necessary for students to internalize the organization to
learn how to function within it; that is, to understand the boundaries of
rule making and rule breaking. Of course, the more habitual knowledge
is, the less conflict is experienced by the worker. On the other hand,
habituation is by no means necessary for successful integration within
large organizations. This is an error common to Marxist and "bourgeois"
social theorists concerned with processes of social reproduction. At one
end, Talcott Parsons's theory of socialization posits the coherent link
between individual family and work place as the necessary condition for
functional completeness.(5)   At the other end, Herbert Marcuse's notion
of technological society requires that its members become "one-dimension-
al"--that is, lose their capacity for critical reflection.(6)   The individuals in both theoretical paradigms are presumed social clones, however
rebellious they may feel.

These modes are reflections of tendencies in social thought that
were dominant in the wake of the rise of rightist regimes in the 1930s.
In the context of liberal and Marxist beliefs that fascism and other
forms of totalitarianism were somehow external or conjunctural to the
history of capitalism, the Frankfurt School insisted that the mode of social and sexual organization produced a new person fitted to the new order. This theory constituted a radical departure from the rationalistic
proclivities of contemporary social and political theory.   The Frankfurt
School sought to explain social domination as a complex of economic, po-

litical, and ideological relations in which the transformation of culture was the crucial condition.   Thus the imposition of a compulsory sexual morality was for Wilhelm Reich a characteristic of the mode of social reproduction, not merely a rule handed down from above to impose a regime of sexual repression.(7)   The individual was always complicit in his or her own oppression to the degree that the option of freedom was foreclosed by the repression of psychosexual needs generated from within as well as externally imposed. Similarly, Max Horkheimer and Marcuse argued that the blandishments of consumer society, particularly its spurious erotic satisfactions, were implanted in the psychic structures rather than being understood merely as the reward for performing prescribed work.

Parsonsian theory asserts the symmetrical relationship between authority and individual action. Students of modern systems theory recognize him as a major predecessor. Parsons claims the fundamental continuity of society and culture as part of a more general theory of the evolution of living systems and argues that the distinctions between personality systems, cultural systems, and behavioral organisms are "merely functional." This position suggests that political and economic dimensions of society are the macrosocial side of a total system in which individual behavior is the microsocial aspect.

Social theory in the period between World War I and the 1960s was obliged to explain the split between advanced capitalist society's and liberal society's tendency to posit the autonomous individual as the bedrock of social life. By arguing the systemic character of power/authority—that it was a function either of social evolution (Parsons) or the inevitable logic of capitalist accumulation and bureaucratic organization (Marx/Weber)—social theory succeeded in abolishing the conception that authoritarianism within liberal society was anomalous. Parsons subsumed the individual under the structural continuity between the individual on the one hand and family, work relations, and the state on the other. The Frankfurt School argued from a utopian position that held up the possibility that people could understand each other perfectly. In order for this situation to come about, there would be no inegalitarian hierarchies of race, sex, or class. Later on, Jurgen Habermas called this a "public sphere" in which an individual in the community possessed communication competence.(8) Wilhelm Reich dispensed with the assumption of putative integrated civilization upon which critique depended. He relied almost exclusively on the historical argument that capitalism distorted the psychosexual structure so that social character became self-repressive and externalized itself as fascism.

More recently, Pierre Bourdieu has invoked the category of *habitus* to explain the subordination of the worker to managerial authority, the student to the school administration, and, by extension, the child to the parents.(9) Like Parsons, he asserts the "specific effect of symbolic relations in the reproduction of power relations." Bourdieu speaks of symbolic violence as the characteristic relation of pedagogic communication that is charged with the transmission of something he calls the "cultural arbitrary" within a framework of legitimate authority. Although Bourdieu remains skeptical that the objects of the cultural arbitrary, the students, are dominated "free agents" such as those referred to in all social contract theories,(10) he does not submit to the view that pedagogic power is imposed by colonizing the unconscious. Power is imposed by a system of social domination by symbolic means through pedagogical authority, but its effectiveness in transmitting the cultural arbitrary is mediated by the strength of oppositional classes and movements. "The relative strength of the reinforcement given to the balance of powers between the groups or classes by symbolic relations expressing these power relations rises with the strength of various classes and the power of the market to confer higher value on the goods delivered by legitimate school authorities."(11) That is, as educational credentials become more central to determining whether an individual may gain access to jobs, good, or economic security, the power of the educational system grows in the system of social domination. The converse is true as long as jobs paying relatively well can be procured without credentials, such as in economic systems marked by technologies employing workers with little or no skill or professional formation.

Under current conditions, students accurately perceive school attendance as a means to enter the power system. To the extent that an oppositional group or class culture generates symbolic relations that constitute a counterlogic to the dominant cultural arbitrary, students may choose to oppose the system of school-induced rewards by fighting authority. In effect, they respond to another authority system, one that places high social and economic value upon factory labor, street life, or participation in the underground economy that is another labor market. Of course, students may not always be aware of the specific options they are choosing, but this is not the same as socialization or technological or psychosexual domination. This lack of understanding of the labor market is particularly acute when job recomposition is under way and new definitions of work and their prerequisites have not yet become "common sense."

Further, the unintended consequences of refusing certain niches in the market system—those linked to school subject matter, for example— cannot exempt most of us from participating in the market system as such. The boundaries of opposition are framed by the system of wage labor, but there is not superior "rationality" associated with choosing to become a part of the prevailing culture, hence the concept of "arbitrary" to connote a particular mode of participation.

In recent years, because proletarian factory labor is becoming less of an option, alternatives to technical/scientific or bureaucratic labor have been similarly narrowed. This does not imply, however, that the technologized "arbitrary" is more than the most "logical" option, given the international division of labor that has assigned certain functions to the United States in which administration and technical and scientific

knowledge play important roles. Paul Willis has shown how students prepared themselves in English comprehensive high schools for factory labor
by doing badly in school; in the midlands region traditional working
class symbolic relations were able, until the 1960s to exert a powerful
influence by producing an alternatiave cultural system, including a rationality of market value among young people.(12)

    Thus, we may reasonably conclude that the decline of the economic,
social, and political weight of the working class movements--trade unions, social clubs, neighborhoods--will tip the balance of power.   These
losses have specific historic preconditions in the patterns of capital
accumulation, past struggles for hegemony at the work place between capital and labor, the political triumphs for the workers' movement, etc.,
but it is the weakening of an alternative cultural system which accounts
for the growth of school enrollment among the subordinate classes. Credentials are now recognized as the only possible way to enter the labor
market system on favorable terms, except for the minority prepared to enter at its margins, spaces that often entail "non-legitimate" economic
relations.

    Higher education is currently at an impasse. First, demand for col-
lege education has increased in the past two decades, especially among
working adults for whom credentials have been identified, correctly, as
the new condition of market survival in an increasingly uncertain situation. This rise of school attendance among the adult population that was
recruited in the 1960s and 1970s for public and corporate administrative
employment has more than offset, at least in the large cities, the decline of the traditional college age population.   These workers entered
school on the heels of a successful struggle spearheaded by black and
Hispanic students for "open admission" to institutions of higher education.   Having established college and schooling as a "right," the hundreds of thousands of minorities and women who streamed into state institutions in the 1970s were soon followed by adults for whom such opportunities had in the past been unthinkable.

    Without doubt, among the most important democratic achievements of
the black freedom movement and the feminist movement of the 1960s and
early 1970s was the hiltherto unheard of policy adopted in many states
that made a college education an entitlement.   Students were admitted to
schools without regard to their high school grades or test scores.   The
college was obliged, by this entitlement, to offer programs, often without credit, to students entering with substandard reading, writing, and
calculating skills.   In effect, open admission was, from the point of
view of administration, a recognition that the United States had become a
credentialed society and that the alternatives of factory and farm work,
which implied a different set of norms, were rapidly disappearing as viable working class options. The academic system was forced to accommodate
a constituency historically considered beyond the pale of the higher

learning.

To be sure, the University of California chancellor, Clark Kerr, the Carnegie Foundation, and other major educators and institutions recognized the inevitability of this change in the 1950s on the heels of Sputnik-generated demands for an increased massification of higher education. The Kerr Plan provided for a three-tiered system that simultaneously provided for mass post-secondary schooling for those hitherto excluded, while preserving the elite character of the major state universities, the private, northeastern Ivy League, and important regional campuses such as Duke, Emery, Chicago, and Stanford. The junior college was transformed from a "finishing school" for young women destined to enter corporate or old ruling class marriages into the community college that became the repository of technical training for specialized skills. The four-year liberal arts college outside the major "multiversities" or the Ivy League remained an anamoly in the new system and seemed to lose its function. Engineering, teaching, medical technology, and industrial sciences were increasingly privileged in the second tier, as administrators and students perceived that the liberal arts, a curriculum traditionally reserved for preprofessionals, managers, and the intellectual elites, had no "use" in an increasingly technology-dominated society.

Consequently, the 1970s were marked by declining enrollments in non-elite liberal arts programs, and concomitant dramatic expansions in technical training at the four-year colleges and the community colleges. In the process, the union of education and training became the emblem of the new era in higher "schooling."

Thus, the crisis of American higher education consists not only of its budget difficulties that have accompanied the world economic crunch, but also in the contradiction between its traditional mission of providing the cadre for ideology, industrial and service production, and the new demand that it become a multilayered mass technical training institute. The market orientation of colleges and universities is the source of the crisis because, with the exception of a tiny group of elite schools, the function of the transmission of Western culture to society's political, economic and ideological cadre has now been permanently displaced. Those fields traditionally associated with the liberal arts—in particular, philosophy, history, and literature—have found themselves technicized in the majority of schools. They have become "breadth" requirements for engineers and business administration majors, subjects to be tolerated because they are not selected voluntarily.

The sign that students no longer see any reason for choosing courses that acquaint them with the liberal tradition was the recent reimposition of a core liberal arts curriculum at Harvard University, one of the schools Clark Kerr envisioned as true repositories of academic learning. Administrators and faculty were concerned that even the elite university had become enslaved to the labor market and also that the signals students had received were distorted. No, said the faculty, large corporations want educated counselors, not only those trained in the law. It is not a waste of time to ponder Plato's *Republic* for Harvard or Columbia students, only for those at Los Angeles State College or Kingsborough Community.

The consequences of this situation extend far beyond the individuals involved to the sphere of international economics and are multiplied by the shifting position of the United States in the world order.   The new conditions of international market competition place the national economy in greater jeopardy than at any time since the turn of the twentieth century.   The United States can no longer rely on its scientific and technological superiority to rule the world or upon the magnitude of its capital resources.   In recent years, government and corporate policymakers have discovered the importance of a sophisticated and literate labor force for setting the cultural environment for rapid capital accumulation.   Although the extreme technicization of schooling was prompted at least partially by the student revolt of the 1960s, as well as by the economic downturn of the following decade, the attempt to bypass the need for broad cultural formation reduces the chance that the labor force will regain its productivity.

On a wider scale, the precipitous decline of cultural formation among the educated cadre, not to mention the general labor force, makes it more likely that policymakers will resort to military options to solve international conflicts.   Lacking the human resources to comprehend the enormity of the changes under way in the new world economic, political, and social orders, we are in danger of reverting to the most blatant use of force to solve our problems.   In this connection, I want to dispose of some popular left and liberal economic arguments.   Conservative attacks on American higher education are motivated by their horror of the 1960s generation that made colleges the base for political and cultural opposition.   The factor of a ballooning military budget should not be dismissed but this was not the reason for the Nixon, Ford, or Carter cuts in higher education.   The Carnegie report of 1971, which argued that there had been an "overproduction" of higher education facilities and services, was made in the context of the still-powerful anti-war movement and anticipation of the coming economic crisis.   Even though large liberal corporate foundations had encouraged the open admissions movement against educators for whom the standards of higher education would be unalterably eroded, by the early 1970s a certain skepticism had crept into organized liberal and conservative intelligence on these questions.(13) The target was not the community colleges or the major research universities, but the state-supported four-year liberal arts colleges for which there was no function, since most of their students were destined neither for the professions nor for management. These were major sites of the new minority and women students and the returning working adults and became a surplus subsystem within academia.   Their only function was to provide credentials, necessary to qualify labor for bureaucratic jobs, but not for an already "overexpanded" system.

Community and four-year colleges, especially those providing no spe-

cialized training or subprofessional credentials, were under attack in
the 1980s both because social sciences and humanities had no specific
function in the market place for mass technical and bureaucratic labor
and because they represented the victory of minorities and women to gain
access to the credential system. This is the basis of the conservative
attack. Saving the nontechnical programs in colleges is a civil liberties struggle, with its implications for the struggle against sexism, racism, and anti-working class bias in the university. Of course, the
fight to save these institutions is linked to the fight to save the liberal arts. For the liberal arts are not only the foundation of the bourgeois claim to be the inheritor of Western culture; they are also the
condition for acquiring critical thinking in a society where the old labor, socialist and radical public institutions that once provided these
amenities have all but disappeared. That is, in the wake of the nearly
complete transformation of the cultural balance of social power toward
the technocratic classes, a new terrain of cultural struggle is within
the universities, especially the battle for the traditional critical curriculum.

At the outset, it must be admitted that the demand for a new curriculum does not currently correspond to the economic and cultural perceptions of the majority of students, especially minorities and women. The
degree to which their aspirations are dominated by labor market considerations can be measured by the proliferation of technical and business
courses in higher education, the concomitant decline of the liberal arts
enrollments in most colleges, and the transformation of social sciences
and humanities departments into service programs rather than having substantial student majors. With each passing year, English and history departments suffer deeper budget cuts; when a professor retires he takes
his job with him to Florida or Palm Springs; in some cases, the absolute
number of faculty in these departments is reduced by layoffs, even among
tenured faculty; and, most egregiously, graduate programs in these fields
decline because they, too, are subject to the shrinking market.

We have already lost an entire generation (measured by ten years) of
humanities scholars. Only those getting their Ph. D. from a major university (especially the Ivy League, the Big Ten, and the University of
California) can hope to find an academic job. Further, many graduating
from these schools can no longer expect to work in their field unless
they are willing to take high school jobs (a path fairly well trodden in
countries like France and Great Britain). Many among the new academic
surplus labor force are women. At the same time, the veritable wage
freezes imposed in many academic institutions, the frequency of layoffs,
and the shrinking number of jobs have discouraged blacks and other minorities from choosing these fields, or almost any academic calling except
administrative, technical and scientific occupations. Until the early
1980s, qualified blacks able to enter elite universities chose law, medicine, engineering, and practical sciences rather than risk less stable
market situations such as the liberal arts professoriate. The partial

exceptions, history and economics, may be accounted for by the persistence of the black tradition of cultural reclamation that has been deposited in the history profession and the many jobs available outside the academic system for economists.

However, the hardest hit have been women, for whom humanities and, more recently, social sciences became an important entry point for professional opportunities during the dramatic expansion of the academic system in the 1960s. The tenure system that assured a lifetime job for selected teachers has resulted in an aging professoriate, overwhelmingly white and male. Given the economic and ideological outlook of the 1980s, these tendencies will accelerate in both the short and intermediate term. Since women are subject to sexism that has excluded a fairly high number of them from the ranks of the tenured in recent years, it is highly likely that their proportion to the tenured faculty will diminish, even as the proportion of women students rises at all levels of the academic system. Absent a strong feminist movement that insists on the full implementation of affirmative action programs, even the "normal" hiring practices in a shrinking job market will reduce women in teaching positions.

American ideology has always tied the struggle for social justice to economic and institutional expansion. Americans have tended, wrongly, to equate equality with equality of opportunity. The argument is that only if the system grows can the excluded demand and get access to credentialed jobs and other cultural capital needed to enter the labor market on a more favorable basis. We have been less interested in programs of redistribution than those that integrate women and minorities into an expanding market. However, during periods of economic downturn that in the United States have been fueled by the rise of conservative ideologies that tend to legitimate exclusion using biological or cultural arguments that place responsibility on the victim, the discourses of exclusion subordinate the discourses of cultural and economic justice. We are now undergoing such a period. Discharged women faculty experience increasing difficulty persuading colleagues, students, and the media that they have been fired unjustly; radicals find unsympathetic administrations are more willing to overrule favorable departmental tenure decisions.

The late 1970s marked a new wave of anti-radicalism on many campuses and, equally important, a massive exodus by students from political and social concerns in the wake of unbearable pressures generated by the economic crisis, the practices of credentialism, and the increasing privatization of social life. To the extent to which the student movement, including black and feminist organizations, constituted a "countervailing" power base against these tendencies in the late 1960s and early 1970s, it was able to impose its will on administrators who nearly everywhere suffered a crisis of confidence.

I do not want to argue that the economic crisis was alone responsible for the changing political climate; ideological tendencies, particularly the rise of neo-conservatism that has displaced liberal hegemony among intellectuals, as well as many workers, were equally powerful in producing a new climate. The attack on the liberal arts gained momentum in part because its various fields had become havens for a new radical professoriate. Thus the conjuncture of various ideological with economic tendencies helps explain both the cutbacks in the university and the substantial number of politically and sexually motivated firings. Even as Marxists and other radicals gained increasing legitimacy within many fields, particularly history and sociology, they found themselves under severe counterattack from a defensive and embattled senior faculty that experienced its own intellectual bankruptcy while, at the same time, being under pressure from women and blacks to support affirmative action hiring at a time of job shrinkage. These questions bring us flush against the contradictions of the tenure system and the pressures for ideological conformity in the academic system.

Tenure has been under attack since the early 1970s. Conservative critics charge that the tens of thousands of dollars entailed in a single tenured academic job violated the pressing need to cut costs in social services. Academic administrators, encouraged by budget cuts, have replaced retiring faculty with a series of part-time employees whose combined salary is half that of the deposed senior professor; or, when the line is not retired with the professor, will hire an untenured, full-time professor. The new teacher earns less than the retiree and may only occupy the job for one to six years, after which they are obliged to look for another "temporary" position. In recent years the pool of adjunct and untenured teachers has expanded and the number of tenured faculty has been reduced.

These conditions, combined with the dramatic slowing of salary increases, have prompted many college faculties to seek and obtain union organization. In 1982, teachers in the second largest academic system in the country, the California State University, chose a collective bargaining agent, the American Federation of Teachers (AFT), in a closely contested election with its competitor, the American Association of University Professors (AAUP) and the AAUP's ally, the National Education Association (NEA).(14)

Unions have won elections in private universities, such as Boston University and Yeshiva University, as well as various Catholic institutions. However, the prospects for new victories in this sector were considerably diminished by the Supreme Court decision in the Yeshiva case holding faculty of "mature" private universities to be supervisors because they share in decision making with the institutional administration.(15)

Naturally, the most notable absence from this record of union advances are the private research universities and the major state research institutions such as the midwest Big Ten members or the University of California. Here most faculty consider themselves part of the directorate of the academic system, clearly identified with the goals and policies of the administration and, more broadly, the state and corporations. To acknowledge that its traditional decision-making power has been progressively eroded both by the subordination of research to the various production markets, particularly the military, and by the increasing centralization of university management would degrade the status of the faculty. Many faculty members prefer to adhere to the ideology of intellectual autonomy that ignores the fact that research grants and facilities are made available only to those able to obtain grants from government agencies, corporations and foundations. While in earlier times faculty determination of tenure was tantamount to appointment, the new situation presents departments with a "higher" authority in the persons of deans, provosts, and college presidents who reserve the right to veto or reverse faculty decisions. Yet, many of these professors are managers of their own research projects that often employ assistants and graduate students, have power over the careers of graduate students, and are the cadre from whom administrators are recruited. As a result, the large research universities have, with almost no major exceptions, been exempt from unionization of their faculties.(16)

In the other systems, faculty unions have fought to maintain tenured positions against constant pressure from above to retire them. The union defends the institution as well because it holds that this is the only genuine way teachers can gain job security. At the same time, the tenure system has effectively excluded the new aspirants for academic positions at a time when jobs are scarce. Job scarcity affirms trade union resolve to uphold the system of institutional racism and sexism, despite union support for affirmative action programs.

But tenure was instituted to prevent state legislatures, other faculty, and outside groups from persecuting faculty for their political or intellectual dissent. Tenure was instituted to protect free inquiry, particularly radical inquiry, research, and views that contradicted conventional wisdom. It was an institution that confined just cause for discharge after a tenure decision to misconduct of a personal nature or gross incompetence that might result in discrimination against students.

There are still good reasons to protect the minority that engages in oppositional inquiry. But the tenure system has been more often employed as a means to secure conformity among faculty to exclude dissenters. Since teaching in universities is a good job, despite recent deterioration of working conditions and salaries, young and new faculty members are encouraged by the market conditions to become more ideologically and intellectually conservative, or at least to remain silent about their dissenting views. As a result of the pressure to conform, the American academy has become visibly less exciting, innovative, and important as a center of intellectual life since the late 1960s. This does not signify the decline of specific ideological tendencies. On the contrary, as has already been noted, Marxism has received a fairly warm reception in some fields and is tolerated in others to a degree unknown either in the 1950s or in the 1930s; but the price Marxism (as only one example of a radical paradigm) has been obliged to pay is that it must cloak its discoveries, methodologies, and its culture in the guise of academic conventions. That is, Marxism has accommodated to the norms of academic life, not made its own way. To a large degree, this conformity is imposed on Marxism and other marginal perspectives by the norms of academic respectability. The Marxist economist must be adept, for example, in mainstream economics and will often try to present his or her position in the codes of the dominant paradigm in order to gain a hearing. Similarly, in philosophy the past decade has witnessed an increasing outpouring of works purporting to demonstrate the commensurability of historical materialism with the canons of analytic thinking.

Analogously, those interested in feminist and black studies have survived to the extent that they conform to the same intellectual norms. The radical feminist who, nevertheless, works in the normal traditions of the historical profession has a better chance for tenure than the feminist who tries to develop a new theoretical paradigm of women's history that entails a critique on either methodological or ideological grounds of conventional narrative history and the absences therein--particularly women.

The arguments become fairly subtle. Some intellectual conservatives (that is, those for whom the positivist traditions of social science research, such hegemonic discourses as those of analytic philosophy or the new criticism, are obligatory norms for scholarship) argue that women's history or black history are not proper objects of inquiry with methodologically valid sets of procedures for obtaining knowledge. These subjects must be integrated into recognized disciplines such as social, economic, or political history. Similarly, Marxist or "post-structuralist" literary critics still have a hard time in most English departments even if they have wide acceptance in the relatively small and marginal comparative literature programs. Again, nonanalytic philosophers of the phenomenological, Marxist, or programmatic schools find difficulty getting jobs in this field, which is dominated almost completely by various schools of language philosophy. When the dissidents succeed, they are relegated to courses in continental or history of philosophy.

These examples demonstrate the degree to which academic departments refuse pluralist practices even as they oppose radicals on the same ground. Their dedication to normal science, in Kuhnian terms, is completely understandable; the problem is that they rarely tolerate those not engaged in research that conforms to the norms established by the "scientific community." Thus, exclusion from tenure is not often announced on overt ideological grounds, but on the quality of the research of the denied faculty member. The concept of quality is articulated in terms of a prefigured conception of normal science. Under these circumstances, overt political repression becomes unnecessary. Anyone engaged in theorizing or research who adopts an anti-positivist perspective or defines an object of knowledge in terms that vary or oppose conventional definitions may find himself or herself out in the cold. Under these conditions the liberal self-perception of the pluralistic academic system is preserved.

Some criteria for tenure are fairly arbitrary. Among them, the most egregious is the statement about whether a faculty member is a "congenial" colleague, helpful in matters concerning department administration, quiet and dependable at meetings, and good at faculty parties. The cultural conservatism of academics often masks deep ideological and intellectual differences with younger or minority colleagues.   Even through the 1960s the biographies of faculty members tended to follow a few patterns. In general, most professors beat a straight line from high school to college to graduate school. Networks established in undergraduate and graduate schools became, as they do for large corporation executives, the crucial foundation for recruitment to academic departments and have only been slightly altered by affirmative action and the inclusion of radical and dissident professors.

Graduation from a particular set of schools, a certain trajectory of career development, and the same intellectual interests are definite signs of probable congeniality.   It is not that faculty consciously seek clones in their young and new colleagues, but they have formed definitions of competence that are framed by well-trodden career paths, as well as by race, sex, ethnicity, and intellectual orientation.   This is the stuff of which intellectual sterility and political conformity are made. Only with the uncontrolled expansion of the academic system is a marginal deviation from the established patterns possible.

It is worth noting in this connection that recruitment below the elite schools reproduces the patterns of their more prestigious counterparts. Until the job crunch, a Yale graduate was regarded with suspicion if he applied to a community or state college unless the school was located in a desirable metropolitan area such as New York, San Francisco, or Boston. Similarly, when I lived in San Diego and did not have an academic job, my application to a local state college was refused because the committee held it was unlikely I would stay. They argued that since I published more than the typical colleague at the school, I would feel uncomfortable in the surroundings. Thus, lacking counterhegemonic social movements, even a buoyant economy may not permit downward mobility just as it denies upward mobility to most women and minorities. The exceptions to this rule only verify this statement, because few teachers in the Ivy League are graduates of universities not reputed to be at the cutting edge of research, and those coming from these universities are rarely found in community colleges or state liberal arts schools that recruit faculty in the image of their social function.

I want to conclude by posing a question raised indirectly in this article: from the point of view of the new relations of industrial and post-industrial society, is the curtailment of the academic system a rational policy? Obviously, for workers, women and blacks as well as political dissenters, the "givens" of American ideology point to a negative answer: since American ideology cannot, at the moment at least, grant

the need for redistributive justice and will only respond to pressures
from below under conditions of expansion, those historically excluded
from credentials must fight for expansion of as well as space within the
critical curriculum. Under present conditions, the critical curriculum
cannot achieve hegemony over the technical and technocratic orientation
but must content itself with affirming pluralism in intellectual inquiry
and hiring against the conformist tendencies that have gained the upper
hand in mainstream instruction.

But what of those who wish to preserve the *status quo*? Are the current setbacks in the size and variety of higher education opportunities
in their interest? This question can best be answered by recapitulating
the argument:

1. In the absence of an alternative such as the romance of the factory or the streets that animated prior generations of working class
youth for whom college was not only unattainable but also undesirable,
today's workers are obliged to get credentials on penalty of dead-end
jobs, lower pay, and economic insecurity.

2. Getting a degree is no substitute for a critical education, which
is barely available in most schools and, in the nadir of the student women's and black freedom movement, is not likely to remain an option.

3. The distance between the new student and the old faculty, each
of whom has been formed in a radically different cultural and social context, is becoming greater. Thus, the quality of credentialed education
is declining, but students learn about authority through being subjected
to pedagogic "violence," knowledge of which prepares them for bureaucratic work.

4. From the point of view of systemic reproduction, the elite university finds itself in serious trouble, mainly because its own uncriti-
cal traditions, its technocratic orientation, and the market orientation
of students who failed to get the message not to worry, conspire to produce a degraded educational and intellectual environment. Tenure has reduced the innovative possibilities of the universities of this type, but
the most important problem remains the canon of normal science which in-
hibits a "scientific" revolution able to comprehend the new world economic and cultural order and provide students with adequate preparation for
that order.   In other words, the old culture that is not being transmitted to the new generations still grips the professoriate. On the one
hand, this culture must be transmitted; on the other hand, it must be
overcome within teaching and learning, in research, and in policy formation. Technocracy as ideology is unable to generate a culture that lives
with the ambiguities of the transition already underway because it reduced problems to types of instrumental rationality.

Taken together these problems suggest not planned shrinkage, but a
bold program of academic renovation analogous to the program that motivated the expansion after 1957. Radical critics of the academic system
that have linked it to the labor market have pinpointed only one side of
its current role in society. Among its other functions, the complex of

ideas and practices that constitute ideology production and politically and economically directed research in scientific and technological fields and the state is vital not only to maintain the prevailing order, but also to solve pressing systemic problems. If Jurgen Habermas is right that modern societies need not only knowledge for the creation of new productive forces to insure their development but also learning mechanisms to revolutionize their communication competence and to solve new problems that lie outside of economic rationalities, then the university, which has become broadly responsible for intellectual renovation, must itself be changed. To the extent that the academic system is confined (and confines itself) to producing technical knowledge, to that extent society itself is deprived of social and cultural knowledge of which power is, in part, constituted. Thus, the formation of a critical cadre able to span a wide area of political, cultural, and social knowledge is an absolutely essential condition for crisis management. The conservative ideology that currently dominates our leading universities, combined with the political- and class-motivated cutbacks at all levels of the academic system, are clearly opposed to the long-term interests of the system, and, it may be argued, are not even consonant with its short-term interests.

Let me give a single example. Business journals, economists, and the daily press agree that among our most pressing economic problems is lack of productivity. In the new circumstances of the world economic order, productivity is intimately tied to knowledge as much as it is to the surplus extracted from manual labor. Just as the Reagan administration and its predecessors unwisely curbed research and development activities that were not linked to the military, so American industries have suffered serious setbacks in advanced technological industries where knowledge production is central. Needless to say, universities have been the main contractor of government-sponsored nonmilitary basic research and have been the major losers in the current retrenchment. By subjecting university programs, faculty, and facilities to the market system, the United States is losing the capacity to respond to those problems not subject to market solutions--for example, the growing ideological and political isolation of the United States in world affairs, not only from the third world but from its erstwhile allies in Western Europe. As United States economic power diminishes, Americans need different skills and understandings to deal with an increasingly interdependent world. This political sophistication was, to be sure, not needed in the post-war era when United States economic power outweighed its sad parochialism. The American academic system is the only place where a new generation of serious scholars about the world economy, diverse political systems, and different cultures can be educated.

Of course, this chapter is not intended to advise the corporate establishment or the political directorate concerning shortsighted education policies. Rather, it is designed to remind liberal and radical critics that the fight to expand educational opportunity is not only oppositional; it may correspond to the system's interest, and some who occupy the commanding heights of political and economic power may recognize this.

A program that fights to expand opportunities for credentials is necessary but not sufficient to defend the interests of those historically excluded. Equally important is to enrich the composition of the professoriate with those whose dissidence exists in their will to carve pedagogic space for critical education. This project entails an ambiguous struggle for the traditional liberal arts in the wake of their marginalization and new curricula that exposes students to the academic system as an object of social and intellectual inquiry. These must be seen in the context of a larger project to deconstruct the hegemonic categories of social and scientific thought. To achieve this program, a new student movement would have to be created. This is the last paradox of liberal and radical practice: there is virtually no likelihood that substantial elements of the powerful will recognize their own self-interest in saving the academic system from decay. On the other hand, those who must save it will help not only themselves, but also their antagonists.

7 The Decline of Literacy and Liberal Learning
BARBARA ANN SCOTT

It has become increasingly commonplace to compare the university to a corporate enterprise, operating on the same mass-production principle and oriented toward economies of scale and bureaucratic efficiency. It is for this reason that the university is often designated a "knowledge factory," a term which owes its inspiration to Karl Marx.(1) A crucial difference, however, is whether this structural convergence between the academy and the corporation is regarded as a blessing or a curse. For the former, we can do no better than Clark Kerr's celebration of the "multiversity" (which he defines as "a mechanism held together by administrative rules and powered by money"), the emergence of which is seen as both "natural" and "irreversible."(2) For an example of the latter judgment, we can do no better than recall the moral outrage with which Thorstein Veblen more than half a century ago warned of the degradation of the higher learning under the impact of "business principles."

In particular, Veblen foresaw how the growth of centralized, bureaucratic administration--and with it a system of "scholastic accountancy" that standardizes and quantifies--would foster mediocrity, vulgar professionalism, and vocationalism. Scholastic efficiency would come to mean that

> learning is a marketable commodity, to be produced on a piece-rate plan; rated, bought and sold by standard units; measured, counted and reduced to staple equivalence by impersonal, mechanical tests . . . [all of which] conduces to perfunctory and mediocre work throughout and acts to deter both students and teachers from a free pursuit of knowledge, as contrasted with the pursuit of academic credits.

Furthermore, Veblen sardonically wrote, scholastic efficiency typically "pushes the member of the staff into a routine of polite dissipation, ceremonial display, exhibitions of quasi-scholarly proficiency and propagandistic intrigue."(3)

For contemporary equivalents, we have only to think of the compulsive search for "FTEs"(4) (which fosters ever more intense internecine warfare among individual professors or academic departments), the calculus of credit hours, contact hours, workloads, student/faculty ratios, numbers of students commandeered as majors and eventually processed (i.e. graduated), and so forth, to appreciate the extent to which quantitative criteria have come to prevail. Mere expediency has, moreover, meant the degeneration of the academic degree into little more than a "meal ticket" or an extra increment of job security.

Scholastic efficiency has today, it seems, transformed professors into "professional entrepreneurs,"(5) students into credential hustlers, and the curriculum into a wasteland of trivia and pseudo-scientific pretense. The result has been the rapid deterioration of standards of excellence and scholarship and the cultivation, instead, of what Christopher Lasch and others have called the "new illiteracy."

None of this, of course, is really new. Veblen in his day was quick to see how the eclipse of the higher learning by the criteria of practicality and accountancy would, at the same time, foster a decline in academic standards and the rise of mediocrity, both among students and professional staffs. As expediency comes to dominate intellectual and scientific inquiry, Veblen argued, "the volume of work done . . . runs chiefly on compilations of details and on the scrutiny and interpretation of these details with a view to their conformity with the approved generalizations of the day before yesterday." He continued, "Practical or utilitarian considerations guide the course of inquiry and shape the system of generalizations in these sciences."(6) Ernest Becker was equally harsh in his criticism of the academic situations fifty years after Veblen. It is a situation, he wrote, in which

> the student has no control and knowledge does not control itself. The result is a fiendish anarchy, viciously competitive, without standards to measure the value of the competition; the loudest voice wins; the grayest temples command the most respect; the simplest and most striking research gimmicks gain allegiance, whether they are intellectually meaningful or not.(7)

Complaints about the decline in academic standards, however, usually center less on the parochialism of professorial entrepreneurs with their "methodological inhibitions" and "pretensions,"(8) and more on the intellectual incompetence of students and their demands for less work at higher grades. In the collective judgment of the National Commission on Excellence in Education, the nation's schools and colleges are now beset by a "rising tide of mediocrity."(9) Symptoms of the new cognitive illiteracy among students are to be found in the decline of their command of their own language, their minimal knowledge of foreign languages and cultures, their impatience with the major literary classics, and their notorious allergy to history and philosophy. Further evidence comes from the deterioration in average scores on college admissions tests. In 1963, for example, prospective college students scored an average of 478 points on the verbal section of the Scholastic Aptitude Test (SAT); in 1987, their average was only 430. Average scores on the mathematical section of the SAT dropped from 502 to 476 in the same period.(10) Internationally, American students are at a competitive disadvantage. Comparisons of student achievement on nineteen different academic tests revealed that "American students were never first or second and, in comparison with other industrialized nations, were last seven times."(11)

Such statistics together with the qualitative evidence of intellectual deterioration cannot, however, be attributed to the influx of minority and low-income students under open admissions and affirmative admissions programs, as conservatives spearheading the "back to basics" movement are inclined to argue. First of all, the proportion of these students in the general college population has remained virtually constant over the last decade. Second, while the decline in scholastic achievement may be more conspicuous at the public colleges, where most of the lower-income students are enrolled, it is hardly confined to this sector. The new illiteracy is, on the contrary, as pervasive as it is perverse. "Standards are deteriorating even at Harvard, Yale, and Princeton," Christopher Lasch declares. According to a study of general education at Columbia, professors have lost "their common sense of what kind of ignorance is unacceptable." As a result:

> Students reading Rabelais' description of civil disturbances ascribe them to the French Revolution. A class of twenty-five had never heard of the Oedipus complex--or of Oedipus. Only one student in a class of fifteen could date the Russian Revolution within a decade.(12)

Lasch further documents the degree to which the new illiteracy is a phenomenon of both public and private higher education: "Every year, forty to sixty percent of the students at the University of California find themselves required to enroll in remedial English."(13) And New Jersey's Board of Higher Education recently announced that at least one-third of of the students entering public and private colleges in the state lack the verbal and mathematical skills needed to do college-level work; without which, the Board said, "learning is impaired, communication is imprecise, understanding is impossible."(14)

In more qualitative terms, C. Wright Mills desribed the "sorry intellectual condition" of so many students in his day. They were, in his view, seldom "caught up in a condition of genuine intellectual puzzlement," nor did they exhibit any "passionate curiosity" to expand their rather limited intellectual horizons. Sadly, Mills found these students to be "less restless, than methodical; less imaginative, than patient; above all, they [were] dogmatic."(15)

The intellectual mediocrity of today's students has its match in the "forceful mediocrity" (in Veblen's words) of many of the faculty who unflinchingly promote the hoax of *higher* education. In hot pursuit of the "higher skilling,"(16) these narrowly-specialized, pragmatic professors care less, it seems, about communicating the higher learning than in cultivating the fine art of grantsmanship. Robert A. Nisbet has derisively called them "academic capitalists" whose notoriety and power are well grounded in their ability to secure substantial foundation and government grants. To Nisbet, the hallmark of their affluence is less a matter of "conspicuous consumption," than (paraphrasing Veblen) "conspicuous research."(17) Distracted by the lure of the R & D dollar, these professional entrepreneurs, when they do occasionally hold forth as classroom teachers, simply become carriers of the new curricular practicality and collaborators in the deterioration of academic standards. Concurring in this judgment, William J. Bennett, secretary of education in the Reagan administration, remarked: "All too often teaching is lifeless, arid, and without commitment. . . . By their indifference . . . and intellectual diffidence," too many educators have abdicated "the great task of transmitting a culture to its rightful heirs."(18)

The vocationalizing of the curriculum and the routinization of intellectual activity, however, have not been merely foisted upon the academic community by high-level corporate and academic planners or even by entrepreneurial hustlers among the faculty. On the contrary, they are readily supported by large segments of the student population. To most observers, however, students' often-heard demands for relevant course offerings and expedient routes to the academic degree are free and spontaneous expressions of their own self-created tastes, desires, inclinations, and needs. Students, in other words, are assumed to be making voluntary choices which, in the aggregate, create the demand for particular educational commodities or services. Yet this notion of the supposedly sovereign consumer—determining, in effect, curricular content and instructional styles—is just as fallacious as its counterpart, the sovereign consumer of orthodox economics. Neither takes into account the manipulation of student (or consumer) taste and the coercion lurking behind the student's (or consumer's) exercise of choice.

Be that as it may, the new rallying cry of "relevance" conveys a pathetic inability on the part of students "to take an interest in anything beyond immediate experience,"(19) or in anything not emotionally stimulating. Such ill-conceived thinking thus embodies, in Christopher Lasch's view, "an underlying antagonism to education itself."(20) Addicted instead to the practical and the personally fulfilling, to the experiential and expedient in the curricular cafeteria, many students reveal themselves pathetically as mere credit junkies on vocational highs. At the same time, the university, accommodating itself to the cafeteria approach, has "boiled all experience down into 'courses' of study—a culinary image," Lasch wryly observes, "appropriate to the underlying ideal of enlightened consumption."(21)

Equally alarmed by the decline of cognitive literacy among today's students, Stanley Aronowitz finds it to be one manifestation of the "gradual but relentless growth of anti-intellectualism in American life."(22) Although partly a result of a chronic antipathy to conceptual and abstract thinking, such a climate of anti-intellectualism is more recently and more significantly traceable to the proliferation of electronic media of communication and, with that, the dissemination of what Aronowitz calls a "visual culture," fixated upon the concrete, the visual, and the literal. The result is an inability to penetrate beyond the most superficial levels of sensory experience, to associate and dissociate concepts, or to engage in systematic debunking and depth-analysis. Mass culture has thus produced, in Aronowitz' view, the "triumph of nominalism in social perception"(23) and, with that, the alienation of reason and the critical imagination.

Under the sway of this collective mindlessness, "enormous stretches" of world history and culture have, in Christopher Lasch's judgment, "passed into oblivion. . . . The effective loss of cultural traditions on such a scale makes talk of a new Dark Age far from frivolous." Paradoxically, he argues, this loss has coincided with an "information glut" stemming from the fragmentary, "specialized knowledge of the experts. . . embedded in obscure journals and written in language or mathematical symbols unintelligible to the layman."(24)

The preoccupation of many faculty with higher skilling and entrepreneurial hustling, however, ought not to be attributed to voluntarism any more than can students' consumption of curricular commodities. Nonetheless, the conventional wisdom insists that students are free to choose the practical and "relevant" over the theoretical and "irrelevant." Similarly, faculty are seen as free to opt for bureaucratic busywork and specialized research in preference to quality teaching. However, the act of choosing, whether on the part of students or faculty, is itself shaped by value orientations and normative patterns in the mass culture with its fixation on practical, pecuniary, and psychological payoffs. Thus, students' choices must, on closer inspection, be seen as subject to both internal and external inducements and constraints, not the least of which is the threat of functional irrelevance in the job market. The same can and must be said of those faculty drawn by the "cash nexus"(25) into the entrepreneurial hustle. In so doing, they become so many "hired heads"(26) compelled to pursue practical research and eventually to market their "captive knowledge"(27) on behalf of foundation or government sponsors.

Curiously perhaps, conservatives (such as Robert A. Nisbet and William J. Bennett) and radicals (such as C. Wright Mills and Christopher Lasch) often converge in their criticism of the deterioration of performance standards and scholarship in higher education today. Curiously too, many conservative and radical critics often agree on another point:

namely, that pursuit of higher learning and rigorous academic standards
is essentially elitist, although for quite different reasons.   Whereas
most conservatives would exile the undereducated rabble from the golden
gates of academia and thus preserve a presumptive meritocracy of talent
drawn from the privileged classes, many radicals would prefer to open the
gates to all comers but refocus the curriculum away from an obsolete literary culture and more toward the practical, relevant, and up to date.

The conservatives' position is, to be sure, conspicuous for its racism and class bias; however, the radicals' position is flawed, too, for
another reason. In seeking to cater to the underprivileged and undaredu-
cated, many radicals frequently fall into the trap of defining radical
pedagogy as the exercise of a benign permissiveness in the classroom and
a great refusal, so to speak, to cooperate in what is seen as a repressive and archaic grading system. Although prompted, no doubt, by a well-
intentioned desire to break down status and power hierarchies by becoming
equal with students, many faculty have come to preside over group raps
instead of lecturing, to trivialize assignments (if they give any at
all), abolish examinations and, at the semester's end, dispense A's to
all concerned. Educational radicalism, in short, has too often degener-
ated into a mere laissez-faire approach to learning.

That approach, however, has often backfired and become quite coun-
terproductive to the goals of an authentic radical pedagogy. On the contrary, intellectual discipline is necessary to the development of incisive critique and, ultimately, radical thought and practice. While a
disciplined intellect may not be advanced by invidious competition for
grades and for access to higher rungs on the educational and occupational
ladders, or by rigid demarcation between expert and novice, it certainly
must involve high expectations on the part of the instructor, and high
performance standards and rigorous evaluations of the intellectual growth
of the students. Authentic radicals such as Thorstein Veblen, C. Wright
Mills, Ernest Becker, Christopher Lasch and Stanley Aronowitz--to their
great credit--have consistently understood this.

In this regard, the observation has been made that the New Left's
political analysis and activity during the decade of the 1960s was bred
in the fertile soil of the post-Sputnik reforms of American higher education. The crusade for national "manpower development" at that time
called forth a systematic tightening of academic standards and a revital-
ization of the curricular core in the more theoretically-oriented liberal
arts and sciences.(28) Political radicalism, one of the unintended consequences of the pursuit of a principled pedagogical radicalism, was at
the same time a logical by-product of the cultivation of more disciplined
intellects and more exacting criteria of scholarship.

Political radicalism, it should also be emphasized, has often been
an intentional outcome of the quest for liberal learning. As Stanley
Aronowitz has documented, a consistent feature of socialist and progressive labor movements here and elsewhere in the world has been the high
priority given to literacy; not simply functional literacy but, more im-

portant, cognitive and critical literacy—that is, the "capacity of people to gain mastery over conceptual and critical thought."(29)   This, in turn, has meant the absorption, not the rejection, of western intellectual traditions (what is often termed, "bourgeois culture") found in the bedrock of the liberal arts and sciences.

Lately, however, the pendulum has been swinging the other way. In the face of the protracted assault on academic standards and the perversion of scholarship to utilitarian ends, it is little wonder that many students, perhaps most, have retreated from political and moral crusades and sought refuge instead in complacency and careerism. The result has been the routinization and depoliticization of consciousness and the privatization of lifestyles among students and academic staffs.   Unfortunately, radicals have often unwittingly aided and abetted this outcome.

Throughout most of the 1980s, considerable attention has been directed to the literacy problem throughout the school system from kindergarten through college. An array of private and public policy planning commissions under the sponsorship of education interest groups, foundations, and government agencies have been seeking to "define the situation," so to speak, and to develop programs for reform. Spearheading this effort was the National Commission on Excellence in Education, appointed by then-Secretary of Education Terrel H. Bell, whose widely publicized 1983 report, *A Nation at Risk: The Imperative for Educational Reform*, caused considerable furor in the educational community. Similar studies, drawing similar conclusions, were released by the Task Force on Education for Economic Growth of the Education Commission of the States, the Business-Higher Education Forum, the College Board, the Carnegie Foundation for the Advancement of Teaching, the Twentieth Century Fund, the National Science Board, and the Commission on International Education of the American Council on Education. A number of prominent educational policy researchers also published book-length studies congruent to the work of the commissions. Among them were James S. Coleman, Robert T. Fancher, Theodore R. Sizer, Ernest L. Boyer, Chester E. Finn, Jr., and Diane Ravitch.

While this first round of policy planning focused on the shortcomings of the elementary and secondary curriculum for the most part, in quick succession came a series of reports addressing specifically the literacy crisis at the college level. Leading the way was the report released in October 1984 from the National Institute of Education's Study Group on the Conditions of Excellence in American Higher Education. A month later came the National Endowment for the Humanities' indictment of the erosion of the humanities curriculum in higher education in a report written by then-NEH chairman, William J. Bennett. In February 1985, the Association of American Colleges issued its own study, *Integrity in the College Curriculum*, in which it charged that college curricula had slipped into a "state of disarray" and "incoherence."(30) Six months later the Commission for Educational Quality of the Southern Regional Education Board lambasted the unacceptably low quality of undergraduate education, stating that "too much of what is credited as college work is not."(31) This was soon followed by a report to the Carnegie Foundation for the Advancement for Teaching (CFAT), written by Frank Newman, president of the Education Commission of the States, (and known as "the Newman Report"): *Higher Education and the American Resurgence*.(32) Still further indictments came in 1986 with the publication of reports by the Carnegie Corporation's Task Force on Teaching as a Profession and another by the CFAT on undergraduate education at "troubled institutions."   "Driven by careerism and overshadowed by graduate and professional education," the report written by Ernest L. Boyer charged, "many of the nation's colleges and universities are more successful in credentialing than in providing a quality education for their students."(33)

The literacy crusade at the college level swung into high gear in 1987 with the publication of two books by pillars of the conservative professoriate: Allan Bloom's *The Closing of the American Mind* and E. D. Hirsch, Jr.'s *Cultural Literacy: What Every American Needs to Know*(34)-- prompting Alfred McClung Lee to caustically ask of Bloom: "What precisely is *the* American mind?" and Leon Botstein to complain that Hirsch's by-now-famous list of tidbits of information for the culturally literate to know was a "typically American quick fix to ignorance" reducing literacy to "superficial word and phrase identifications."(35) (See the Coda, "Confronting the Conservative Literacy Crusade: Dissenting Voices," for further discussion of these issues.)   If Hirsch and Bloom are especially keen on targeting students for their wrath, the 1988 jeremiad by Charles Sykes titled *Profscam* blames professors, by and large, for the "demise of higher education" that, in Sykes' view, is "no longer higher or much of an education."(36)   Unlike the rather staid (and temperate) policy commission reports, that typically reach only a finite academic audience, the media attention and celebrity these three books and their authors commanded (especially the rather flamboyant and outspoken Allan Bloom) guaranteed the literacy crusade a place in the national limelight and gave it a decidedly conservative cast.

Taken together, the assortment of policy reports and mass-marketed bestsellers that articulate the agenda of the literacy crusade range the ideological spectrum from conservative defenses of "back to basics" and the traditional academic curriculum to liberal apologia for increasing educational spending as the key to upgrading educational quality.   Their common denominator, it would seem, is a call for tightening standards by: (1) developing a core curriculum with emphasis on some of the once-neglected basics--English, history, mathematics, science and foreign languages; (2) upgrading instructional quality by more efficient teacher training and retraining programs, decreased workloads, increased pay, and improved working conditions so as to boost teacher morale; and (3) demanding more of students with tougher textbooks, more homework, and longer time spent in the classroom.

Reminiscent of the attention paid America's educational shortcomings in the last great literacy crisis of the 1950s and 1960s following the Soviet Union's launching of Sputnik, new momentum is being generated to upgrade the performance of our educational institutions. On the premise that all programs for educational reform convey a tacit political agenda, how then are we to understand this new literacy crusade?

Whether the ideological hue is conservative or liberal, the main motive behind demands for literacy coming from the ranks of educational officialdom seems to be a concern for national security and economic stability. The National Commission on Excellence in Education fired the opening salvo with its talk of "the rising tide of mediocrity" generating a "nation at risk," and threatening our "prosperity, security, and civility."(37) The Carnegie Foundation for the Advancement of Teaching (CFAT) concurred, noting that, "Today the push for excellence in education is linked to economic recovery and to jobs," especially in the high-technology fields.(38) On the often-explicit premise that economic productivity is a direct function of educational productivity, the policy agenda of the new literacy crusade is, evidently, the crisis management of the American capitalist economy.

Integrally connected with the economic agenda are important military and political payoffs: securing preeminence in the high-technology military and aerospace field in order to ensure the hegemony of American power in the world. As a panel of the American Council on Education emphatically declared, "Nothing less is at issue than the nation's security."(39) The CFAT concurred, "Clearly, education and the security of the nation are interlocked. National interest must be served. . . . At stake is . . . the place of the United States in the world."(40)

To be sure, any effort to direct public attention to the implications of the "new illiteracy" for personal and social survival is commendable. Yet, the various reports from pundits and policy planners in the academic establishment have some significant shortcomings. First, in their attempts to define the situation, there is little, if any,(41) acknowledgment of the connection between the "rising tide of mediocrity" and the technicization of education, even though such a connection, as I emphasized earlier,(42) is crucial to understanding the reasons for the literacy crisis. In fact, some of the leading architects of the crusade for career education (vocationalism, by any other name) are now spearheading the effort to tighten standards. Among them are Ernest L. Boyer, president of the Carnegie Foundation for the Advancement of Teaching (CFAT) and former U.S. commissioner of education; sociologists James S. Coleman and Amitai Etzioni; Terrel H. Bell, former U.S. secretary of education; and past and present officials in the U.S. Department of Education, the American Council on Education, the CFAT, the Education Commission of the States, the National Science Board, the Ford Foundation and the National Institute of Education.

Second, the educational establishment's version of the literacy crusade puts greater emphasis on the extrinsic rewards of a high quality education--for example, the high-paying jobs allegedly available for high-technology workers in industry, business, and government.(43)   As the National Commission on Excellence in Education bluntly declared, "Learning is the indispensable investment required for success in the 'information age' we are entering."(44)   More fundamentally and macrosocietally, an extrinsic payoff is the successful crisis management of the American capitalist state.

Finally, such an instrumental approach places certain limits on the agenda for curricular and pedagogical reform. "Back-to-basics" is essentially a demand for functional literacy and, to a degree, cognitive literacy within the bourgeois tradition.   It is not an explicit and purposive quest for critical literacy, at least not for the mass of students in the educational system, as has been amply demonstrated by public statements of former U.S. Secretary of Education and NEH chief William J. Bennett.(45) The main concern of the mainstsream literacy crusade is the short-term, extrinsic payoff, both for the individual and the society, not the intrinsic, long-term pleasure to be found in educational excellence.

Thus, the literacy crusade currently being mounted by the educational establishment is fundamentally anti-radical and anti-democratic. An authentic (and, consequently, radical) concern for literacy starts with the assumption, in Stanley Aronowitz's words, that "critical thinking is the fundamental precondition of an autonomous and self-motivated citizenry."(46) This means, in turn, appropriating the bourgeois tradition of liberal learning in order, ultimately, to transform it in the interest of intellectual and social empowerment. Critical literacy, in short, is the essence of the radical democratic agenda.

But does this mean that radical educators should dissociate themselves from the back-to-basics movement just because it appears to have been captured by representatives of the educational establishment? No. On the contrary, a concern for literacy--in whatever form and on whatever level--should be welcomed, as should any effort to contain the technicization and trivialization of education.   Yet at the same time, radical educators need to recognize the shortcomings of liberal and conservative approaches to educational reform, take care to avoid cooptation, distinguish short-term from long-term agendas (e.g., the progression from cognitive to critical literacy), and be eternally vigilant in defending and extending the liberal arts and sciences curriculum. They need, above all, to remember that the broad tradition of bourgeois culture and liberal learning has often yielded--unintentionally, or otherwise--a "radical" payoff: namely, the liberation of critical thought and democratic action.

Part II
Toward Recovery of the
Higher Learning

Introduction to Part II

No one defined the central purpose of a college education more clearly and cogently than John Stuart Mill writing more than a century ago:

> Universities are not intended to teach the knowledge required to fit [people] for some special mode of gaining their livelihood . . . but to make capable and cultivated human beings.
>
> Doubtless the consummation of a liberal education is that the pupil be taught to methodize his [or her] knowledge; to look at every separate part of it in its relation to the other parts and to the whole.(1)

The Enlightenment ideal of the university saw it as the place where independent reason and the synthesizing imagination, social criticism, and self-criticism are nurtured. It demanded passionate curiosity and a dynamic restlessness that, in C. Wright Mills's words, "compels the mind to travel anywhere and by any means to remake itself if necessary, in order to *find out*."(2) It called forth a special sensitivity to the great moral and social problems of the day. Above all, the intellectual's search involved a process of attaining a *gestalt*--a unified vision of what is and was and what might be. Richard Lichtman elaborates the point: "A mind in pursuit of knowledge is one in which the various facets of awareness are active, cumulative and mutually relevant, wherein observation, inference, imagination, and evaluative judgment inform each other. It is a process which depends upon creativity and reason."(3)

The reason of which these philosophers speak is, however, no abstract "ivory tower" conception of *pure reason*. On the contrary, the liberal arts tradition, properly understood, has always held knowledge "to be a function of the good life," as one observer explains: "Pure reason has no place in this tradition, for there is no use of reason that does not have some emotive base and some moral payoff."(4) This is so because reason "cultivates the human spirit" and this, Lichtman adds, provides each person with the capacity to transcend his or her present context "for the sake of a more comprehensive, articulate and worthy" self-understanding.(5)

Today, however, that transcendant vision--that dialectic between the world as it is and what it might be--is jeopardized by the rise of captive knowledge and the new breed of academic pragmatist (as was explained and underscored in the previous section of this book). In that case, we might ask, is there any hope for the recovery of the higher learning?

The contributors to this section rekindle that hope as they provide

a reaffirmation of the meaning and value of liberal learning.   Leon Botstein, Henry A. Giroux, Huel D. Perkins, Elizabeth Briant Lee, Rosette
Liberman, Henri Peyre, Gilbert J. Sloan, and Ronald Colman each, in turn,
offer some workable guidelines for reshaping academic curricula and performance standards in the spirit and substance of the liberal tradition.

    Leon Botstein's examination of the current state of education and
the liberal arts begins with a look at what he regards as the myth of the
time when education really worked.   He contrasts the 1960s with the
1980s, specifically the contexts in which education existed in these two
periods.   The context of the 1960s was one of widespread challenges to
educational traditions that culminated in the belief that education was
not independent of culture and society, as it had often been conceived in
the past. Moreover, along with the critical examination of culture which
arose in the 1960s there came a critique of culture's prime vehicle of
transmission: education.
    The 1980s, by contrast, represented a reaction to the failure of
that reform effort. Botstein points to several sources of this failure:
(1) literacy, it turns out, has no substitute; (2) the political ideals
of the 1960s were far too unclear; (3) it was a delusion to believe that
education was really an instrument of change; (4) the status of teachers
was not upgraded; and (5) because it became "fashionable," higher education received more attention from reformers than did secondary education.
    In examining the decade of the 1980s, Botstein sees the context as
quite different: the country was in a "conservative mood," there was a
renewal of international hostilities, and the economy became a major concern. Given such a context, it is understandable, perhaps, that reformers now call for education to return to goals set in the nineteenth
century: that is, to train people for positions in industry and the military. It was, after all, literacy which allowed people to function economically. Only later did it contribute to their becoming citizens of a
society.
    While our contemporary ideals may appear to be the same as those of
the nineteenth century, as Botstein points out, there is one fundamental
difference: in the nineteenth century, we admitted that our actions fell
short of our goals. Today, we are reluctant to do so, as we graduate
students grossly deficient in skills.
    In addressing the questions which face education, both higher and
secondary, we must tie our reforms to our larger national goals of democracy and equal access to the society's valued resources. What reforms
relate to these goals? Botstein suggests several. In the first place,
there must be far greater emphasis on the development of literacy in high
school. We must have greater expectations of students in the sciences
and in mathematics. Equally essential is knowledge of the world and the
nation, which implies the study of foreign languages and cultures. Finally, we must improve students' abilities to reason and think.

In conclusion, Botstein insists that educational reform is in our own self-interest. We are responsible for the education of citizens who will be capable of dealing with a world that in another twenty-five years will be dramatically different from the world we know today. We must stop deluding ourselves that we are doing all right.

Radical approaches to the analysis of education in a capitalist society have, according to Henry A. Giroux, made enormous contributions in contesting conservative and liberal paradigms. Yet they have several shortcomings, in Giroux's view, each stemming from an overreliance on orthodox Marxist discourse.

The first such shortcoming involves a simplistic effort to find a structural and cultural correspondence between the school system and the factory system, with class domination as their common logic, to the exclusion of factors that might differentiate them and better illuminate the dynamics of both domination and emancipatory action. A second shortcoming, according to Giroux, involves a reduction of the concept of ideology to merely the legitimation of capitalist class interests, neglecting its positive role in mobilizing people on behalf of progressive social change. Third, radical educators have often "failed to develop an organic connection to community people or to critical social movements." As a result, they are prevented from being "actively educative"--a process that involves learning from the experiences and practices of excluded majorities. Finally, there is a need to view the teaching and learning process dialectically, as part of a set of activities that "both enable and restrain the development of collective identities among teachers and students."

A solution to these several shortcomings, Giroux asserts, is the reconstruction of a radical pedagogy. Essential to this reconstruction is the recognition of the distinction between schooling and education. The former takes place primarily in state-supported institutions that transmit the legitimating ideologies of the dominant society and have a functional and instrumental relationship to that society. Education, on the contrary, takes place beyond established institutions and "represents a collectively-produced set of experiences organized around the issues and that allow for a critical understanding of everyday oppression," as well as the task of creating alternative cultures and an active, democratic citizenry.

Reflecting on the work of Stanley Aronowitz in this regard, Giroux presents a model of pedagogy that advances critical literacy and cultural power, while "simultaneously presenting a strong defense for schooling as a public service." Essential to critical literacy is its linkage to "self and social empowerment, as well as to the processes of democratization." Thus, it means an effort to interpret the relationships of self and society "critically and relatedly," to secure a deeper understanding of "how knowledge gets produced, sustained, and legitimated" and, most important, to develop modes of "social action and collective struggle."

An authentic radical vision must recognize the distinction between schooling and education, between instrumental and critical literacy, and, on the basis of this distinction, must advocate and develop organic alliances between educators and organizations within the community.   The goals of such alliances are as modest as the need to gain some control over the content of schooling, and as broad as to nurture the development of alternative public spheres in the service of democracy and public welfare.

The relevance of the humanities to black students and other racial minorities, who of late have flocked to the more "relevant" vocational curricula, is the focus of Huel D. Perkins.   He reminds us that any discussion of the place of humanities in the education of minority students must regard them as both potential consumers and producers.   Minority students, no less than any others, have experiences in life that form the seeds of literature, the arts, and philosophy.   To not educate them in the humanities, either by neglect or by design, is to deny them the opportunity to reflect on that experience and to make something of it. Minority students need to be able to experience truth and beauty, "not for purposes of information, but the elevation of their own lives."

Exploration of one's own life, while possible with no education at all can be greatly enhanced by examining the records of the self-explorations of others--an important objective of humanistic learning.   This is no less true for black students than it is for white ones.   As Perkins points out, the "big questions of life" have been asked since the days of the ancient Greeks; they must be asked by all people, minorities included.

In this essay, Perkins reminds us that all education, no matter what the subject matter, involves reading, writing, and thinking. The humanities can contribute to the development of these skills.   Reading, he argues, must be required of all students, no matter how poor their background.   Only through reading can one develop a sense of appreciation for the beauty of language. Writing is "the way civilization talks to itself about itself." Cultures record their experiences primarily through writing.   This is no less the case with the culture of Harlem of the 1920s than it is with Renaissance Italy.   It was, incidentally, only the writings of those in the Harlem Renaissance which made possible the belief that "black was beautiful." Such a flowering of pride could have happened only because writers such as W. E. B. DuBois, Wallace Thurman, and Jessie Fauset could transmit their experiences to others in the form of writing.

A culture, Perkins concludes, especially a minority one, must know where it came from, both literally and figuratively.   It must have a sense of identity. It is only through the humanities that such an identity can develop and be passed on.   The humanities are relevant to all

people of *all* ages because they capture and transmit the experiences of
being human.

   Sociologist Elizabeth Briant Lee begins her essay by connecting the
crisis of the liberal arts with the crisis experienced by women striving
for liberation from cultural and institutional forms of discrimination
and oppression. Both crises, she insists, "reflect growing and decisive
changes in the world's social economy," although seldom are they perceived as such.
   Historically, the education of women has been fraught with contradictions. Although defended as a means of securing personal and social
liberation, the provision of even a "liberal education" has been no guarantee of any significant alteration of women's social status and self-image; nor have there been significant advances in their economic and social power as a result of the expansion of the numbers of educated women.
   Lee sees as part of the "present crisis in women's higher education"
the renewed emphasis upon more practical and vocational studies at the
expense of the liberal arts. The mere acquisition of marketable skills
"as preparation for immediate entrance into a narrowly defined current
job market," Lee contends, "sells women short." Higher education for
women has historically functioned to equip women for limited secondary
roles in the labor force and in society. Regrettably, the present curricular and pedagogical trends are "scarcely an advance beyond the last
century." The options open to women nowadays, in her view, still tend to
be "limited and limiting."
   Given the higher expectations that women have come to experience as
a result of their strivings for liberation, we as educators, Lee insists,
have "all the more responsibility to nurture in them cultural tastes and
satisfactions along with marketable skills." These, of course, spring
precisely from an education in the liberal arts.
   Lee closes her essay with some guidelines on how education can be
made more liberating for all, women and men alike. Central to such an
enterprise is the liberating of creativity and imagination--qualities
that are developed only by the purposive "stimulation of thinking, of
doubt, of criticism, of experimentation."

   In her essay titled "Foreign Languages and Humanistic Learning,"
Rosette Liberman decries those educators who attempt to "sell" the study
of foreign languages in terms of their commercial value. Whenever education is so narrowly construed as mere training in a marketable skill, the
result, Liberman contends, is the trivialization "of both the student and
the skill."
   Despite the alarming pattern of enrollment declines in the past two
decades, the study of foreign languages must be promoted for its intrinsic value. Perhaps the two most important reasons for learning foreign

languages are, in Liberman's view "to realize one's identity as a member as a member of the human family and to contribute to the welfare of that family." These goals are not to be accomplished solely through the skills of listening, speaking, reading and writing foreign languages, but in the same way that all humanistic education contributes to identity formation and the safeguarding of human welfare, "by developing in people balance, maturity, judgment, wisdom."

Drawing upon her knowledge and experience as a language teacher, Liberman discusses some of the new pedagogical techniques (such as "immersion" programs) for stimulating student interest in and learning of specific language skills. But instruction in the language itself, Liberman argues, must be accompanied by introduction to linguistic theory and "exposure to the cultures of the countries whose languages are being taught."

"Language is perhaps the chief way," she contends, "that people and nations are either drawn to or alienated from one another." Understanding the universalities in both form and content that grounding in linguistics provides, together with the appreciation of the universality of the human experience through the study of diverse cultures and peoples, are among the intrinsic benefits of foreign language education.

As such, the study of language is an essential component of humanistic learning, even as it is a prerequisite for civilization itself. Its discipline is a component of the general discipline of the mind that a general education in the liberal arts and sciences provides. Drawing inspiration from Mark Van Doren's classic defense of "Education by Books," Liberman concludes by saying that it is only through that "profound comprehension" of languages, peoples and cultures that "humanity can attain the maturity by which it can save itself . . . from an atomic and ecological abyss."

Henri Peyre, whose academic career has spanned over fifty years in the United States and in Europe, presents a multi-faceted defense of the liberal arts. In a world made increasingly small by technological advances, it becomes even more important for us to become aware and conversant with different kinds of people and different ways of life. The vehicles for such an understanding are represented by the area we call the humanities: languages, history, art, philosophy. In the light of the prominence of the United States in the world today, this demand for understanding is even more pressing.

Contrary to popular belief, the humanities are not a mere frill to be tacked to a basic curriculum of technology and vocationalism. They represent the link between the past, present, and future. Their timelessness contrasts markedly with the rapid turnover of technological knowledge. An education based primarily on the examination of the currently popular may produce marketable workers for a short time, but it will fail to produce citizen, both of a specific nation and of the world as a whole.

Third, the humanities, properly taught, enhance our ability to enjoy ourselves and our leisure time. This makes them, in Peyre's view, essentially democratic, more so than the highly specialized fields of computer science or business administration to which students currently flock. Any education which narrowly prepares students only for their first jobs will have cheated them out of the opportunity to explore other aspects of their lives.

Finally, several other facets of education characterized by an emphasis upon technology are examined, among them excessive isolation and and excessive precision. The former takes the form of increased specialization, such that even within disciplines, there may be little hope for cross-stimulation. The latter takes the form of reliance upon quantification, however premature it may be.   Together these two tendencies conspire to produce people who know a great deal about one small subject area and little of much else. Such an education cannot do justice to the broader aspects of our lives or to our responsibilities as citizens.

In examining the unity and utility of learning, Gilbert J. Sloan addresses the historical antagonism between the humanities, on the one hand, and the sciences and technology, on the other. This antagonism derives in part from the tendency for humanists to practice their art within the confines of academic settings while science and technology are practiced, by and large, in industry. Moreover, a corollary of this logistical difference is the assumption that the spirit which infuses the pursuit of beauty characteristic of the humanities is absent from the "crass" activities of the scientist. In Sloan's view, nothing could be further from the truth; and to endorse this position not only demeans science, but also limits the humanities.

One only need look at the lives of the greatest scientists of history to see that the passion they experienced in their work is the same as the artist's passion. Citing the work of Poincare as an example, Sloan points to the scientist's pursuit of beauty in the examination of nature. It is simply arrogant and incorrect to assign the pursuit of beauty to the poet alone.

It is not, however, only in the attitudes of scientists and humanists that this antagonism becomes a problem. As Sloan points out, traditional academic curricula reinforce a related distinction between vocational and academic tracking in secondary schools. The assumption, of course, is that whose who intend to enter the world of work following high school will neither have the time, the intellect nor the inclination for the humanities.   It is arrogant to make the latter two assumptions and incorrect to hold the former.

Moreover, the humanities as a vehicle for teaching thinking, in contrast to mere technical ability, are of increasing importance in the world of rapidly changing technology. Job-oriented students and the industries ultimately employing them will benefit from an education that encourages them to examine the humanities in addition to more specialized and technical programs.

In conclusion, Sloan argues that the content of courses taken in schools and colleges is far more transcient than the context in which the learning has taken place. The endurance of this context and the spirit common to both the humanities and the sciences are essential to a truly liberal education.

Ronald Colman argues that the issue of academic standards is central to the crisis of the liberal arts curriculum. Among the functions of high standards are the enlargement of the student's intellectual capacities and, in addition, the assessment for the student's benefit of his or her competency within the academic environment as well as the larger society. While some might be satisfied with only the former, Colman contends, the latter is equally essential, since individuals are inextricably linked to society.

But both of these functions require the acceptance, rather than the elimination, of status and power hierarchies, and this acceptance runs counter to many of the educational innovations of the 1960s that are still, for the most part, with us today. Those egalitarian innovations, in Colman's view, are considerably misguided in that they result in the confusion of an individual's performance in an academic setting with his or her overall value as a person. The two are not equivalent and academic ability, like mechanical or physical ability, is not distributed equally across the society. To pretend otherwise is to foster a dangerous delusion. Viewed in this way, the appeal to defend high academic standards is no more elitist than, say, for the National Football League to require that its players meet the standards of great size, strength, and speed.

Colman continues by discussing certain structural constraints which make the goals of a liberal education difficult to attain. First of all, by the time a student reaches the university, he or she has been exposed to a history of schooling which far too often fails both to spark curiosity and to set rigorous standards. For the most part, high school diplomas today merely reflect attendance, not academic achievement. A second structural constraint is the amount of time the instructor has to devote to individual students. With decreasing support for education and an increasing emphasis on the productivity of educational institutions, instructors have less and less time to devote to individual students. A third constraint, one that arises from the liberal arts themselves, is the increased specialization of fields of study. To the ancients, education meant not only the exercise of the intellect but the development of moral character. In contemporary education, not only is the intellectual severed from the moral, but even specialists within the same general field (e.g., biochemists and geneticists) have difficulty in communicating. All of these constraints operate to subvert the goals of a liberal education.

Colman concludes his chapter by offering some practical approaches to pedagogy to assist the instructor in the classroom.

8 Reclaiming the Tradition: Educational Reform in Historical Perspective
LEON BOTSTEIN

Recent advances in historical research and in thinking about the nature of historical argument have led us to be cautious about making claims about the past insofar as those claims purport to be objective or factual. They show the biases in method and ultimate values of the observer. This is especially true in the history of educational reform, because the issues are precisely those issues that reflect on our sense of the future, our polemics against the present. We seek to use history in our own behalf by the way we describe and analyze educational history.

For example, when we talk about the reform of American higher education, one of the most persistent myths is the nostalgic myth of the past, of a time in which higher education really worked, in which people received a serious education, in which the basics were taught. In the 1960s, this idyll was shattered by the radical reforms which reflected a disillusionment with the very past we are now nostalgic about. One can marshal evidence for the existence of such a prior Eden, but I defy anyto make a serious case. Clearly, however, the absence of such a noble past in no way justified the equally wrong-headed claim of the "irrelevance" of the past charged in the 1960s.

Take the example of literacy, in which we now see a decline. There is no doubt that there is a decline, but it is not exactly historical in nature. It is perceived in relation to today's needs and the demographic requirements education must meet. There is no lost golden age of literacy, nor did the past at any recent time believe itself to be one. The issue now revolves around the question of mass literacy. The people we educate are different, the numbers more extensive, and the practical standards (perhaps not the ideal ones) different.

Now that a new era of reform is under way, it is important to point out that the contextual problems we now face are radically different from those we faced in the 1960s. The 1960s were a time of increasing afflu-

ence allied to a notion of an expanding nation, internationally and nationally. The context in which educational reform took place then was a
lessening of the Cold War, and included the early missile gap discussions
of the 1960s which took place on the heels of a concern about the arms
race, Sputnik, and a race for outer space. These rivalries seemed to diminish as international cooperation increased and as the United States
made substantial progress. Domestically, there was the concern of an expanding population, racial equality, generational conflict, tradition,
and changing values. The conviction emerged that one could establish new
values and create a new society. The name Students for a Democratic Society and their various reforms, radical and moderate, all were presumed
on the expanding economic and technological capacities of the United
States.

A very important aspect of those presumptions was the notion that
the traditional modes of learning and the traditional substance of learning could perhaps now legitimately be called into question. The old notion that learning is, by definition, cut off from the economic, social,
and political character of the world in which education takes place was
set aside. Thinking in the 1960s doubted knowledge for knowledge's sake.
Social critics, after all, have argued that learning to read and write is
essential for an economic world that requires rules and rational procedures in work. These skills are critical where individual incentive, en-
trepreneurship, the ability to learn technical information for a highly
industrialized economy, and the performance of bureaucratic tasks are expected. (Here Marshall McLuhan needs to be remembered. His work was an
extreme version of a serious attempt to look at literacy, to look at traditional book-learning and essential modes of ritual behavior in cultural
communication that only appear to be based on certain *a priori* values.)
This sociological argument posits that the kinds of literacy we have put
forth in our schools are really handmaidens of the economic system we
have built and require.

Therefore, along with the expanding critique of our economic system
two decades ago came the expanding critique of learning. Critics argued
that the "establishment" wanted growing numbers of working- and middle-
class people to behave the way an upper class wanted them to behave.
What better way to accomplish that objective than to teach them rules and
manners of behavior and call that education, call that culture. The context of educational reform in the 1960s, therefore, was economically ex-
pansive, culturally critical, and politically optimistic about some radical unformed notion of the future that could replace a corrupt present.

What we have inherited in the 1980s and the 1990s is the intense
failure of that reform effort. Its failure lies not only with the people
involved, but in the conception of and the attitude toward that reform.
The failure has to do, first, with the inability to substitute serious
alternatives to the ideas of literacy and to the content of the cultural
tradition. Second, the failure was grounded in the ineptitude and bankruptcy of hazy political ideals, many of which could be dismissed as

merely Oedipal from a social/psychological point of view. The older generation was seen as corrupt, but there was no particular answer to that
corruption, and therefore the political vision remained empty. Third,
people deluded themselves that at a time of substantial social unrest and
heightened political expectations, education was somehow an essential instrument of change. The university became a surrogate arena for social
change. Since the 1960s, the works of Christopher Jencks and others have
pointed out the extent to which education is a useful tool for social and
political reform. The power of education has been case in serious doubt.
Major reasons for that view clearly relate to family structure and regional mobility. The interaction between the work place, the family, and
the school has changed considerably since the 1950s, and school is perhaps no longer the best instrument for political and social change. Accordingly, exclusively political agendas transmuted into the school system are in many ways misplaced. Similarly, considerable historical study
over the past ten years indicates that the myth of school as the major
instrument for social mobility before 1945 may not be true. Consequently, much of the optimism and character of the reform in the 1960s has not
been sustained in the economic and political climate of the 1980s.

One of the serious issues of the 1960s and before, inspired by
James Bryant Conant's research during the 1950s, was the poor training of
teachers in our school systems. The unionization and professionalization
of teachers--perfectly legitimate ends in terms of job security and their
place in society--brought about an attitude in which work ceased to be a
vocation and became merely a job like any other bureaucratic or industrial employment. The failure of society substantially to reward and upgrade the status and character of the teaching profession followed on the
heels of the cultural critique in the 1960s and our persistent national
anti-intellectualism to weaken the teacher's identity and role in the educational system. With the expansion of higher education, a large portion of the major talent that might have gone into secondary teaching
went instead to higher education. They, too, soon discovered that there
were no jobs. Consequently, the status hierarchy and reward system for
teachers from elementary to graduate education have not significantly
been altered since the 1960s.

Finally, the arrogance of higher education was manifested in the
1960s in a critical way. When the secondary schools and the elementary
schools failed to upgrade their quality under the pressure of Sputnik
and with the impetus of new federal funding (especially for science education), the post-secondary institutions were smugly confident of their
ability to pick up the pieces. With the massive expansion of access to
higher education in the postwar period and the 1960s, educational wisdom
concurred in the presumption that higher education institutions would essentially carry the ball if it were fumbled by the secondary sector.
This arrogance gave the post-secondary institutions a much larger claim
to national attention and to national resources. They undertook a task
strengthened with community colleges, expanded state systems, and private

institutions which they alone could not fulfill. One of the primary reasons for this shared view was the coincident expansion of graduate facilities in many institutions which turned the attention of undergraduate
faculty in the 1960s away from the classroom into graduate training. A
false and broadly-based professionalization of college faculty resulted
which cut against the traditional character-building and curricular agenda of the liberal arts colleges and the priorities of the older state institutions with a strong tradition of undergraduate teaching. Quality
would be achieved by a rigorous professionalization from the top down.
Sadly, the hoped-for improvement in our schools after the "why can't
Johnny read" crisis of 1956 (together with Sputnik) never materialized.

After two decades of intense public preoccupation with education,
one problem we face now is the tremendous boredom on the part of the public regarding education. Yet that boredom might be an opportunity. A
major concern in the present day is economic. How much does it cost to
educate? Second, the conservatism of the Reagan and Bush administrations
and whatever new populism has emerged have raised for the first time a
serious challenge to the liberal separation of church and state. With
that, the possibility has arisen that public education must be rethought,
recast, and defended in a new way. Further, with the rise and popularity
of sectarian institutions in the South and West come the possibility that
there will be an effort to create a two-tiered system which will be supported by the public: one private (some sectarian) and the other public.
The hegemony of compulsory schooling through public education may even be
seriously questioned.

The conservatism of the current mood in international politics will
also have an impact on education. This is where the pressure for change
will be most intense. Despite the apparent easing of Cold War rivalries
between East and West, many of the ideas that were current before the
Vietnam war are coming back. In the wake of the United States's 1989 in-
vasion of Panama and the increased deployment of American troops and
military forces to the Middle East following Iraq's annexation of Kuwait
in August 1990, military preparedness and economic strength may, once a-
gain, become a major rationale for stepped up educational reform.

This was the original impetus for mass education in the nineteenth
century. Consider Thomas Gradgrind in Charles Dickens's *Hard Times*. He
wanted to educate everybody in Coketown because he wanted them to be able
to function better at work; to be improved in their moral sensibilities;
again, to stabilize a life organized around economic production. There
was a merger of economic effectiveness, moral rectitude to be a good citizen, and the capacity to read and write.

The vision of the nineteenth century reformer comes home to roost in
the twentieth century when we have people who cannot perform the basic
functions of industry and national defense. Given the comparative weak-
ness of our educational system, can we compete with Japan and a newly
united Germany in the market place? Therefore, the sense of international crisis in the United States becomes stronger and provides a basic

agenda for President Bush. Eventually, these critical issues will transcend the politicians and fall right on the doorstep of our schools and
challenge the way educators train people.   Many of us may not like or
share these political agendas, but those of us in education are familiar
with philanthropists who lobby for the teaching of capitalism and with
the often narrow views held by school boards and those who vote on bond
issues.   Whether we have an aggressive foreign policy or a passive one,
the United States faces the major source of its decline as a primary
technological, intellectual, and political force in the world in the deterioration of its educational system.   That deterioration is not trivial. It is severe in a way that is no longer merely the classic problem of
why Johnny can't read.   Now, not only can Johnny not read, but he has a
diploma to show that he can read, and he's been in school twelve to fifteen years. Not only can he not read, but he doesn't admit that he can't
read; and his teachers don't admit that he can't read; and his employers
don't admit that he can't read; and what he can't read and now produces
is the standard of literacy.   There is a self-deceptive fraud going on,
and we are the heart of that fraud.   We are earning our living partly
through that fraud; we reluctantly perpetrate it, and we find no route
out of it. We are in a situation of extreme seriousness.

     The definition of what is sufficient education has significantly
changed.   This is not to say the standard has declined, but it has
changed.   The ideal of mass literacy in the nineteenth century was initially a very primitive one.   It was not based on a vision of people reading Plato. It was based on the need to have a population that could read
signs in stores and simple primer literature.   In the era when the level
of the cheap entertainment literature that preceded television was raised
the concern was that literacy had to do more than simply allow people to
function economically.   The moral argument aspect of literacy took hold.
Finally, there followed the cause of common schooling, one which was man-
ifest in the ideals of the late nineteenth and early twentieth centuries,
and again in the 1930s, a peculiar and wonderfully American vision which
sought to raise the standard of literacy sufficiently to make the individual an autonomous thinking citizen.   Although this ideal was implicit in
the rhetoric of the founding fathers, it is in the progressive era and in
the 1930s that it took serious hold.   At this point, the plate of education enlarged from one R to two Rs to three Rs, and finally to the range
of curriculum that we see in the grammar school that includes the civic
and cultural teaching aimed at developing fully-fashioned individuals.
This was clearly part of Horace Mann's dream as well.   But as the ideals
were raised, the expectations were raised. They attained their peak in
the period right after the second World War and have now reversed themselves in an obvious way. We talk the same way but define achievement in
a simplified and trivialized manner.   No one has called the bluff. No
one has said that the emperor has no clothes.

     Many people are concerned about current problems in the educational
system, but they fail to realize that there has been a divergence between

the certification function of an institution and its educating functions. Education is a national social bureaucracy that expanded rapidly because of demographic pressure. Now we fear economic retrenchment, and we therefore become very protective both as administrators and as teachers within organizations and unions. The possibility of real change, consequently, seems evermore unlikely. There are also fewer economic resources. No one wants to conclude that we are not doing the right thing, because every administrator knows that in change, even curricular change, lurks the possibility of a budget reduction. Educational reform and economic efficiency now seem to be linked objectives. And insofar as they are linked, they are resisted even more strongly than they were in the 1960s when educational change was concomitant with an expansion of resources. Reform means reduction not addition.

How do we manage educational change at a time when it means less and not more? One of the major issues that educational reform needs to address is the larger vision of the society toward which it seeks to work. Our national ideals are not trivial. The idea of democracy in the American system of education presumes equal access; equal access ought perhaps to presume some modicum of equal exposure and even, one might hope, equal outcome. The reason we don't have an overtly pyramided system, as many Europeans have, is because we believe that age eleven or twelve is too early to determine a person's career, and we also believe that there is a certain basic level of education to be achieved in high school that every citizen is entitled to have even if it takes sixteen years to obtain it. We believe in second chances for education in a person's career. We believe in challenging the individual to think autonomously.

With the growth of lifelong learning, the obligation of education over a lifetime also becomes a right in a democratic society. A central question concerns the level achieved through equal education. An easy and obvious answer is the elitist one. We have all been asked, "Aren't there more people going to college than should be?" One answer is yes; that there is no doubt that the tested capacities of many individuals are far lower than our institutional expectations. Nothing is more demoralizing to teachers in secondary or higher education than to see serious material which has inspired their own best work chewed into banalities by generations of students. They wait, often in despair, for the one or two students cast in the teachers' own self-image who can cause them to say, "Now, there is a student who can really grapple with this question." The sciences have a somewhat easier time. Because talent in the sciences is frequently discovered early, there seems to be no widespread obligation to provide any significant general education in the sciences. Therefore, the agenda of the science teacher is the relatively easy teaching of the pre-professional. Scientific language is self-contained, and therefore the teacher does not face the continuing translation problem to a mass audience as severely as a teacher of English or a teacher of history. Clearly, the standard of general education in the sciences must be upgraded radically.

But it is merely facile to say, "Well, there just are not enough people capable of following the highest agenda of education." Considerable psychological evidence coming forward today through research on artificial intelligence and biological development shows that we know very little about potential and achievement. Pseudo-scientific arguments on nurture/nature or genetic endowment are not very useful. When one raises the moral questions of living in a political community, theoretical speculations about cognition and learning theory are no longer germane. Ability is not the issue. The issue is whether those people who perhaps do not have the ability or, for whatever reason, have not developed the tested ability or the visible ability to follow a high agenda of education ought not to be exposed to it nonetheless, whatever their final level of attainment might be. The elitist argument is neither scientifically nor politically appropriate. There are good reasons for the American premise that reform toward better education should have a broad base and a broad impact in the 1990s. They are rooted in the future of a participatory democracy in a technical, scientific and internationally interdependent world.

In the 1990s reformers in education will be limited to specific institutions and will perhaps touch a very small sector of the population. But what each individual does, and how he or she does it, must be thought about and done with a view to the solution of the larger problem for a large percentage of the population. Many in the educational and professional communities are defensive and hostile toward the democratization of access. We should remember that even now only slightly more than 50 percent of the population goes on to college, and the attainment of serious learning is still achieved by a very small group of people. Given this democratic posture and the vision of a society where people get a serious education in their youth, what is the benefit of designing and assembling a high standard of education for a broad sector of society?

There are two primary benefits. First, it allows individuals to assume a position in the work place which is serious and effective and, from an international point of view, competitive. It gives them the capacity to perform and to innovate in the technological, political, and social service sectors of our society. The minimum standard will rise.

The second benefit is inextricably bound up with the moral and political fiber of the nation. Education should produce people who are capable of making sense out of democracy. What is required in the twentieth century is a capacity to reflect on and judge issues which involve more technical matters, more expertise in a particular technical language or science. The minimum level of necessary education rises with the advancement of science, technology, economic systems, the interdependence of the world, and the necessity for the United States to understand it. There is the irony: the minimum education necessary for a democracy is going up, and yet the actual quality is going down. If we fail to meet the required level, we will be forced to consider the extent to which we may have to abandon democracy to an aristocracy of economic, technological, or political experts. Despite all the diplomas on the wall, the extent to which we may recede into passivity through national ignorance is a serious problem. The extent to which in the 1990s we accept and certify inadequate knowledge and experience as a surrogate for education makes the solution of the problem even more difficult. Mere ignorance is more easily diagnosed and cured than the illusion of education.

What can we do? Let us consider the obligations to reform. If we are not simply going to rail against the current system but ask how we can change it, the task becomes enormous. First of all, the economic constraints are an opportunity. Precisely because we cannot continue to support the system the way it is now, it must be changed. Therefore, let us take leadership in the economic crisis and be a force for constructive and serious change. Let us cease being a lobby. For example, the posture of the unions must change considerably in their own self-interest. Teachers and other academic personnel have become involved in the political process not as expert citizens but as a parochial pressure group. This is a serious problem. We should make clear that education is not only a profession but a task which we have undertaken as a vocation for the common good. It is one in which we have some experience and knowledge but is not one which assumes a language or an approach in imitation of a computer scientist or a nuclear physicist. A paramount issue has to do with the language we use, the research we do, and the professional self-image we develop. Educators must take care not to employ jargon in calling for reform in the 1990s. The agenda must be clear in content and delivery.

The following seem to be the major areas for action: (1) radical improvement in the level of literacy that is achieved by the end of high school; (2) massive redefinition of the expectations for all students with respect to familiarity with mathematics, science, and technology; (3) substantive change in the knowledge of world and national geography—physical, political, economic, and climatic; (4) improvement in the standard of knowledge of foreign languages and cultures; (5) revision in the extent and character of a student's capacity to reason and employ logical argument.

Within this agenda for reform subsidiary goals exist. For example, the teaching of history and the nature of historical argument need to be improved. But most important are two dimensions that run through the entire agenda. First, one cannot assume that our intellectual and cultural tradition has sustained its own momentum. The generation that is coming to school does not, by reasons of its political past, family or culture, maintain the traditional interest and attitude toward learning. This is not to argue the merits, for example, of television. It is merely to stress the presence of a radical cultural discontinuity in the post-World War II era. A major example of this discontinuity is the effectiveness of past approaches to the problem of literacy. One might want to teach grammar and spelling and rules of paragraph construction in the old way directly from the outset. But there is considerable evidence that this

generation and future generations must first reconnect with language as
the sole instrument of thought.   Future generations of students must
first learn that language is more than an external, cosmetic requirement.
By new techniques of free writing, collective exercises in revision and
editing, stresses on reading aloud and on generating the habit of using
writing to express private feelings, we can come to the moment of teaching and legitimating the absolutely valid rules of grammar and construction.   Education is, no doubt, a conservative enterprise; it preserves
our view of the past and transmits it to a younger generation. If, however, we are going to conserve tradition in the best sense, then we must
learn that the imitation of tradition is not merely a matter of style.
Serious imitation and traditionalism require originality and a vital re-
invigoration of the past.   That vitality within tradition must be gained
by educational reformers through contact with a clear, critical, and honest recognition of what has changed in our contemporary social and political culture.

Second, what runs through this entire agenda of reform is the possibility that the institutional patterns of education can be altered with
good results. In particular, one open area of reform for the 1990s is
the possibility, as many are now suggesting, that we start school earlier
and end high school sooner. The early college idea has gained a curren-
cy, and in an age of more mature and wordly adolescents it makes eminent
sense. By restructuring the patterns of education, many of the substantive goals cited above could be achieved more easily.

In the specific case of a particular experiment and effort at structural reform, the question of reform was in a way easy.   Started in the
1960s, Simon's Rock represented an old idea, not a new one: the early
college.   It takes students out of high school where adolescents often
encounter barriers to becoming inspired. The secondary school, because
of its large centralized structure, the nature of its teachers, or the
necessity to gear the material to lower levels, often loses the student.
The idea that there are students who might do better by accelerating the
progress of their education is an old one. It was a turn-of-the-century
idea of Charles Eliot's, an idea that Robert Maynard Hutchins had in the
1930s, and one that Elizabeth Hall from Concord Academy put into practice
in 1966 at Simon's Rock. She had the best way of accomplishing a reform.
She had people who cooperated with her, people who supported her, people
who encouraged her; but she did it herself.   It was a charismatic act of
reform.   She was fortunate enough to have had the funds to do it. She
was not dependent on any multiple triplicate form to the National Institute of Education. She had to answer to no one.   She was an old-style
warrior. If we could go back to it, we should. Critical, however, was
that her effort at structural change was deeply traditional and has resulted in the present in a better, more coherent, and vigorous curriculum
for high school age children. Reform was imitative, but in a radical fashion.

The issue of educational leadership and the extent to which we become too private in our sense of ambition are important.   Very few people are willing to take more than rhetorical risks in what they do.   People are forever building   careers or nest eggs   for a future that may not exist.   The extent to which people are demoralized from taking leadership except when calculated to provide a reward by the standards which already exist (which is really a false reform) is a severe problem.   I challenge one to look   at superintendents,   principals,   or college and   university presidents and regularly find real   leadership, charismatic or otherwise. It is not only because   they are chosen   in the wrong way.   It has to do with the disinclination   of truly   qualified people   to want to take such jobs, make the effort, accept the burdens, and suffer the restrictions on possibilities that those jobs contain.

The contrast   is with   consensual reform.   Consensual   reform takes different interest groups in an organization and tries to come to some a-greement to change.   Clearly, consensus is extremely difficult to reach. The idea behind any reform   can all too easily be   lost in the process of compromise.   We live in   a society with high   social mobility and diver-gence.   It is very improbable   that in a community   in Boston or New York or Washington,   San Francisco or   Phoenix,   you will   find a   majority of like-minded people.   Perhaps consensus   is possible in   isolated places where there are shared values despite differing   individual stakes in the economic or structural position of an institution.   In general, however, the consensus becomes compromise in the   absence of uniformity or charis-ma; what comes out is old wine in old bottles.

The idea of restructuring education   holds some hope if we are will-ing to abandon the   ineffective pilot project and   instead, seriously re-juggle the structural pieces.   To reorganize, in a structurally signifi-cant way, the new lines   and redistribution of   authority and power might in fact create   the condition   that will force people   to think about new wayhs of   delivering education and about its   content.   Here is where the national economic   situation is critical.   Pragmatics and politics might generate a redesign of the   fundamental premises of   the educational sys-tem, without a particular ideological view,   simply because reform promi-ses that education   will be more   efficient and better.   I think that is shown by the   growing public attraction   to earlier schooling and earlier graduation evident in New York State.   What is   important about the early college idea is not that it   has a particular view of   liberal education. It tries to do liberal education as well if not   better than other insti-tutions.   But its need to do so comes   out of the fact that it is dealing with young people with different levels and kinds of preparation.   Facing a new reality, often unpredicted,   forces an institution   into rethinking the methods and   content of teaching.   Experiments with new   age groups, even   experiments with the   time of day,   experiments with   the calendar year, may seem   like structural   changes of no   substantive   import; yet, they may be one way of   introducing change toward the   substantive agenda for reform.

Experiments work too often as enclaves.   Our intention   ought to be to do more than that.   The obligation of reform is to create national change. We must be willing to risk in many ways some assets in our institutions, risk our own image of how our careers will develop.   Beyond that, the easiest thing for successful, experimental enclaves to do would be to say smugly, "We're a model, we're terrific, we'll break even, we'll put aside a nest egg, we'll build an endowment, we'll build a bell tower" --all things that have been done already.

We need to extend reform in the 1990s to a broader range of individuals and young people. We want any reform undertaken in any of our institutions to have extension. The early college concept, for example, is elite only in the sense that each unit of an early college can touch only a small number of people. As we attempt to accomplish extension, we need to link hands in a serious way across the country in unobvious alliances, unhindered by the card we carry or the role we have, or, in the case of the unionization of higher education faculties, whether we are managers or not. We need to generalize the benefits of, for example, the early college.

To what end do we make this effort? We ought to invoke a very basic reason for the vocation of what educators do.   When young people reach physical and personal maturity in the 1990s, it will be in a very radically changed and yet unclear social, personal, national, and international context. The empowerment of the individual to control his or her life, and therefore all of our lives, becomes a primary and serious matter.   Marginal literacy, false literacy, stupidity, ignorance, dependency on media, incapacity to read and to think are too critical to bemoan as the decline of civilization. They are issues that cut at the very root of our future security; our own personal, economic, and political future self-interest.

Educational reform is not a moral crusade. It is a vital matter for reasonable survival. The level that we must achieve for the best of our students and for the worst must be significantly raised. We must be absolutely clear about being able to distinguish between rubbish and serious teaching. We must be able to convince our fellow citizens that the primary issue for educators is delivering quality to a nation that in the next twenty five years will have to exercise a major role internationally and will have to confront an awesomely changed technological, medical, and biological reality that will encompass moral questions in ways we have yet to see. We must educate citizens who will be capable of answers to those questions and who will not leave them in the hands of a few experts, who may themselves be products of our own inadequate institutions.

The strongest card left to educators is their impact on the amount of time that young people spend in school. We need to start with something we know about, can influence, and that will likely sustain itself into the future. That starting point is the buildings, the bricks, the institutional network we call schools and colleges.   The only way to begin is to stop cheating ourselves, the public, and our students by pretending that what we do now is adequate. We must be quite clear and sim-

ple about the objective: a standard of excellence and achievement, asserted by ourselves, and made available to all citizens.

This objective has been the rhetoric, if not the substance, of educators for generations.   The tradition has been to sustain the level of
civilization, technique and practical learning sufficient to stabilize a
particular era's view of itself.   In the dialectic of the transmission of
culture and learning, often the young who inherit the state of the art of
learning and scholarship rebel against it.   Revolution and reform are, in
that sense, children of tradition, the offspring of a process of education rooted in the imitation by the young of the habits of the old.   Educators use reform often to restore and to renew.   Their efforts can be
reactionary or conservative.   Reactionary efforts would be the futile attempt to recreate a mythic or real past.   A conservative effort at reform
in the strictest sense would be to preserve the present against the possible erosion of values and standards in the future.   What the 1990s require in educational reform is neither conservation nor reaction.   Reform
requires the restoration of essential principles of quality and rigor, of
imagination and originality; reform demands the renewal of the principles
of the tradition of learning and teaching.   This can be accomplished only
by transcending conservation and reaction and by reaching for a fundamental change in the way we recruit teachers, train them, organize the curriculum, teach students, and set the content and standards of education.

9 Critical Literacy and the Legacy of Marxist Discourse

HENRY A. GIROUX

Within the last decade, radical theories of schooling have borrowed heavily from the traditions of Marxist theory in order to reveal the deep-rooted class inequalities that characterize both the schools and the wider society.(1) Radical educators of various theoretical persuasions have made it clear that schools share a particular relationship to the class structure and economic order of capitalist societies. The nature of this connection has been explored in great depth through the concept of the hidden curriculum with its emphasis on the political logic underlying classroom relations and the social relations of the workplace.(2) In addition, radical educators have focused on the ideological nature of classroom knowledge and school culture, and the role these play in legitimating the class-specific nature of capitalist societies.(3) More recently, radical educators have focused on how class domination is formed within the processes of resistance and struggle, and how the school setting acts as a terrain for both promoting and containing such resistance in the interest of working class defeat and failure.(4) These various radical traditions have not only fundamentally challenged liberal and conservative views of schooling, they have made visible to educators a plethora of critical discourses that illuminate the various ways in which schools participate in the social, economic, and cultural reproduction of a class system. The central argument presented in this chapter is that radical educational theories that have developed primarily within the contours of a Marxist framework, while having made enormous gains in contesting conservative and liberal accounts of schooling, have outgrown their theoretical and political significance as the basis for a radical discourse. Since the development of the diverse radical traditions that currently inform educational theory have been reviewed and criticized by a number of theorists recently, they need not be repeated here.(5) Instead I will illuminate those theoretical failures directly related to the overreliance by such theories on a Marxist discourse.

First, *hegemony*, as used by radical educators, is almost exclusively referred to as *class domination*. For instance, in more orthodox readings where schools are seen primarily as a reflex of the economic system, the nature and meaning of domination is explored through studies of the relationship betwkeen the workplace and the school. In some cases, classes represent not only the single referent for domination, they also become simple extensions of the relationships of production. Schools, in turn, seem to be driven by a logic that is simply an extension of the logic of capital accumulation. Gilbert Gonzales's Marxist study of progressive education typifies this approach. He writes:

> The social sphere, in the final analysis, corresponds to the social relationships of production. How people come together for the sake of production will determine how people relate to one another in the political and social sphere. Furthermore, the prevailing ideology of any given society is ultimately a reflection of a particular system of production.(6)

Similar accounts have tended to shy away from the simple economic reductionism and class analysis of schooling that Gonzales provides, but they still remain trapped within a paradigm that argues that education is organized along lines that correspond to the relations of the work place and that schools are primarily sites of class domination. This can be seen in the studies of Bowles and Gintis, Mickelson, and a number of others who work in the political economy tradition.(7) The restrictive nature of class analyses is also found in theorists who explore the role of schooling through areas other than the workplace and economic structure. That is, a number of Marxist theorists have used the categories of culture and ideology to explain how the internal workings of school contribute to the reproduction of capitalist societies. In this case, radical educators have used the notion of ideology to specify the way classroom knowledge and social practices function to legitimate capitalist rationality and values, but in most cases the rationality in question is reduced to the reproduction of class relations.(8) This becomes clear even in those socialist critics who reject the ideology of simple determinism in radical educational theory. Proefriedt is representative of this position:

> The genius of socialist criticism is to have worked through the Marxist understanding of the influence of production relations on other aspects of society and to have spelled out specifically how school policies and practices mirror those production relations. At the same time, however, the critics have become imprisoned in their own paradigm. Their concept of ideology obscures the fact that school policies and practices are also informed by working-class interests; the present muddled *state*

of education in this country is a product of class conflict.(9)
(Emphasis mine.)

That the conflict over schooling might be informed by other forms of struggle appears lost in this position.   But such an omission becomes even more glaring in those studies of schooling that attempt to interrogate the ideological nature of school ideology and culture. For example, the work of Pierre Bourdieu and his cohorts in France portrays school knowledge as the privileged cultural capital and experience of dominant classes.   Jean Anyon, Michael Apple, and myself have too often viewed school knowledge as either a representation of specific class interests or as fulfilling the productive needs of the economic sector.(10) Moreover, the transition from radical critiques of schooling to the development of radical educational strategies has often been marred by a similar form of class reductionism. For example, the extremely important ques-question of what constitutes really useful knowledge in radical pedagogy for many on the left is often reduced to what is useful exclusively in terms of working class students and culture.   The notion that other cultural logics may prevail in constituting the lived experiences of both dominant and oppressed groups is lost in many Marxist accounts of schooling. This failure to understand how race, gender, and other cultural logics work across a range of political and educational discourses severely limits the possibility for developing pedagogical strategies that can critically illuminate the dynamics of both domination and the processes by which social groups engage in emancipatory action.(11)   This leads to my next criticism.

Radical Marxist educators have, furthermore, reduced the concept of ideology to either the processes of domination or to forms of critique which attempt to unveil how the logic of domination works in the interest of capitalist rationality. The notion of ideology as a positive moment in the formation of cultural forms and social movements has been largely ignored within a Marxist paradigm on education.(12)   While the notion of ideology as a form of domination is crucial to understanding how social and cultural reproduction work in and outside of schools, it must be extended to include analyses of how it functions to empower specific groups to engage in social change.(13) Moreover, the complex and dialectical nature of ideology must be stressed in order to understand human agents as multilayered subjects; that is, as human beings who are more than merely class subjects, who exist as complex agents who live in different "nows," and who are both formed and act out of a variety of ideologies and cultural experience. In the most immediate sense this would necessitate developing a view of critical pedagogy around a notion of how lived experience is forged in a dialectical tension between elements of domination and reproduction, on the one hand, and elements of critical social formation and resistance, on the other. If radical pedagogy has to become meaningful before it can become critical and emancipatory, the concept of what is meaningful to oppressed groups will have to be extended to include more than the notion of class experiences.

Third, radical educators have failed to develop an organic connection to community people or to critical social movements. This is evident in both the theoretical work that characterizes educational theorizing, as well as in the absence of major alliances between radical educators and other progressive social groups. Most theoretical work on
schools focuses on either what goes on in schools or on ideologies about
schools. For instance, there are theoretical critiques of the curriculum
in use, the hidden curriculum, and the role of the state in schooling.
But what is generally excluded from these perspectives is any acknowledgment of the historical and contemporary development of either oppositional public spheres and their views on education, or any attempt to
seriously understand and learn from popular experiences of schooling.
Radicals need to develop theories of *practice*, rather than theories *for*
practice. In this case, theory is not reduced to a technical instrument
for change, an instant set of radical recipes for social action, but begins with a dialectical reflection on the experiences and problems of excluded majorities. Of course, this is not to underestimate the material
and ideological forces that isolate and threaten radical educators, forces that limit their political effectiveness or, worse, incorporate them
into the security of safe tenure systems and the rewards of academic promotion; it is simply to suggest that an overreliance on Marxist discourse
has also prevented such educators from taking the cultural capital and
concrete struggles of various social groups seriously. It has prevented
radical educators from becoming what Richard Johnson terms "actively educative."

> Being actively educative is not just a question of "carrying a
> policy to the public" or "destroying myths about education."
> It involves learning too. It involves really listening to pop-
> ular experiences of formal education. It involves research,
> centering around particular struggles and local issues. It in-
> volves making links with other local agencies--researchers,
> community activists, black groups, women's groups--not to take
> them over, but to learn from their experiences and practices.
> It involves creating a real branch life at the level of ward
> constituency, something actively to look forward to, energizing
> rather than deadening, developing socialist understandings and
> commitment. It involves extending this activity beyond a nar-
> row local membership, organizing events and activities on a
> more open basis, not requiring immediate political commitment
> from those attending.(14)

Finally, Marxist discourse has failed to interrogate either the role
that teachers play as organic intellectuals who come out of specific sets
of class, gender, and racial experiences, or as part of a specific work
force that bears the historical logic and ideological weight of the domi-

nant societies of which they are a part.   In the first instance, Marxist ideology has presupposed that an allegiance to Marxist discourse exempts one from the societal contradictions that become an object of research and work. The problem is always out there. Thus, there is little under- standing of research on how our own backgrounds either bear the weight of the existing society or contain emancipatory moments that speak to new forms of social relations. Domination runs deeper than alleged rational- ity and discourse.   A critical view of depth psychology and an extended notion of Gramsci's view of the organic intellectual would be useful in moving beyond this impasse.(15)   In the second instance, there is a need to view schools and the process of teaching as part of a set of economic, ideological, and cultural practices that both enable and restrain the de- velopment of collective identities among teachers and students.   In both instances, the link between the individual and the wider society, on the one hand, and the individual and the dynamics of collective cultural for- mation, on the other, become central concerns for understanding what is being produced in schools beside relations of production.

While the above criticisms of radical educational theory contain elements that can be incorporated into a new critical theory of educa- tion, I want to finish this chapter by briefly analyzing some of the ele- ments of critique developed by Stanley Aronowitz and others(16) in light of the relevance they might have for the development of such a critical theory.

The work, in particular, of Stanley Aronowitz points to three major theoretical tasks that must be addressed in the reconstruction of a radi- cal theory of schooling. First, it is necessary to articulate a new cri- tical view that recognizes the political and strategic relevance of dis- tinguishing between education and schooling. Second, it is imperative to develop a discourse and set of concepts around which this distinction becomes theoretically operational for developing more viable forms of po- litical pedagogy. Third, theoretical work that focuses on social and cultural reproduction has to be developed in conjunction with analyses of social and cultural production, particularly in relation to studies of oppositional public spheres and the emergence of critical social move- ments.

If radical pedagogy is to become conscious of its own limitations and strengths within the existing society, it must be viewed as having an important but limited role in the struggle for creating a more just soci- ety. This suggests that radical teachers not only reevaluate the materi- al and ideological conditions under which they work, but also raise new questions about the educative role they may undertake outside of schools. At stake here is the need to extend the possibilities for developing edu- cational work by redefining the distinction between radical forms of schooling and radical forms of education. Moreover, at the present time there is an urgent need to create a new discourse regarding the debate

over the nature of education and what it means as a process of self and
social formation. Underlying the call for a new discourse about educational theory and practice is a dual concern. On the one hand, radical
educators have to reconsider the content and purpose of school reform.
On the other hand, they have to construct organic links with community
people around the injustices found in and through the schools; furthermore, radical educators have to actively involve themselves with social
movements and groups working to develop oppositional public spheres outside of schools around broader educational issues.

The dual role for radical pedagogues implicit in this analysis can
be clarified by providing a distinction between schooling and education.
Schooling, as I use the term, takes place within institutions that are
directly or indirectly linked to the state through public funding or
state certification requirements. Institutions that operate within the
sphere of schooling embody the legitimating ideologies of the dominant
society; they generally define their relationship to the dominant society
in functional and instrumental terms. *Education* is much more broadly defined and, as it is used in this context, takes place outside of established institutions and spheres. In the most radical sense, education
represents a collectively produced set of experiences organized around
issues and concerns that allow for a critical understanding of everyday
oppression as well as the dynamics involved in constructing alternative
cultures. As the embodiment of an ideal, it refers to forms of learning
and action based on a commitment to the elimination of forms of class,
racial, and gender oppression. As a mode of intellectual development and
growth, its focus is political in the broadest sense, in that it functions to create organic intellectuals and to develop a notion of active
citizenry based on the self-dedication of a group to forms of education
that promote civic courage and democratic principles.

For radical teachers, it is imperative that strategies be developed
that start with an understanding of how knowledge and patterns of social
relations steeped in domination come into being in schools, how they are
maintained, how students, teachers, and others relate to them, and how
they can be exposed, modified, and overcome, if possible. I suggest that
such a strategy can be organized around a pedagogy that argues for a notion of critical literacy and cultural power, while simultaneously presenting a strong defense for schooling as a public service. In the first
instance, critical literacy would make clear the connection between knowledge and power. It would present knowledge as a social construction
linked to norms and values, and would demonstrate modes of critique that
illuminate how, in some cases, knowledge serves very specific economic,
political and social interests. Moreover, critical literacy would func-
as a theoretical tool to help students and others develop a critical relationship to their own knowledge. In this case, it would function to
help students and others understand what this society has made of them
(in a dialectical sense), what they no longer want to be, and what they
need to appropriate critically in order to become knowledgeable about the

world in which they live. Thus, critical literacy is linked to notions of self and social empowerment as well as to the processes of democratization; in the most general sense, critical literacy means helping students, teachers, and others learn how to read the world and their lives critically and relatedly; it means developing a deeper understanding of how knowledge gets produced, sustained, and legitimated; and, most important, it points to forms of social action and collective struggle.

As a form of critique, critical literacy would raise questions about modes of discourse and organization in schools that reduce learning and social practices to their technical dimensions. In other words, it would it would make problematic the instrumentalization and technicization of American education. Such a critique would analyze the technocratic ideology that dominates teacher education, the empiricist and technical thinking that governs state certification policies, and the "methodological madness" that generally characterizes curriculum theorizing, classroom social relations, and the technicist modes of evaluation and selection. Of course, the reduction of thought to its strictly technical dimensions is only one aspect of how schools promote forms of political and conceptual illiteracy. At another level, schools disempower students, parents, and community members by disconfirming their histories, experiences, and, in effect, their role as historical agents.

The point here is that the concept of critical literacy moves beyond the call for counterhegemonic knowledge and social relations by acknowledging the need for educators to incorporate in their pedagogies the experiences and social practices that give a collective voice to specific individuals and groups, whether they be racial minorities, women, working class people, or alienated members of the dominant classes. Put another way, critical literacy interrogates the cultural capital of the oppressed to learn from it; it functions to confirm rather than disconfirm the presence and voices of the oppressed in institutions that are generally alienating and hostile to them. But the call to take the cultural capital of oppressed and oppositional groups seriously should not be mistaken for the traditional liberal argument for educational relevance. The latter makes an appeal to a pedagogy responsive to the individual interests of students in order to motivate them. Critical literacy responds to the cultural capital of specific groups or classes and looks at the ways in which it can be confirmed and also at the way the dominant society disconfirms students by either ignoring or denigrating the knowledge and experiences that characterize their cultural capital. The unit of analysis here is social, and the key concern is not with individual interests but with individual and collective empowerment.

It must be remembered that many students grow up within the boundaries of a class culture, popular culture, and a school culture. It is on the terrains of class and popular culture that students develop an active voice. On the other hand, for many students school culture has little to do with either their histories or their interests; instead it becomes the culture of dead time—something to be endured and from which to escape.

Of course, school culture is really a battleground around which meanings are defined, knowledge is legitimated, and futures are sometimes created and destroyed. It is a place of ideological and cultural struggle favored primarily to benefit the wealthy, males, and whites. But it is precisely because there is room for struggle and contestation in schools around cultural and ideological issues that pedagogies can be developed in the interest of critical thinking and civic courage.

Struggles within the schools have to be understood and linked to alliances and social formations that can affect policy decisions over the control and content of schooling. In effect, this means that radical teachers will have to establish organic connections with those parents and progressive groups who inhabit the neighborhoods, towns, and cities in which schools are located. Such an alliance points to the need for radical teachers to join with feminists, ecology groups, neighborhood organizations, and parents in order to question and influence school policy. Critical literacy, in this case, points to forms of knowledge and social practice that take seriously the notion of school democracy. Moreover, it points to the need to develop a real defense of schools as institutions which perform a public service, a service defined by the imperative to create a literate, democratic, and active citizenry—in this case, citizens who would be self-governing and actively involved in the shaping of public welfare.

The concept of radical education suggests a different role for radical pedagogues. It points to the necessity of struggle in sites other than those influenced and controlled by the state. It points to developing and working in oppositional public spheres aimed at achieving forms of collective power. Radical educational reform cannot rely on existing institutions to promote emancipatory change. The power of such institutions to set the agenda for debate, the disrespect they exhibit for the oppressed, and their willingness to take economic and political action against oppositional voices make them unreliable as primary institutions for social change. Oppositional public spheres, on the other hand, provide the possibility for using collective aspirations and criticisms in the development of an alternative culture. One reason for the development of oppositional public spheres would be to help people develop what Stanley Aronowitz calls a healthy narcissism. That is, to provide the conditions through which

> people who have been excluded from making political decisions were able to recover their self, to find the basis upon which to validate their own pleasures, as well as their own work. . . . To intervene politically on the basis of a reflexive recognition of common needs that are systematically denied in the culture is a means of recovering a collective narcissism as a moment in the process.(17)

For radical educators, it means working with community groups to de-

velop pockets of cultural resistance based on new forms of social relations and practices. It means working with adults around those issues
directly related to their lives, and acting as educative citizens struggling to establish a social and economic democracy.   As radical educators, we can help to destroy the myth that education and schooling are
the same thing, we can debunk the idea that expertise and academic credentials are the distinguishing marks of the intellectual.   Equally important, such educational work would also promote critical analyses of
schooling itself and its relations to other institutions included in the
state public sphere.   Furthermore, radical educators could provide, discuss, and learn from historical and contemporary examples in which various social groups have come together to create alternative public
spheres. Clearly the elements of a democratic pedagogy can be exhibited
through an examination of historically specific examples of alternative
public spheres in the various organizations, clubs, cultural activities,
and media productions developed at the turn of the century by, for example, the nationality federations associated with the socialist party.
Aronowitz provides some sense of what form they took:

> These federations, organized among nearly every major group of
> foreign-born workers, were veritable "states within a state."
> They formed burial societies, social organizations and, with
> the collaboration of socialist-led trade unions, [taught] hun-
> dreds of thousands of workers how to read and write along with
> elements of politics, economics, and socialist ideology.(18)

One of the most important purposes for creating alternative public
spheres is to provide the conditions for the development of what Antonio
Gramsci has called *organic intellectuals*. That is, intellectuals who are
part of a specific class and who serve to "give it homogeneity and an
awareness of its own function, not only in the economic, but also in the
social and political fields."(19) Gramsci's notion of the organic intellectual is important for radical educators because it broadens our understanding of the role of intellectuals by highlighting their social function as mediators between the state and everyday life.   In this definition, the concept of an intellectual is politicized. It rejects the current meaning of the term which restricts it to scholars, writers, etc.
Moreover, it suggests that oppositional groups have to form their own
leadership rooted in and committed to the history, experience, and set of
goals they share with the people such intellectuals represent. This concept is important because it lays the theoretical ground for radical educators to examine their own organic connections to specific groups; at
the same time, it points to establishing social relations with social
groups in concrete institutional contexts such as neighborhoods and trade
unions.   Furthermore, its logic argues for democratic organizations in
which intellectuals and the masses coalesce around building their ascen-
dancy as groups fighting the material and ideological forces of domina-

tion, while simultaneously and self-consciously educating every member of the community to develop the general skills, knowledge, and capacities to govern.

Of course, at the present time only shadows of a left public sphere exist in the United States. These are organized mainly around journals, magazines and academic publications. Some counterinstitutions also exist in the form of alternative schools, but generally the left has given little political attention to creating cultural sites where people who share a common language, set of problems, and cultural experience can come to argue, learn and act collectively to transform their lives.   The obstacles against the development of alternative public spheres are enormous. The media, the power of corporations, the culture industry, and the state all function to keep oppositional groups on the defensive. Under these circumstances, it becomes difficult to establish new agendas that can examine the preconditions for establishing a left public sphere. Aronowitz provides the starting point for such a task, and it is worth repeating in full:

> [The left's] independent role is primarily to create a left
> "public sphere;" that is, to find the basis for enlarging the
> left political culture in ways that address existing conditions
> but also to find ways of going beyond them. This task has several practical specifications: (1) a major effort to study the
> formation of intellectuals in the American context, both those
> who were destined to serve the prevailing order and those who
> attempted to define themselves as the opposition; (2) recognition that mass communications is the mainstream public sphere
> in which political and social ideas are disseminated and sometimes debated—mostly among the organic intellectuals of capital; (3) investigation into the relations between economic, political and ideological spheres in the United States as a specifically "late" capitalist society; and (4) a concrete and unsentimental analysis of the evolution and devolution of the
> American working class—particularly its ideological formation
> and changing composition—and the trade unions.   This would
> deepen our understanding of the centrality of race, sex and
> ecological politics in both the discourses of domination and
> the political culture of the left.(20)

In conclusion, it seems imperative that radical educators recognize the limits of orthodox and neo-Marxian discourses. This is not a call to abandon Marxism as much as it is to critically appropriate what is relevant to the present historical and contemporary juncture and to develop it as part of a new radical social theory which points to existing possibilities and more expanded opportunities for radical educational work. Of course, what I have provided is a broad theoretical sweep that draws primarily from the work of Aronowitz and other critical theorists.   The point has been to make a small contribution to rethinking those ideologies that have traditionally informed radical educational theory and practice and to provide some theoretical contributions to creating the basis for a new and more viable radical educational discourse.   If ever there was a time for such a task to be undertaken, it is now.

10 Humanities in the Education of Minorities

HUEL D. PERKINS

In the summer of 1975, George Bonham, then the editor-in-chief of *Change* magazine, convened a symposium on the plight of the humanities. In setting the stage for that forum, he observed, "We now see the rapid flight of students out of the humanities. In some places it has become a rout. In a growing number of colleges the question is no longer what ought to be taught, what curricular improvements ought to be made, but what one must do in order to survive."(1)

In 1977, the American Association for the Advancement of the Humanities was formed to promote public understanding of the humanities and increase the contribution of the humanities to national life. In 1978, the Rockefeller Commission on the Humanities was established to undertake an exhaustive study of the status of the humanities in American life and culture. The recommendations of that commission, which are now public, are destined to have a far-reaching effect on how the disciplines of the humanities are perceived. In that same year, 1978, an editorial appeared in the *Washington Star* newspaper titled "Graduates Without Jobs." It said, in part, that the market for college graduates seemed to be surprisingly good that year for just about everyone, except humanities majors. "If your field is computers, the world is your oyster. But if your field is English or history or comparative literature, you may find yourself pumping gas--if there is any gas to pump."(2)

When the National Humanities Center was opened in North Carolina in 1979, Steven Marcus, who had been instrumental in its planning, wrote, "We cannot predict what has not taken place, and we have no blueprint for the future. What we are certain of is that the humanities are in trouble and that serious work has to be undertaken to help them renew their indispensable functions in American education and society."(3) And in 1981 the National Endowment for the Humanities (NEH), which was established in 1965 and had supported numerous curricula and course projects in the humanities, was in danger of having its funding substantially reduced upon the recommendation of the president of the United States to Congress. This rethinking of federal support to the humanities came at a time when the NEH was celebrating its fifteenth anniversary--trying to bring to pass what was written into the enabling legislation of the Endowment: "A high civilization must not limit its efforts to science and technology a- lone, but must give full value and support to the other great branches of man's scholarly and cultural activity in order to achieve a better under- standing of the past, a better analysis of the present, and a better view of the future." The bill continues: "A democracy demands wisdom and vi- sion in its citizens. . . . It must therefore foster and support a form of education designed to make men masters of their technology and not its unthinking servants."(4)

If the humanities are in trouble nationally, the problem is doubled in the black higher education community. Two decades of over-riding em- phasis on science and technology, coupled with years of economic depriva- tion among black people, have worked havoc in the area of the humanities. Black students are, understandably, job oriented. They are attracted to the fields that offer immediate and lucrative employment.

In recent years, the financial support available to students in the science fields has all but left the humanities with the most meager of enrollments. Socio-economic status (SES), family educational attainment, family income, size of hometown, and imagined difficulty of the field of study are all factors which appear to affect the choice of a student's major field in college. In a study undertaken by James A. Davis several years ago concerning graduate career decisions, he found that there was: (1) a high correlation between education majors and lower SES and smaller hometowns; (2) that more men than women chose business as a major, influ- enced by the idea of "making a lot of money," and (3) that while no firm conclusions could be drawn from this data, blacks appeared to avoid the humanities.(5)

In 1972 Frank Newman concluded in the federally commissioned *Report on Higher Education* that black students are concentrated in a few ma- jors, principally in business, education, the social sciences and the non-M.D. health professions.(6) These career choices have not changed significantly since the report.

There is a story which goes something like this: A small lad who liked to read children's stories was struck with the fact that while the lion was the king of the jungle--ferocious, mean, unafraid--no matter how frequently the lion fought with man, man always emerged victorious. This disturbed the boy, so he asked his father about it. His father's reply was at once sagacious and instructive. He said that the lion would al- ways lose in any encounter he has with man--until lions learn how to write books. The implications of this anecdote are at once apparent for the study of the humanities as they relate to the minority experience in American colleges and universities. Books about this experience must be written and must be read if the minority experience is to have any validity in the larger context of the American higher education system.

We are speaking, in short, of persons of minority status becoming both producers and consumers of the humanistic tradition; not all of them on the model of an Alex Haley or a Toni Morrison or a James Baldwin, but producers who have the empathetic relationship with experience; who have the ability as well as the emotional imperative to set down the unique paths which have been traveled by minorities to get to this moment in history.

The humanities must also produce consumers of humanistic learning—both from the ethnic point of view and from the more embracing, over-arching consideration of what it means to be a human being. We must produce students who are impelled to draw closer to sources of beauty and truth—not for purposes of information, but for the elevation of their own lives, the fulfillment of their private dreams, the sharpening of their aspirations, and the honing of their imaginations. Nothing, save the humanities, has the capacity to make men and women civilized, to have them become keenly aware of their continuing stake in all of civilization, to cause them to live above the level of brute force, instincts, and appetites. The humanities can do this because they are concerned with our experiences, failures and successes, hopes, and fears. They are not concerned with things but with people. They are not concerned with analysis but with synthesis. They are not concerned with humans as tool-using animals, but as rational, thinking, feeling, spiritual beings. Their special function is the distillation, preservation, and application of the wisdom of humankind to the problems that human beings must continually face as they try to fashion for themselves a civilized existence. As one writer has put it, when one studies architecture, one should be better able to understand, design, build, or repair structures. When one studies the humanities, one should be better able to understand, design, or repair a life—one's own.

The humanities serve yet another very important function in our lives. They cause us to ask the big questions which must be asked again and again—with each age, with every generation. We honor the Greeks of classical antiquity for just that reason. They asked some difficult questions which led to some startling conclusions: How do things come into existence, have their being, and then pass away? What are our duties and purposes upon this earth? Is this universe a cosmos that can be studied and conclusions drawn therefrom? When human beings were utterly at the mercy of what they must not try to understand, the Greeks made the humanities important vehicles for understanding themselves and the world about them. If it worked for the Greeks, it should also work for minorities.

The humanities, then, must be used both as catalysts and models in the teaching of minority students. They may serve as models because they represent the best that has been thought or written about. They may serve as catalysts because they say to minority students that as others have done, they might do likewise. Frederick Douglass, for example, was born a slave, learned how to read his alphabet by following a carpenter's markings on pieces of lumber, and went on to become the most articulate spokesman imaginable for the cause of the abolition of slavery. He was able to stand before a gathering on the Fourth of July in 1852 in Rochester, New York, and declare "that you might rejoice at this day but I must weep. . . . go where you may, search where you will, roam through all the monarchies and despotisms of the Old World, travel through South America, search out every abuse and when you have found the last, lay your facts by the side of the everyday practices of this nation, and you will say with me that for revolting barbarity and shameless hypocrisy, America reigns without rival."(7) If an ex-slave could learn to use such mellifluous language, then certainly our children who have had eighteen years of schooling should be able to make a verb and subject agree. The humanities can catalyze--can open new vistas--can irrigate deserts--can cause the soul to find new ways to look upward and outward--if given the opportunity.

A fine example of the humanities being used as a model can be found in a passage from W. E. B. Du Bois's *The Souls of Black Folk*, which indicates how beautifully language can be used. Indeed, some of the writing in this group of essays borders upon sheer poetry. Consider the essay titled "Of the Passing of the First Born," where he writes on the death of his only son in these words: "If one must have gone, why not I? Why may I not rest me from this restlessness and sleep from this wide waking? Are there so many workers in the vineyard that the fair promise of this little body could lightly be tossed away? . . . Sleep then, child, sleep, until I waken to your voice--above the veil."(8)

It can perhaps be said that all of education is reading, writing, and thinking done at varying levels of difficulty along the academic ladder. And likewise, the humanities, especially the three handmaidens: philosophy, history, and literature, have the capacity to contribute to the refinement of these skills. If a man or woman has not read the great thoughts of the ages, cannot put his or her ideas down in a written form for others to peruse and profit therefrom, cannot see relationships among discrete bodies of knowledge, is that person really educated? Mastery of these skills is indispensable for success in any field. College students need to be told this again and again. And they need to know that the humanities can greatly assist in this mastery.

Consider first, reading. Reading must necessarily be a part of every humanities course. If there is no reading involved, then the course should not only be eliminated from the humanities division, it should not be offered in college. Granted that minority students often come to college with poor reading skills and read at an interminably slow rate; this does not excuse the necessity for the inclusion of the great books of the world as an undebatable requirement in any humanities course offered.

And students must be told why they are reading certain materials. Does a student really know the unlimited and infinitely possible nuances of the English language if he has not read some James Baldwin, Toni Morrison, Henry Fielding, Nathaniel Hawthorne? These writers demonstrate how beautifully the English language can be used, even as they increase passive, if not active, vocabularies. An extended contact with good books forms the basis of a student's feel for language for years to come.

Someone has said that only after one has read and read and read does one achieve the ability to express oneself effortlessly. Reading is a psychologically difficult process and one that requires continual practice. The only alternative to extended reading is that of osmosis, and oft-times the absorption can be faulty. One reads novels to cultivate the imagination; one reads biographies to build character; and one reads nonfiction for purposes of information. Students must be told this. Nowhere have I encountered this "imagination" aspect of the humanities so poetically stated as in the words of Jacob Neusner, professor of Religious Studies at Brown University, when he asks:

> But where in your scheme of education is there a place for
> imagination? To feel with Othello, to weep with Achilles, to
> admire and be awed at the nobility and wisdom of Socrates? And
> this we do in the only way open to us: by showing what humani-
> ty has been and has made and has thought. This is how people
> have become more than what they are, and why you, the future
> and the hope, can feel and do and be and think. Some men and
> women have known how passionately to care and to dream. These
> we teach: the creations of their caring and passions.(9)

This is what reading is all about: imagination, character, passion, caring. Significant contributors to this universe are vociferous, voracious, insatiable readers. Hardly anything else matters in a humanities course if no reading is taking place. There must be sustained contact with the written word in the education of minorities.

And what about writing? Writing is a way of thinking by placing words on paper. It is the way we make ideas permanent and give shape to our insights and our concepts. It is the way a civilization talks to itself about itself. People are revealed in their writings. What they are will be there indelibly imprinted. If a civilization has not written very much, that alone expresses a lot about it. Civilizations and ethnic groups carve niches for themselves in history precisely by their writings.

To underscore the importance of writing in the education of minorities, consider the effect of the monumental book, *Roots*, by Alex Haley. In all the hoopla of the television version and the subsequent acclaim given it, the fact that Alex Haley first *wrote it down* was overlooked. Or put another way, Mr. Haley wrote rather than rapped. The results: an enduring account of a race of people preserved for untold generations to study and analyze and finally build upon. About the singular achievement Alex Haley wrote, "Overall, I'm just glad that it was possible to see the

book explode the pervasive old myth that black material couldn't hold a
major audience."(10)   The moral? *No writers—no roots.* Write it down!

When black became fashionable in the sixties ("black is beautiful,"
black pride, black studies), one had to wonder where we would have been
had not someone before the sixties taken the time to write things down.
We were especially indebted to a period called the Harlem Renaissance
which occurred briefly between 1917 and 1929.   This period, which in a
dozen short years produced more creative efforts by blacks than had been
produced in the preceding two hundred years, became a veritable gold
mine. Here we found the entrepreneurs of the movement, men like W. E. B.
Du Bois, Charles Johnson, Alain Locke, who encouraged the creative talents of Countee Cullen, Claude McKay, Langston Hughes, and Jean Toomer—
producers of a golden legacy. Here we meet the first black female novelists—Zora Neale Hurston, Jessie Fauset, Nella Larsen.   From this period
we can read the short stories of Wallace Thurman, Rudolph Fisher, John F.
Matheus, Eric Walrond.   This was an exciting period in the history of
black arts and letters, and it was all written down.   We must keep this
tradition alive. History must not write that it died with the minorities
who came along in the last half of the twentieth century—who preferred
"The Young and the Restless" to Shakespeare, "Barnaby Jones" to Ralph El-
lison, rapping to writing.

This is summed up in a passage from an article written in 1922, near
the beginning of the Harlem Renaissance. Alice Dunbar-Nelson, writing in
The Southern Workman, said:

> The ancient Greeks wishing to impress upon their children the
> greatness of Hellas, made the schoolboys memorize Homer. The
> Romans saturated their youth with Roman literature, history and
> law. The French child recites La Fontaine, even before he can
> read. Spain drives home the epic of El Cid to the youth of the
> nation. The reason for this is obvious. If a people are to be
> proud or self-respecting, they must believe in themselves.
> Each rising generation must be told that it possesses a history
> and a literature and this history and literature must be made a
> part of life.(11)

This is why the humanities are eternally important in the education of
minorities.

When Bartlett Giamatti, then-president of Yale University, testi-
fied before a Congressional committee concerning a bill on education, he
addressed himself to the value of the humanities. He said:

> A curriculum must have at its core the teaching of the humanis-
> tic disciplines, here broadly defined as centered upon versions
> of the Word. That means any education wishing to do more than
> simply accumulate and transmit information must pay attention
> to the value-laden languages within it.   That means that the

need to teach students to respect language and its power, its
capacity to shape themselves and their fellows, is an essential
part of an education for citizenship. It means clarity, grace,
and logic in written expression is at the heart of the matter.
Without a decent regard for what language can do, and a love
for its variety and some awe before its brooding reach, without
that, in some deep and authentic way, our humanity will not be
summoned and shaped and made civil.

He concluded his testimony with this simple theme: that a curriculum embody the regard for languages, written or spoken, in order to reassert
the civic, not technical purposes of an education. "Only if a curriculum
sustains a shared core of values held by educated people through language
can a free and mutually supportive people continue to flourish.(12)

No other disciplines, save the humanities, have quite the potential
for bringing about this mastery over these essential skills. Whether the
humanistic disciplines are defined in a narrow sense and include only
philosophy, literature and history; or whether they are defined more
broadly (as the National Endowment for the Humanities does) to include,
in addition, the study of languages, linguistics, archaeology, jurispru-
dence, criticism of the arts and music, ethics and comparative religion,
the fact remains that they represent the distilled wisdom of humankind's
best thinking and writing and thereby can serve at once as models and catalysts.

The human species is the source and substance of the humanities. As
long as we remain human beings, we have need for the study of these disciplines. They let us know who we are and make it possible to understand
what has shaped us the way that we are. As W. E. B. Du Bois once wrote,
"Herein lies the tragedy of the age; not that [people] are poor--all
[people] know something of poverty; not that [people] are wicked--who is
good? Not that [people] are ignorant--what is truth? Nay, but that
[people] know so little of [one another]."(13) Humanities education
seeks to remedy this void by providing access to our culture as well as
the culture of others. A people, and especially a minority people, has
to know that it came from somewhere. A people, and especially a minority
people, needs heroes, myths, legends, stories. Refuse to acquaint them
with this past and they began to believe themselves incapable of going
anywhere. A hero looms twice as large in a minority culture because that
hero becomes "Exhibit A" of one who has made it out of the bondage of
race and circumstance.

For too long, there have been two routes out of the depths of poverty for minorities in this country: athletics and entertainment. There
is a third route that must be emphasized, and it is education. Within
education, there must be a strong component of the humanities--those disciplines which civilize us. They must be taught with passion and with
conviction.

Human wisdom has been the study of the humanities time out of mind, and to the extent that we deny the chance to share that study with any significant portion of our population or to the extent that we do not vigorously and aggressively find ways to keep this area of study alive, we court moral, spiritual, and intellectual bankruptcy.

A passage from Greek antiquity seems to distill why the study of the humanities is so important and underscores the ultimate possibilities of of the species. Sophocles' *Antigone* is a rapturous song that glorifies humankind.

> Wonders are many on earth, and the greatest of these
> Is man, who rides the ocean and takes his way
> Through the wind-swept valleys of perilous seas
> That surge and sway.
>
> The use of language, the wind-swift motion of brain
> He learnt, found out the laws of living together
> In cities, building him shelter against the rain
> And wintry weather.
>
> There is nothing beyond his power. His subtlety
> Meeteth all chance, all danger conquereth.
> For every ill he hath found its remedy,
> Save only death.(14)

The humanities are eternally relevant to all people of all ages. They are relevant because they deal with the study of humankind. They are relevant because they represent the best that has been thought and written. The humanities are needed in the education of minorities as never before. For it would seem that in the years ahead, race will no longer be the mitigating factor against minorities becoming part of the mainstream of America. Instead, it will be education, and the quality of this education, therefore, must be uncompromised. One essential ingredient in this uncompromised, quality education must be the inclusion of the disciplines known as the humanities, taught with vigor, purpose, and commitment. They have the power to transform this world. And as Sophocles would have us believe: There is nothing beyond our power--save only death.

11 Reflections on the Education of Women

ELIZABETH BRIANT LEE

The frequent discussions of liberal arts being "in a time of crisis" do not often enough link that crisis with the related one in the strivings by women for liberation. Both crises reflect growing and decisive changes in the world's social economy. Those changes are now being used to excuse the reduction or manipulation of both educational funds and the employment of women and other disadvantaged groups.

Although educational opportunities for women have greatly expanded, there is a long way to go. In that context, the current crisis in the liberal arts is a recurrence of a longstanding and chronic condition. In particular, we need to sharpen the clarity of our realization of past conditions, of subsequent changes relative to women's education and social situation, and of what can be gained in social guidance from those experiences. Contrasted with the present state of women's aspirations and problems, that realization might help us to see the differences between where we have been, where we are now, and where we might or could be going.

Where have women been, educationally speaking? On this, biographies are illuminating. Only 817 women appear among the 16,004 persons included in *The Dictionary of American Biography (DAB)*, a distinguished twenty volume reference work.(1) Women thus number only about 5 percent of those thought to be sufficiently eminent or notorious for that work. Since the *DAB* contains biographies of only those outstanding Americans who are no longer living, its most recent supplement is updated only to the end of 1950.

To highlight the changing situation for women, let us look at the lives of the twenty three women social scientists who were considered prominent enough to be contained in the *DAB*. Of them, eleven were anthropologists or archaeologists, seven were psychologists, and five were more or less sociologists. The latter category is stretched a bit to involve a social economist. All were born between 1847 and 1887. That none among those profiled was born sooner is understandable, because the social sciences as such were only coming into being in the middle to late nineteenth century.(2)   That there were no more than twenty three among the 817 reflects the social history of the times. Social scientific work requires systematic training and study, and women were long discouraged from attending college. They were frequently denied admission to graduate schools.

With the increase in the number and quality of institutions of higher learning for both men and women in this country, women began to have access to the training necessary for scientific work. Custom and culture continued for some time to raise barriers against women's participation in many disciplines, barriers far from lifted as yet. Perhaps it is more to be commented upon that there were as many as twenty three women social scientists of eminence.

The education of these select women is colorful in detail. If they were lined up in a row, as it were, with their training indicated by the color of their clothes (running from the palest tint for the less formally educated to darker shades for the more advanced degree holders, the effect would be a gradation heavily weighted with the deeper shades. By the middle of the nineteenth century, female academies or seminaries, equivalent to mediocre high schools of today, were numerous. By the end of the Civil War, female colleges offering instruction comparable to that given in men's colleges had begun to appear in appreciable numbers.(3) Thus, earlier women like Sara Yorke (1847-1921), archaeologist, a banker's daughter who attended only an institute for women in France while living abroad with her parents, had no further formal education. Through her interest in a school for Indians, she went on to teach herself, and to work within an archaeological institution in Philadelphia that became a museum, largely through her efforts and her family's financial backing.(4) Three other women had only finishing school educations. As their birth dates appear further and further along in the decades of the nineteenth century, the level of highest educational attainment rises rapidly. Three became college graduates, one attained a master's degree, and fifteen earned their Ph.D.'s.

It is indicative of the times and of the attitudes toward women in graduate work that, although Christine Ladd-Franklin qualified for the doctorate in 1882 at Johns Hopkins University as a psychologist and logician, she was not granted the degree until 1926, forty four years later.(5)   The psychologist and philosopher, Mary W. Calkins (1863-1930), had similar problems. She got her A.B. degree in 1885 and her M.A. in 1888 from Smith College, one of the earliest women's colleges. In 1890, she was appointed an instructor at Wellesley. While she was teaching there, she began her studies at Harvard and worked with William James, Josiah Royce, and later Hugo Munsterberg. Within six years, she fulfilled the requirements for the doctoral degree with distinction, but Harvard could not and did not grant degrees to women.(6)   About the same time, Ellen Semple (1863-1932), anthropogeographer, after graduating from Smith in 1882 and doing graduate work there in history, went from 1891 to 1892 to the University of Leipzig, where she studied under Friedrich Ratzel. He was regarded as the greatest anthropogeographer of his time. She was his first woman student, the only one among some five hundred men. As a woman, she was not permitted to matriculate, but she was allowed to attend lectures by sitting in an adjoining room with the door ajar. Ratzel's influence changed her field from history to anthropogeography, in which she came to excel.(7)

By the turn of the century, women did receive Ph.D.'s from such universities as Columbia, Chicago, Wisconsin, and even in 1896 from Yale—but not from Harvard. From then on, for women social scientists as for women in any other of the learned professions, advanced education became the rule.

Outstanding performance in the learned professions calls for learned people. Of the earlier professional women, those who made the greatest contributions were those who had had the opportunity to study and work in universities with men who were leaders in their fields. This might have been a situation of the times, when there were only beginning to be women college professors as role models. Speculation arises as to what the story will be fifty years hence, with women now entering practically all the professions.

Among all 817 of the DAB women, the most significant motivation was found to be economic necessity, with no other stimulus nearly so strong. Many found it possible to continue with their chosen vocational interest only because it provided the basic sustenance they needed. Single women, whether unmarried, divorced or widowed, worked to support themselves and their young or old dependent relatives. Married women in the list often had improvident or sickly husbands and felt pushed at least to supplement the family income. In those days of inadequate insurance and at a time when public welfare assistance was only for some of the most poverty-stricken and was considered shameful for the bourgeoisie, widows turned their hands and minds to anything "respectable" that would provide the necessities.

Out of this kind of situation came any number of "rags to riches" tales of women who at least in part supported their families by their writings, their business acumen, their school teaching, and school founding. They did not all make fortunes, but many did remarkably well at whatever work they came to do, mostly because they--like so many men--had no recourse but to keep on with it.(8)

In the social sciences, economic motivation is not so readily apparent. It combined often with a strongly felt need for intellectual development and self-expression. Women who later became famous in this area grew up in families who prized education as a desirable cultural refinement in itself. Beyond that, higher education was thought of as a desirable training for self-support if, by unfortunate chance, that became necessary--if no proper provider in the way of a husband were available.

These bourgeois families were in the main economically comfortable, at least sufficiently so that they sent their daughters to be educated in the colleges of the day.

Once a taste for higher education was roused, women of an earlier era had, they thought, a choice between either a career with its requirements or marriage. Most of the ones who chose only marriage are, for our purposes, lost. Others chose a career. Some did manage both a career and marriage, but they were few.

Parental families of single career women were not or could not always be supportive. More than once are there stories like that of Esther B. Van Deman (1862-1937), archaeologist, who for several years alternately taught in colleges and did graduate work; she thus financed her own advanced training.(9) On the other hand, husbands of married women graduate students appear to have been supportive, financially and otherwise. For example, Harry L. Hollingworth, a University of Nebraska classmate and fellow psychologist of Leta Hollingworth (1886-1939), married her two years after graduation from college, and gave her the opportunity to take graduate work. In 1909, he joined the staff of Barnard College of Columbia University. Thus she had the chance to take her master's degree in 1913 and her doctorate in education in 1916 from Columbia. There she also taught for many years in Teachers' College and became a recognized authority on the psychology of adolescence. That was a long step from being born in a Nebraska prairie dugout, living in a sod house, beginning her education in a one-room schoolhouse, and, after college, teaching in a local school.(10)

Both single and married women also benefited from fellowships to help them jump the degree hurdle that stood between them and the regular practice of a profession. Harriet B. Hawes (1871-1945), archaeologist, illustrates this. She was enabled by her grant in 1896 as Agnes Hoppin Memorial Fellow to the American School of Classical Studies in Athens to be original. When she discovered that there was evidently no opportunity for a female student to take part in the school's excavation program, she decided to use part of her grant to underwrite her own excavations and went to Crete to look for a site. At Kavousi in eastern Crete, she discovered eearly Iron Age houses and tombs and a few years later, at Gournia, a Bronze Age town. Through these findings, Harriet Hawes became the first woman to be responsible for the direction of an excavation and for the publication of its results. This also brought her her master's degree from Smith College in 1901. In fact, her archaeological work won her international fame.(11)

That women social scientists at the beginning of this century should have experienced gender discrimination in their efforts to obtain higher education may sound antediluvian to some persons. But let me point out that that was not so long ago as to be beyond memory. In 1937 when I was granted my Ph.D. at Yale University, there were fewer than 2,000 women with earned doctorates in all fields in the whole country. In contrast, between 1970 and 1978, about 1,500 doctorates *in sociology alone* were

granted to women.(12)   More recently, there are signs of a lowering of
those figures because of economic stagnation, the higher costs of advanced education, reductions in financial aid, and the stress laid by many colleges on the practicality of technical training.

The present crisis in women's higher education arises in large part
from the emphasis upon technical skills as preparation for immediate entrance into a narrowly defined current job market that sells women short.
It is a bare amplification of women's roles as they have long been considered. It is in fact scarcely an advance beyond the last century. It
says, in effect, that of course you are welcome to go to college and of
course you can prepare for paid employment afterward, but the courses offered and the emphases in counseling are upon skills and techniques that
prepare most women for limited jobs.   The preparation is not training in
a broad field and not thorough as though for a budding expert who will go
on to a lifetime of participation in a science or an art.

All too often higher education for women fits them for secondary
roles--for example, interior decorators, not fine artists; dental hygien-
ists, not dentists; paramedics or nurses, not physicians;'law librarians,
not attorneys; choir leaders and piano teachers, not solo performers,
conductors, or composers; bank clerks, not bank officers.   In my own
field, women are taught statistics, the computerization of data, grant-
writing to fund research on a problem set by someone else, and sociology
as though it were a cut-and-dried, fully understood science, explored
long since by master minds.   The future for most students--for males but
especially for females--promises the merry-go-round of a modest teaching
position or the limited scope of a governmental or industrial bureaucratic post.

That education plays a large role in promoting the full development
of women's potentials is generally accepted nowadays.   To be sure, no
amount of stimulation and refinement through education, training, the influence of role models, and the presence of opportunity can change a
genetically limited individual into a talented, intelligent person es-
teemed by her peers. In the process, too, the creative individual needs
to find ways to transcend the conformist pressures of so much formal education. As part of this, society is much more likely to benefit, as are
women themselves as individuals, if they are reared from infancy, as people with as much potential as men. If women are educated with the expec-
tation of their fullest development and given a wide range of opportunities to explore that potential, they will far more often rise to that ex-
pectation.

If this point appears obvious or labored, it is emphasized here because investigation of the literature on women and achievement shows that
in many parts of the world popular opinion still holds to the position
that women are innately more limited in their abilities than men, contrary to scientific findings.(13)

We need to do a better job of child rearing and child training in
order that women themselves, their families, their teachers, and all of

society *expect* them all of their lives and as a matter of course to go on learning, thinking, and developing. Society and educators in particular, not only in the interest of individual women, but also in the interest of the enrichment of all social life, would benefit by providing a wide range of cultural opportunities for all of its members.

Currently emphasized educational alternatives are more than anything else limited and limiting. Marketable skills quickly learned lead to low-level jobs that might or might not be available for a dependably long period, as the economy and technologies change. If the jobs do continue, the routine of their duties and the dead-end nature of the work involved dulls the mind and the senses to no one's benefit. For that matter, such routine jobs are now more and more being entrusted to the growing range of mechanical instruments. For example, it will not be long until dictation will be taken directly into typewriters, and computers are already taking over many kinds of filing.

When women respond to higher expectations with the claim that the present high cost of living makes any paid work immediately imperative, then, with that limitation built in so far as work goes, we as educators have all the more responsibility to nurture in them cultural tastes and satisfactions along with marketable skills. We still can and should emphasize much more the joy of living to be derived from a cultivated appreciation of the arts. Beyond that and most importantly, we can teach the elements of design that are the same in painting, in photography, in music, in theatrical design, in sculpture. We can teach not just the reading but the writing of poetry. We can teach not just the history of art and literature but the sense of satisfaction, of fulfillment, and of self-expression to be had from any artistic endeavor, even if limited. Such effort, carried on as a collateral activity to the main occupation, is possible in fragments of time and limited energy, even while other parts of the mind are preoccupied or the hands are busy with routine operations. This is important to make clear to the many women who in later life will otherwise find the days spent and the years gone by in taking care of endlessly repeated detail and without a sense of accomplishment.

We can add enormously to the sensitivity of all students, men *and* women, through helping them to realize that creativity is a natural quality within each individual, springing from imagination. That quality can be developed and helped into expression through instruction not only in the use of concepts and techniques but also in the stimulation of thinking, doubt, criticism, and experimentation. Its habitual exercise can be a lifelong source of gratifying self-expression in the arts, in the sciences, in the humanities, in life itself.

In sum, limited perception of women's roles is a major problem to women themselves and to society in its waste of capacities unused. Great enrichment would come from making accessible to women the full range of opportunities to explore their individual and collective potential.

12 Foreign Languages and Humanistic Learning
ROSETTE LIBERMAN

Not long ago, the school board of a town on the Connecticut shoreline met to decide on what they euphemistically called a "realistic" budget for the following year. This meant, of course, that they were planning to cut the humanities budget and, in particular, to make cuts in foreign languages. A number of people protested the elimination of foreign languages, and did so on the grounds that foreign languages are economically useful.

One person said that foreign language study is of particular importance to Connecticut students because of the many international and multinational corporations based in the state that could employ Connecticut graduates. Another person pointed out that in the light of the importance of foreign markets, foreign language study could prepare students for careers in advertising. Thus, American advertising slogans would at last be translated accurately into foreign languages so that the General Motors Flemish division would never again announce "Corpse by Fisher" instead of "Body by Fisher," and so that when the Chinese are encouraged to "Come Alive with Pepsi," they are not instead promised that, "Pepsi Brings Ancestors Back From the Grave," as happened recently.

These speakers could have added other similar information. Knowledge of foreign languages can undoubtedly get one a good job. According to the Educational Testing Service, 100,000 language-related top jobs go unfilled each year because Americans are not qualified for them.

The United States Chamber of Commerce notes that in New York City alone, 10,000 Japanese businesspeople speak English, while of the same 900 American businesspeople in Japan, only a handful speak Japanese, and then in the most rudimentary way--which probably means that Japanese goods have a far greater commercial future here than American goods do in Japan. The examples could be enumerated at great length. And there is nothing fundamentally wrong with the premise of the speakers at that school board meeting. There is nothing wrong with learning a skill in order to derive from it financial gain. The problem is that this was *all* that was said, that this was the only basis for their objections. Financial profit as an academic motive is fine. However, financial profit as the sole or chief motive trivializes both the student and the skill. It transforms one's life's work into merely a salable commodity. It strips one's profession of pleasure and satisfaction. It asserts the sovereignty of business over people. It implies that education needs to be justified as a commercial benefit.

The obvious absurdity of this attitude is illustrated by a story told about a pupil of Euclid. This young man, upon learning a geometric proposition, inquired, "What shall I get by learning these things?" Euclid turned to a servant and said, "Give him a copper coin, since he must needs gain by what he learns."

Studying a language simply in order to gain a foreign service post or to write a winning advertising jingle in Chinese is like pocketing a copper coin, while ignoring the gold. What then is the gold that is overlooked? Why study a foreign language if not for financial gain? Perhaps the two most important reasons for learning foreign languages are to realize one's identity as a member of the human family, and to contribute to the welfare of that family. To accomplish these a foreign language program must include teaching the language itself, introduction to linguistic theory, and exposure to the cultures of the countries whose languages are being taught.

The number of American students taking foreign languages has sadly declined during the past half century. Before World War I, 36 percent of all high school students studied a foreign language. By 1980, the enrollment had fallen to 15 percent, with fewer than 5 percent of all students reaching the third year of study. At present, approximately one-third of all American high schools offer no foreign languages at all. The common justification offered for this academic poverty is that there is no demand for foreign languages, since only 8 percent of American colleges and universities require a foreign language for admission, which is down from 34 percent in 1966.(1)

Despite the reduction in enrollment, fascinating and viable new techniques are being implemented in the teaching of foreign languages. These include at least two of the three elements that I recommend: teaching the language itself, by concentrating on the four language skills of listening, speaking, reading, and writing, and exposure to the culture of the country whose language is being studied. The third element, an introduction to linguistic theory, is missing from most curricula probably because most language teachers are ignorant of it. Two of these noteworthy techniques are: Total Immersion programs, and the Dartmouth Intensive Language Model.

Total Immersion programs are those that for at least half the school day teach various academic subjects in a foreign language. These programs--some partly government funded--have been proliferating in many

New York State and New England communities along the Canadian border. The language in these schools is, quite naturally, French. There has also been an upsurge of Total Immersion Hebrew language programs at Hebrew day schools in both the United States and Canada. In fact, the demand for competent Hebrew language teachers is so great, and the supply so small, that at least one Hebrew day school in Ottawa was offering upwards of $35,000 a year to fill its faculty slots.

In my own experience as a language teacher, total immersion has proven quite successful with elementary school youngsters from about grade three through grade six. Mine was a program with an original twist, the objective of which was oral fluency. The students began by learning the verb "to be" in the present tense (and its negative), followed by insults that have English cognates, making them easy to remember; and they proceeded vigorously to communicate in a foreign language. Their dialogues sounded something like this:

"Tu est stupide."

"Non, je ne suis pas stupide. Tu est imbecile!"

"Idiot" and "repulsif" were also pretty popular. French fluency was attained by my students at a terrific rate of speed. In fact, they were so charmed by their success that they promptly mastered the present tense of the verb "to have" and enthusiastically accused one another of harboring everything from the plague to bad breath. And by the time that game had paled, they were hooked on French. They had realized that they could communicate fluently and usefully in a foreign language.

At the college level, the most successful innovation in recent years has been the exciting Dartmouth Intensive Language Model. It was developed and is taught by Professor John Rassias. There is no homework. The students spend fifty minutes daily with a master teacher, another fifty minutes with an apprentice teacher, and usually a third period of fifty minutes in a language lab.

John Rassias specializes in dramatic teaching that is teacher-centered but that also demands continuous and active student participation, to the extent that each of twenty-two students (the maximum allowed in class) is expected to participate sixty-five times within a fifty minute period. And, while they are participating, Rassias is teaching, directing, and exhorting them by cavorting, falling, dancing, shouting, and hugging the students, all while speaking in a foreign language.

The vocabulary drills are directed by a lead sentence. The teacher will say, "I haven't slept, therefore I am tired." Each pupil, in turn, modifies the sentence, as in, "I haven't eaten all day, therefore I'm hungry." Instead of translating, Rassias acts out meanings. He stresses grammar, but rather than teach it traditionally, he acts it out using skits and props. These skits are perhaps most valuable in exposing students to the culture of the country whose language they are studying.

Something marvelous happens to people who learn to communicate in more than a single idiom, and who become thoroughly familiar with the customs of other people. They are enlightened by the understanding that definitions are not absolute. They are broadened by the realization that their social and religious traditions are not the only viable expressions of human experience, and that these traditions are neither right nor wrong, but merely idiosyncratic. They become cosmopolitan by learning to accept (not merely to tolerate) the customs of other people. They do not consider the Nepalese custom of saluting their lords by ceremoniously sticking out their tongues any more odd than the Western custom of snapping hands to foreheads on similar occasions. They are not shocked that mourners in Madagascar dance and sing instead of weeping or keening. This marvelous something which happens to people is part of the process of becoming cultured, of transcending geographic and political limitations by learning to identify oneself not as a member of a narrow group but as a member of the human family, which is the first of the major reasons I originally offered for studying foreign languages.

The sense of oneself as a member of the human family would be greatly heightened in students if they were to be introduced to linguistic theory, and specifically to the theories of Noam Chomsky. I have no intention of defending the Chomskyan suppositions, but I do stress their valuable implications.

Chomsky's hypothesis of a universal grammar specifies the principles that make a possible system of grammar into one that is humanly accessible. It points out that languages are not developed and regulated arbitrarily or fortuitously, but according to a priori determinants that have universal application.

Dr. Chomsky equates the study of universal grammar with the study of the nature of human intellectual potential. This grammar establishes the conditions that a system must fulfill to be considered a human language. He maintains that these conditions spring from an innate capability for language among people, that human minds throughout our planet are equipped at birth with an archetype of this grammar. His theory thus explains the speed with which children learn language and master its myriad transformations. The fact that children accomplish the intellectual feat of language mastery at the earliest stage of development when they possess virtually no general competence or life experience further supports Dr. Chomsky's theory of a priori and universal language determinants.(2)

It is this stress on universality that would help students of foreign languages to see themselves as members of a single human family. Language is perhaps the chief way that people and nations are either drawn to or alienated from one another. The ancient Greeks, for example, scorned their non-Greek neighbors primarily because of differences in language, not in customs. They called those neighbors "Barbarians"-- meaning those who expressed themselves by making noises that sounded like "brrr, brrr," instead of speaking proper Greek, as civilized people did.

Just as differences in language alienate, so similarities attract. In 1960, when I lived in Ibiza, I became close friends with an elderly English couple of aristocratic pretensions only because I shared with them a more or less common language. Russians living outside the boun-

daries of the Soviet Union feel a similar closeness to anyone who speaks
Russian, particularly if the person does so in a reasonably decent ac-
cent.   Total strangers approach one another and enter into conversation
at the first sound of a Russian syllable.   I have made friends with people in that way on the streets of Paris, Madrid, New York, New Haven.

This sense of belonging, of common identity, can be fostered in foreign language students by suggesting to them the frequent and exciting
similarities between words of even ostensibly unrelated languages.   My
students experience an ineffable sense of satisfaction when I point out
to them these similarities. For instance, in a timely comparison between
English and Iranian, they found strong similarity between the words identifying members of a family.   The English word "mother" in Iranian is
"modar," with only a minor shift from "th" to "d."   "Father" is a little
more distantly related to "pedar," but still recognizable. "Daughter" is
almost identical to "dochtar," with "gh" very logically equated with
"ch," as in the "Channukan." These are fascinating similarities for two
languages in which only one has Latin roots. By realizing these similarities, my students felt a greater sense of kinship even with Iranians.

This sense of kinship is most vividly felt by people when they can
communicate with others in the same language.   Communication is the purpose of language. It is the transmission through words (spoken or written) of events, insights, longings, and aspirations by human beings to
one another. Accurate transmission is doubtful even when a writer and
reader, or speaker and listener, share a time, a set of assumptions, a
language. Human experience is elusive, evading definition.   The human
languages are inexact, with meanings disguised by analogy and discerned
only intuitively in metaphor. Taking liberties with Thornton Wilder, we
might say that the only people who ever realize language while they speak
it "every, every minute," are "saints and poets, maybe" and Noam Chomsky.
How much more difficult is it to understand an author or a speaker when,
in addition to time and geography, language itself mitigates between that
person and the comprehension of the reader or listener.

Understanding one another and feeling a kinship with one another
must not apply exclusively to communication among modern people. We cannot become cultured without access--ideally direct access in the same
language--to the observations of thinkers who had preceded us.

As an undergraduate at Barnard, I heard my favorite professor, Barry
Ulanov, mention that he studied foreign languages to read great books in
the language of their authors. He learned Spanish to read Cervantes and
Italian to read Dante. He also read at least French, Russian, and German. Apparently, he was not about to be denied literary immediacy even
by Scott Moncrieff, Constance Garnett, or Helen Lowe-Porter. For all of
us who respect great artists and thinkers, such literary immediacy is an
imperative, and can only be gained through multilingual fluency.

This fluency not only gives us unobstructed access to the thoughts
of others, but it infinitely increases our own capacity for the pellucid
expression of our ideas.   Knowing many languages provides a speaker or

writer with linguistic options.   No doubt many of us are familiar with
the aprocryphal tale of Charles V, emperor of the Holy Roman Empire,
which illustrates such options. Charles was asked if he had a favorite
language of the many that he spoke. He is reported to have replied as
follows: "I have no favorite language. I suit my speech to my audience.
To my God I speak in Spanish, to my mistress in Italian, to my ministers
of state in French, and to my dog in German."   We who love the work of
Goethe, Heine, and Thomas Mann disagree with his conception of an ideal
canine tongue, but being multilingual, we ackowledge the truth inherent
in that imperial summation.   Each language is rich in a unique way.   I
find that English is rich in vocabulary; Russian is better able to express shades of feeling; French is precise; Yiddish is the language of
bitter-sweet humor. Swahili has, by one account, more than thirty syno-
nyms for the word "cow;" and probably, of the 4,000 or more languages
spoken by the human race, at least one is the language of regret.

One's choice of language can also define interpersonal relationships. The American student who speaks only a modern, egalitarian English devoid of distinctions between "thou" and "you" realizes a new world
of social distinctions expressed by the familiar and polite pronouns of
other tongues. Conversely, Oriental speakers can find new social dimensions in addressing one another in that democratic English. Korean, for
example, has six clearly defined levels of politeness. The level selected by each speaker depends on perceptions of rank vis-a-vis that of the
other party. There is a story about the contradictory circumstances that
prevailed when a male Korean graduate student and his female faculty su-
pervisor became lovers. In the laboratory, he spoke with a courtesy bor-
dering on the deferential, while she was familiar.   In private, however,
their relationship was equal. It was an equality between male and female
that could not be accommodated in Korean.   Thus, in private, they spoke
to one another in English. By choosing to speak in English, these two
people transcended their national limitations and acknowledged themselves
to be simply and splendidly human.

I had suggested two main reasons for the study of foreign lan-
guages--the first to realize one's identity as a member of the human family, and the second to contribute to the welfare of that family, not specifically through the foreign language discipline, but generally in the
way that all liberal arts contribute to the safeguarding of human welfare
by developing in people balance, maturity, judgment, and wisdom.

For the past century and a half or more, the world has gaped in a-
mazement at the marvels of industrialization, has worshipped at the
mighty altar of applied science, has entrusted its soul into the keeping
of multinational apparatchiks. In their anxious scramble for physical
comfort and military and material security, people and nations have lost
their sense of value and perspective. These losses are still not irrevo-
cable. A balanced perspective is the result of intellectual and emotional maturity, a maturity that is developed specifically by a strong humanistic education.

Some time ago, I came across a short essay by Mark Van Doren titled "Education by Books" that strongly affirms the value of a humanistic education; and I wish that all those school board members who view intellectuals with misgiving and who are inclined to eliminate the humanities from budgeted curricula could read this flashing riposte to their insularity. It asserts the value of a strictly prescribed curriculum to tune the mind to universal, timeless verities. Thinking is a developed skill and, as with other skills, the degree of proficiency depends largely on the amount of practice, on the stringency of discipline, on the challenge of the materials. Dr. Van Doren's way may not be the only one to so tune the mind, but it is a superlative and time-tested way, and, unfortunately, a way that in modern education is too often shunned due to fear, ignorance, or superficiality in both teachers and students. His observara are eminently relevant to the focus of this book.

> Let us assume that an institution was founded for the sole purpose of requiring its members to read certain books. These members were called students, for the institution was something like a school or college; and there were a few exacting elders on hand who after announcing their authority began to teach.
>
> The teaching in this institution, like the studying, was at the same time simple and difficult. It consisted in the first place . . . in requiring the students to read certain books. It consisted next in requiring that an intelligible account be rendered of the contents of each book. And it consisted last of all in requiring that the readers be able, in the course of discussing a given book, to prove that their memory of all previous books was accurate and complete.
>
> It was as simple as that, and as difficult. The books were the acknowledged masterpieces of the past three thousand years—masterpieces of poetry, of history, of philosophy, of fiction, of theology, of natural science, of political and economic theory. There were two hundred or so of them, and none of them was read in an abridged edition. Neither were any of them approached through a digest or a commentary, or through a biography of the author which told how many wives he had and what the biographer believed to be the modern significance of his mind. No, these books which the teachers selected for the students to read . . . these authors . . . were read naked and entire; and understood.
>
> A few students—some say a good many—had got into the institution by mistake. They complained about the lack of freedom to read what they pleased; some of these books, they insisted, were not suited to their personalities, and they had supposed that what one went to college for was to develop one's personality. Precisely, answered the head preceptor, closing the door behind them with the most obvious and feckless relief.

Others proved to be helpless once they were face to face with an author's original sentences; they had been brought up on outlines, introductions, histories of literature and thought, and collections of excerpts, and so had long ago lost whatever ability to read they had been born with. Still others had expected to learn a trade or a profession. Then there was a final group of pedantic youngsters who snorted at the reading list because it was not contemporary. They wanted as swift an introduction as possible to the civilization about them. To the reply that this was that, they were very scornful as they scurried off to become freshmen in some up-to-date college where field trips to factories alternated in the weekly schedule with lectures on large and immediate subjects.

These gone, the others settled down to the task that had been so arbitrarily assigned them. At regular intervals they met in small groups with two or more teachers who questioned them closely concerning the contents of the required, the inevitable book. If they revealed by their answers that they had read it badly, they were forced to read it again. There was no going forward until Aristotle's conception of the individual, or Grotius's theory of natural law, or the unity of "King Lear" was clearly stated. No excursions were made into the culture of the Greeks or the domestic life of the Middle Ages; merely the books themselves were read, discussed, and understood. And so on for four years.

At the end of which time, a generation of students was set loose upon a world with many of whose aspects they were not at the moment prepared to cope. The only thing, indeed, to be said in their favor was that they were educated. They were e-quipped, that is, with so much understanding of what the best human brains had done in three thousand years that they realized without difficulty how few contemporary brains--naturally--were of the best. They were so competent in the recognition of theory that they felt strangely at home in a world most of whose citizens lived by theories without knowing it. They were able to reduce a kind of order out of the childish chaos which they slowly recognized contemporary literature to be. They missed a great many ideas and distinctions which they knew had been fruitful in past centuries, and some of them set about considering the possibility of restoring these to an intellectually impoverished world. Whether they succeeded is not yet known. But it can be said of them that in their own minds they continued to be fairly secure. For never would there be written a book which they could not understand simply by reading it from the first word to the last. They might not save the world. They might not change it. But they would comprehend it.(3)

I think that it is only through that profound comprehension that humanity can attain the maturity by which it can save itself.   We are like a precocious child capable of marvelous technological inventions, but without the good judgment to handle those inventions discreetly, without the wisdom to control and circumscribe their consequences.   We are like precocious children juggling our creative playthings on the brink of an atomic and ecological abyss. Mark Van Doren may have been right.   Intellectuals, students of the liberal arts, might not change the world; but it is only through their vision and their wisdom that the world can change and save itself.

13 Revitalizing the Modern Humanities

HENRI PEYRE

One of the most respected apostles of humanistic architecture in the United States, Lewis Mumford, remarked at the beginning of his volume, *Art and Technics*, that "when a Chinese scholar wished to utter a withering curse upon his enemy, he said: 'May you live in an interesting age!'"(1) In Western terms, that would mean an age of moral landslides and bitter recriminations. The humanities, in that sense, are particularly "interesting" in the United States in the last quarter of the twentieth century. Commencement orators praise their excellence and the benefits they may bring to our minds, and are duly applauded. Occasionally, foundations, endowments, or institutes step in to provide modest funds to assist and encourage humanists. Yet not a few college administrators, while paying lip service to those disinterested studies, tolerate them as a venerable museum piece, "a kind of marble hall shining on a hill," as William James once called them.

Humanists might deserve part of the blame for that sad state of their vocation, by fixing their gaze too insistently upon the past and mourning for the bygone days, instead of vigorously rethinking the whole of education in an era of mass attendance in schools and colleges and of fast-expanding technology. A humanist in the United States and in Europe today has little in common with the Renaissance humanist or with a seventeenth century member of the leisure class in Bologna, Paris, or Oxford. Yet the right and duty exists to proclaim and explain that he is serving all of society rather than his own ilk and an inherited tradition. The humanist's concern is with the future. The burden of guiding, perhaps even of saving, the world has fallen upon American society. Is it content with becoming a nation of accountants, lawyers, technicians, advertisers? In politics, at home, and in our dealings with a complex world, in science and technology, in trade, in labor relations and social problems, never has this country stood in greater need of a vast pool of educated citizens, conversant with modes of thinking other than the "Anglo-Saxon" ones, willing to persuade and to understand people with a sensi-bility and a sensitiveness not necessarily attuned to ours. Brandishing the threat of force and promising "agonizing reappraisals" have not con-spicuously succeeded in rallying friends to the leaders of several admin-istrations in Washington. The coolness, if not the indifference, with which the celebration of our bicentennial was received outside our bor-ders in 1976, should have showed us what gulfs of incomprehension separ-ate people in an age of mass media, air travel, and the near-universality of the English language. If ever the modern humanities, in which the knowledge of foreign languages and cultures is central, should be deemed vital to the most powerful nation on earth, the time is now. Statesmen, journalists, and educators have uttered many a warning lately. A profes-sor of language and literature, with more than fifty years of familiarity with American universities, may in his turn repeat them and explain why.

The humanities, which are called in other countries "human sciences" and are less separated from social studies than they are in the United States, cover a broad range of disciplines: English, ancient and modern languages, philosophy, religion, art, and even history to a large extent. One of their functions is to provide young people in school and college, and adults as well, with some acquaintance with the past and with a tra-dition which has remained very much alive in and around us. Through that study, the young generation may gain a perspective on the experience of the human race and some awareness of the forces which have molded their predecessors. Few things are more essential in the process of education than the broadening of the shrunken world of the child and the acquisi-tion of historical imagination. An educated man or woman of our time can hardly afford to remain the person of one age alone and the citizen of one country.

It requires little ingeniousness in the teachers of humanistic sub-jects to depict the past, in T. S. Eliot's words, not as what is dead, but as what is already alive.(2) The present can only artificially be severed from the past. The ideal of the French child, as Matthew Arnold once defined it after visiting schools in France, is also that of an edu-cation worthy of the name anywhere--namely, to understand oneself and the world. Science, political studies, economics, and anthropology stress the knowledge of the world at large, in which the American reach-ing adulthood is certain to be involved. Philosophy, literature, and language are more concerned with the equally necessary insight into our-selves.

What is called the present is but an ever-shifting and tenuous link between the past and the future. No less than the sciences, the humani-ties aim at preparing young people to face the future, to anticipate it, and to some extent to mold it. The mortality rate of what is taught in courses in physics, biology, medicine, economics, and international rela-tions is considerably higher than in humanistic studies. Few science teachers are as candid as the proverbial scientist who modestly opened his course with the warning: "Half of what I am going to teach you this term will soon be proved false, but I don't know which half."   One thing may be stated with certainty about the economics of 1999, the genetics or the microbiology of 1999: they will be radically different from what was taught in the colleges in 1989.   Any textbook of physics, chemistry, embryology, or mathematics written thirty years ago is ludicrously outdated. Robert Maynard Hutchins, never much impressed by the deceptively practical bent in college teaching, once wondered if we were educating our children for the wrong future. For the world two decades hence is sure to appear very different from what it is today. Homer, Dante, Goethe, and Shakespeare will have lost little of their timelessness. The obsession with the practical and the immediate has been harmful to the training of intelligent citizens. The most relevant subjects are often those that the young hastily and superficially deem irrelevant.

Lastly, if properly taught--that is to say, if lived and presented with fervor--humanistic subjects should also enhance our sense of beauty and our enjoyment of life. If not reduced to purely intellectual analysis and to learning dates and facts by rote, they appeal to the imagination and perhaps stimulate the impulse to create and to feel.   Scientists, economicsts, physicians, city planners, and ecologists are no less aware than humanists of the woeful havoc we have inflicted on our environment and of "the shame of our cities," as it was called and denounced fully a century ago. They are aware of the role that literature, archaeology, music, and the fine arts can play in enabling us to enjoy the world while we have it. Such benefits to our lives are in no way elitist or reserved for the best and the brightest, who often are also the greediest and the busiest. The modern humanities are, in fact, more democratic a pursuit than the study of the arcana of corporate law or of computer science. It is the duty of education in a democracy not to deprive anyone of opportunities for mental or spiritual growth and to train young people not only for, but also *against* their future profession or trade. The inability of too many people to enjoy leisure is one of the pathetic sights of our civilization in its addiction to the oral and the visual.

These goals are noble and lofty; they are not easily reached. Those who are entrusted with the teaching of the humanities may well wonder, with no little anxiety and soul searching, whether they come close to fulfilling them. There are poor teachers of foreign languages and literatures just as there are mediocre engineers.   There are also poor students, whom the best of instructors do not always succeed in inspiring. An unreasonable claim is too often put forward by adults who, twenty years earlier, were exposed to Latin or French or German in school. They remark that they have forgotten most of it--as well as English grammar or much of American history, calculus, or chemistry. But the benefits to their whole personalities and to their understanding of people different from themselves cannot be measured by what they remember in terms of declensions or conjugations, syntax, or pronunciation. I have observed the teaching of language and literature in the United States for half a century, visiting scores, if not hundreds, of colleges. I have been able to compare the American achievement in this field with that of the older institutions of Western Europe. Now retired, there is no reason to flatter younger colleagues or forsake objectivity. At a time when pessimism is the order of the day and the former—and often merely formal—arrogance of Americans has given way to an inferiority complex to the countries the United States defeated in World War II, it is nevertheless justifiable to declare that the best institutions in the country compare favorably in the teaching of the modern humanities with the most prestigious ones abroad.

Innovation has been the key to most of this country's successes, in education as well as in industrial and political life. But the ability to innovate is not bestowed once and for all. The bold forward moves effected by one generation have a perilous tendency to turn into sclerosed traditions, unless the spirit that originally animated the creation of a tradition remains alive. American education once had hoped to part for good with scholasticism and with the pedantry that had been the bane of the humanists of sixteenth-century Italy and France. In the eighteenth century, Bishop Berkeley, a better philosopher than he was a poet, boldly composed a piece, "Verses on the Prospect of Planting Arts and Learning in America." He hailed this blessed land as "Happy climes/ Where man shall not impose for truth and sense/ The pedantry of courts and schools."(3) Pedantry and the flight away from simplicity and clarity have since prevailed, not the least in criticism and linguistics where specialized language is less indispensable than in more esoteric disciplines. Too many professors of would-be "humane letters" appear to wish to address themselves only to a select minority of their colleagues and no longer to those who might find pleasure (a word repugnant to those new and solemn Puritans) in the reading of novels and poetry or even of essays. Too many critics appear to have forgotten their role as intermediaries between the difficult and challenging works of literature, history, or philosophy and the men and women of good will who could well accede to those works if encouraged.

The result has been a steady lowering of the verbal scores on the Scholastic Aptitude Test (SAT) in the most prosperous and once best-educated sections of the United States. On a campus as selective and renowned as that of the University of California at Berkeley, nearly half of the freshman class failed the placement examination. At two of the best schools of journalism, Wisconsin and Minnesota, 30 to 50 percent of of the applicants had to be rejected for inadequate spelling. Gene Lyons reported these missed educational opportunities and many similar ones in an article titled, "The Higher Illiteracy."(4) He blamed the indifference and the selfishness of too many scholar-teachers. As a result, even those students who might have something to express "produce only a mass of confused and puerile nonsense." Kingman Brewster, the former president of Yale University, deplored the sloppy writing that professors tolerate and that students indulge in, seemingly unaware that they are

"using an atrocious style to spoil what might otherwise have been a mediocre idea."(5)

One of the most regrettable fallacies has been, in the syllabi for
English courses as well as for those in foreign languages, the excessive
stress on very recent texts, often of bare journalistic value and seldom
offering models of prose. That has been due in part to an absurd competition of material read in classrooms with what the young people will
probably watch on their screens later in the evening. It has led many of
our teenagers to stress their affinities with other young people and to
isolate themselves from adults. The trite phrase, "generation gap," has
served as a dubious excuse to separate the young from their elders, and
the loss is gravest for the former. As soon as they enter the world of
public affairs, of law, industry and banking, these same young people
will have to work with persons twenty or thirty years older. They had
better have learned how to cooperate with them. Through them and through
their teachers, they might have gained a little of that sense of the past
in its bearing upon the present which endows an otherwise fleeting and
vacuous present with substance and density. The disappearance of almost
all classics of literature from schools and even from some colleges is a
woeful calamity. It prevents the growth of a sense of cultural community
in a society which is not only pluralistic, but made up of more diverse,
if not antagonistic groups than any other. No less harmful has been the
alienation from history in even the most respected of establishments.
Jeffrey Record in an article titled, "The Fortunes of War," deplored the
shift that, at West Point and Annapolis, has stressed technology, mathematics, and logistics at the expense of history. Yet that very same emphasis on technology brought our leaders bitter disappointments in the
Vietnam War. It would not prove any more efficacious in Iran, El Salva-
dor, or Angola. The study of history and some understanding of the mental processes of nations different from us might have saved us dismal errors. We have examples of great military men who knew better: Napoleon,
Clausewitz, Mahan, MacArthur, and Patton learned much from history, including respect and allowance for the role of chance and imponderables in
war. They knew that technologies could become a liability if not util-
ized with intelligence and flair. Record concluded that "the proper
study of war is the study of history."(6)

The advance in most scientific disciplines has resulted in the growing use of quantitative data. Statistics, word counts, linguistic laws,
even the construction of models and the reduction of dramatic plots or of
folk tales to a limited number of patterns have some usefulness in humanistic research. However, the sectors in which resorting to measurable
factors can be rewarding are few. It is debatable if even political science and structural linguistics have gained substantially from the generalized practice of such methods. It is even more doubtful that the humanistic or sociological studies have been served by them. Not a few eminent social scientists who had once been seduced by the lure of quantitative measurements, from Pitirim Sorokin to Gordon Allport, subsequently

deplored the reductionism prevailing in their discipline and denounced the peril of its "galloping empiricism." The obsession of some political thinkers with statistical data and precise methodology has not always enhanced their ability to predict the future and to prepare for it.   In 1976, a well-known social scientist widely read in philosophy and art history, Robert A. Nisbet, published a book with the challenging title, *Sociology as an Art Form*. He contended that the most significant achievements of modern sociology had been accomplished outside the scientific method--statistical analysis, for example, problem design, verification, theory construction, and so forth. The fertile concepts (community, progress, alienation, anomie) were reached through imaginative processes similar to those which are at work in art. "Science and art in their psychological roots are almost identical. . . . Sociology is also one of the arts." Several of its greatest practitioners, Alexis de Tocqueville, Georg Simmel, Emile Durkheim, Max Weber, Thorstein Veblen, Claude Levi-Strauss, Raymond Aron, and Sir Peter Medawar, have been men trained in philosophy and sensitive to literary values. It is ridiculous, Nisbet submits, to allow students to believe that "a small idea abundantly verified is worth more than a large idea still unsusceptible to textbook techniques of verification."(7)

The rage for ever narrower specialization has indeed worked havoc in many a realm of study in our time. Humanities have not remained totally immune from it. Fences and watertight partitions separate a chemist from another chemist, a microbiologist from another biologist with slightly different interests. Mutual enrichment might well accrue from diverse points of view if closer relations could nevertheless be maintained. "Chance favors the prepared mind," a famous scientist was reported to have quipped, and the best prepared mind is seldom the narrowly specialized one. Claude Bernard started with literary studies, and even with the writing of a tragedy, before turning into one of the greatest physiologists; he became a faultless experimenter who could also write a beautiful classic on experimental medicine. Sigmund Freud was at least as much influenced, when he started his career, by Shakespeare, Goethe, and minor French novelists, as he was by those who had analyzed neuroses and interpreted dreams before him.

In the fields that we call humanistic, the refuge in specialization has become a form of timorous laziness. A scholar specializes in one writer or in one dozen years of a century. Doctoral candidates are encouraged to limit themselves even more narrowly, getting to know, as the cliche goes, more and more about less and less--hence the atomization of knowledge about which we all ritually complain, but seldom attempt to remedy. New universities are founded every twenty years; but none has mustered the audacity to modernize the Ph.D. training in English and other literatures. It is as untouchable as the antiquated system of electoral colleges and of primaries in presidential elections.

Yet the complaints are loud and the warnings against excessive specialization in education and research have been uttered by the wisest and most far-sighted people for a hundred years. "You are not good musicians because you know only music," Debussy admonished his younger contemporaries. Henri Bergson, in the first address he gave in Angers, France, in 1882, spoke on and against "la specialite."   Specialization, he warned, is a feature of animals which, like the ant, the bee, and the beaver, can do one or two things to perfection, but nothing else, and fail to develop through trial and error.   Almost a century later, Sir Julian Huxley, speaking as a scientist who was also a broad humanist, in *New Bottles for New Wine*, declared that "one-sided adaptation to a particular mode of life leads to an evolutionary dead end."(8)   Business enterprises have been just as outspoken in their laments over the narrowness of engineers, chemists, managers, and economists trained by the universities; deans of medical schools have echoed their complaints when observing the blinkers too complacently adopted by future physicians.   A prominent political scientist and university president, Stephen Muller of Johns Hopkins, has repeatedly stated that highly technical training in college, superseded within ten years, does not serve the graduate as well as a liberal arts education. "Liberal arts graduates leaven the society with generalists who are eminently employable. . . . The choice of possible jobs open to them is usually wider than that opened to the graduate of a vocational or technical curriculum."(9)

If one of the aims of education is to prepare the young for life in society (and the not-so-young, too, for continuing education is more and more a *sine qua non* in our fast-changing world), it should also assume another purpose: to ready the educated citizens to be on their guard against the deficiencies and the perils of their society. A humanistic training, with an emphasis on languages other than our own and on the most valuable experience of the race as embodied in works of literature, may assist us in eschewing what I consider three common pitfalls. They may be summarily designated as narcissism, reluctance to mature, and the lack of a constructively critical spirit.

Narcissus was once sung by poets as one of the most graceful and touching figures of mythology. From poetry and painting, he has in our century been reduced to the symbol of a neurosis on which psychoanalysts multiply papers. A skillful popularizer and vigorous polemicist, Christopher Lasch diagnosed narcissism as one of the corroding ills of American culture today. His widely read volume, *The Culture of Narcissism,* bore as a subtitle, *American Life in an Age of Diminishing Expectations.*(10) The author deplored the lack of interest in the past and in the humanities, which has had as a consequence the loss of faith in our future. Philosophy consents to be truncated and shorn of much that was formerly meaningful in it. Its practitioners would blush to be viewed as speculating on the good, the beautiful, and the true. They refuse to address themselves to the people in the "market place," as Plato, Epicurus, Montaigne, Bacon, Pascal, Descartes, Spinoza, and Hume did; none of them was a university teacher. Literature that, for a time (with the existentialists, most notably), had invested philosophy with a seductive liter-

ary garb, has become a mere epiphenomenon of language abstractly analyzed. Jogging as a means of salvation has become the motto and the "so-
teriological" value of literature, once proclaimed by Proust and Camus,
is derided. Little do typical narcissists care for the masters of fore-
gone literature, or even those of the present; they are unable to iden-
identify with anyone else, except as extensions of themselves.

Such a woeful dearth of inner resources is a form of obstinate in-
fantilism. The divinized heroes of the masses, such as Elvis Presley,
Jerry Rubin and Eldridge Cleaver, become pathetic figures seen in retro-
spect or when looking at their own selves after reaching the fatal age of
forty. The phenomenon is not exclusively American. The haste with which
formerly radical leaders of the youth in France (Jean-Francoise Revel,
Bernard Henry Levy, Philippe Sellers) have repudiated their revolutionary
idealism to become champions of traditional values and idols of the middle class has bewildered their followers. Their American counterparts
are more disarming in their ingenuity. One of them, Jerry Rubin, titled
his palinody, *Growing Up at Thirty Seven*. At thirty, he was repudiated
by his admirers, abandoned by his girlfriend. He naively discovered that
"followers of heroes have a hidden desire to see their heroes die." Pathetically, he concluded, "If you're unwilling to grow old, you are unwilling to grow up. . . . Much of my life, I have been running away from
myself." Somewhat late, he came to the modes avowal: "As I grow older,
I am learning how much I do not know about life."(11) Better late than
never, no doubt. Some French veterans of the abortive 1968 revolution
have, fifteen years after their utopian illusions were deflated, committed suicide. Their American counterparts appear to be endowed with, at
the very least, resiliency--the privilege of an incessantly mobile society. Still, one may be optimistic enough to believe that a more solid
practice of the humanities and some vicarious experience of life as a ma-
turing process (an experience gained through literature) might have
spared twenty years of fumbling to the youth raised during the 1950s and
1960s. Some of us thought of adopting as a motto for the study of ancient and modern European literatures in the New World the three words
that, in his tragic resignation, Edgar utters in the final act of *King
Lear:* "Ripeness is all."

Critical spirit cannot be claimed to be the monopoly of the students
of languages. Lawyers, social scientists, and physical scientists are
obviously not lacking in it. Still, the latter have, more enthusiastically or more resignedly than the humanists, fallen for test questions to
which the examinee must answer "yes" or "no." It is as if one were asked
which of the Ten Commandments one elects to observe. Those of us who
suspect that there are no absolute standards of taste or of truth in elusive humane subjects fret at examinations that must elicit only mechanical answers. "Life is an offensive against the repetitive mechanisms of
nature," remarked scientist-philosopher Alfred North Whitehead.(12) Ask-
ing the right questions is, on the part of students and of teachers a-
like, more profitable than giving what textbooks or dull and conventional

common sense may take to be the correct answers.

If the training in ancient languages proved for so   long a valid one
for future statesmen and scientists, it was   precisely because wrestling
with difficult tasks in a language other than our own sharpened the critical spirit. Deciphering Thucydides, Tacitus, Dante, or Pascal required
an unflagging power of attention.   With the cult of images invading our
culture today and the role of reading questioned and perhaps shrinking,
the cultivation of a certain tenseness of our active attention should be
more than ever necessary. A conspiracy of all the means of publicity and
of the mass media is at work to bring about a systematic "decline of attention," in Clifton Fadiman's words.(13) It should be the purpose of
education at all levels to train the young to resist that repetitiousness
of the publicity slogans that attempt to turn them into passive and un-
discriminating consumers; the fleeting succession of entertaining images
should be offset by harder cogitation.   The reading of Joyce, of Proust,
of Wittgenstein, even of a serious daily newspaper demands it.   Indeed,
Henry James complained, as early as 1902, to William Dean Howells that
their readers were but few because "the faculty of attention has utterly
vanished from the general Anglo-Saxon mind."(14)

A number of events have occurred since 1902 that have increased the
urgency of that warning.   Physicist and Nobel prize winner Dennis Gabor
advised us, in these crucial times, to "invent our future."   He bluntly
asked the question: "Can we survive our future?"(15)   The inventor of
holography and member of the faculty at London College of Science and
Technology, warned us that humankind is not well prepared for technology.
We should first, in some degree, control our own activities, learn how to
understand others, and realize that "economic growth pursued as an end in
itself has become senseless." It should be offset or supplemented by
other values--in part, humanistic ones. "The path to peace is often more
difficult than the road to war," a wise secretary of state warned us not
long ago.(16) Winning the respect and the collaboration of other nations
through an understanding of their languages, their aspirations, and their
spiritual needs might well, in the long run, prove a more profitable enterprise than threatening or bribing their leaders.

14 The Unity and Utility of Learning
GILBERT J. SLOAN

In his 1959 Rede Lecture at Cambridge University, C. P. Snow analyzed the
breakdown of Western culture into two noninteracting segments.(1) Adherents of the "two cultures" speak different languages and each actually
takes pride in its remoteness from the other. In the original lecture
and in a reevaluation in 1963, Snow acknowledged that two might not be
the right number. Perhaps three or some much larger number of cultures
could be identified. In American society, at least, one must in fact
think of three separate cultures. These can be associated with science
and technology, commerce and finance, and arts and letters. To be sure,
there are points binding pairs of cultures. Some areas of philosophy
bridge physics and humanities faculties, and some segments of engineering
are equally rooted in technology and in commerce. Nevertheless, the
three cultures are discrete and tend to view each other without mutual
comprehension and often with hostility. This is not to say that each of
the three cultures, as defined here, is homogeneous. There is plenty of
hostility between science and engineering, and one need only look briefly
at *Commentary* or *Partisan Review* to know that humanists squabble. Nonetheless, affiliation with one or another of these goes far toward defining an individual's outlook, beliefs, and lifestyle--transcending even
religious, ethnic, and class ties.

  Science and technology have transformed life since the industrial
revolution. These disciplines have been responsible for the enrichment
of the developed countries. In turn, the developed countries have nurtured science and technology as a treasured resource. The enrichment of
our lives by technology is so deeply embedded in Western culture, that we
take it for granted. We assume that most of us will live seventy or more
years in reasonably good health and that our children will survive birth
and infancy. These prospects were alien in Europe and the United States
until technological times, and remain remote for two-thirds of the

world's people today.   The practitioners of science and technology see
the results of their collective effort as profoundly humane.   Even without detailed historical analysis, they sense the forward thrust of technology and look more to the future than to the past in a generally optimistic way.

Certainly, there is a dark side to science and technology, and increasingly scientists and technologists are recognizing that it simply
will not do to attribute misapplication of technology to someone else.
Scientists are viewing their own work in the broad context of how it contributes to evolving social goals and human aspirations.   This mode of
thought was well expressed by Glenn Seaborg: "In our complex twentieth
century world, we must recognize that the capability of our Earth to sustain certain kinds of growth is limited, so we must recalibrate our traditional vision of a world with an unlimited supply of material resources, at the same time making sure there is no limit to the growth of
knowledge or of beauty in our lives."(2)

Social structures must be designed to make use of technology and to
distribute its products, and resources must be allocated in a rational
way among competing claims.   These functions must be performed whatever
the socio-economic structure of a technological society.   The culture of
commerce and finance should act in concert with science and technology to
maximize the physical wealth of society.

While both commerce and finance and science and technology have academic connections, the preponderance of both lies outside the colleges
and universities.   Still, their practitioners see their own work as essentially intellectual.   The degree of abstractness and the symbolic content might vary, but the work has or can have substantial intellectual,
aesthetic, and emotional content.   The chasms that separate the cultures
are so deep and so broad that many humanists cannot concede, or are unaware of, these aesthetic and emotional contents.   The late Bartlett Giamatti, a former president of Yale University and specialist in Italian
renaissance literature, talked about the cultural divisions as a "ballet
of mutual antagonism." The metaphor is an apt one, and Giamatti enlarges
on it: "There is in the notion of a ballet something choreographed,
deeply satisfying and almost luxurious.   What I wanted to indicate is
that people in the academic world and people in the corporate world have
each derived real pleasure out of insulting the other in an ordered and
stereotyped way for years now."   Giamatti commented upon the question of
how humanities faculties should respond to vocationalism:

It is stupid, foolish, to induce in students who have a vocational impulse a sense of guilt for it.   You cannot ask highly
competitive young men and women to compete, to make a contribution, and then deny them their desire to locate that in something useful. We should be trying to shape that vocationalism
rather than deny it. You shape it by affirming not the "morally corrupt" qualities of students for wanting a job, but by af-

firming the principles of education along a broad spectrum as
the best way to prepare a person for the types of jobs opening
up now. Rather than asserting the virtue of a broad education
because it denies vocationalism, it is much more to the point
to speak of it as the proper base for preserving occupational
flexibility.(3)

Scientists believe that humanists see science and technology as mechanical and without a spirit of adventure, joy, and beauty. Scientists
have quite a different view of what impels them. In an essay on "Beauty
and the Quest for Beauty in Science," Subranmanyan Chandrasekhar quotes
Poincare as follows:

The scientist does not study nature because it is useful to do
so. He studies it because he takes pleasure in it; and he
takes pleasure in it because it is beautiful. If nature were
not beautiful, it would not be worth knowing and life would not
be worth living. I mean the intimate beauty which comes from
the harmonious order of its parts and which a pure intelligence
can grasp. . . . It is because simplicity and vastness are both
beautiful that we take delight now in following the giant courses of the stars, now in scrutinizing with a microscope that
prodigious smallness which is also a vastness, and now in seeking in geological ages the traces of the past that attracts us
because of its remoteness.

Chandrasekhar goes on to discuss some examples of what scientists have
responded to as beautiful and mentions situations in which mathematicians
perceive arcane truths with no apparent reason. Thus, one reader of the
works of Ramanujan recalls an earlier mathematician's response to Her-
mite's papers on modular functions: *"On a la chair de poule."* He also
cites Boltzmann's reaction to paper of Maxwell: "Even as a musician can
recognize . . . Mozart, Beethoven or Schubert after hearing the first few
bars, so can a mathematician recognize . . . Cauchy, Gauss, Jacobi, Helm-
holtz or Kirchhoff after the first few pages."(4)
    Lest you think that these sentiments fly around only in the loftiest
circles of the higher mathematics, a recent survey of M.I.T. physics undergraduates, most of whom intended to study for a Ph.D., showed that
most studied physics because they found it interesting, not because they
expected it to be valuable in their future employment. Further, Jacob
Rabinow, holder of more than two hundred U.S. patents, said, "Invention
is an art form and must be supported like an art form." He described how
he felt an "emotional reaction to beautiful inventions."(5)
    A personal illustration might clarify this point. My son learned
about crystals at school when he was about ten. Knowing that crystal
growth is one of my scientific interests, he asked if we could grow some
crystals at home. After spending a couple of hours in the kitchen heat-

ing salt solutions and cooling sugar solutions, he asked, "Do you really get paid for doing this?" Skills and constructs for which there is a commercial market are not necessarily drudgery and can even be fun. Humanists will do well to consider this fact very carefully.

Many people will have wondered, "Who are Ramanujan and Poincare?" which leads to the next point. The cultural gaps that exist in our society arise largely from the scientific illiteracy of humanists. To expect scientific literacy is not to expect that humanists should be able to do science or even to follow its results in a quantitative way. What is expected, however, is that humanists not consider themselves cultivated persons of the twentieth century without knowing at least the methods, qualitative results, goals, nonlinearities, and discontinuities of science and technology. Certainly they should refrain from charges of Philistinism or a lack of intellectual content against persons and disciplines they hardly know, much less understand. Even more certainly, they should shrink from the role of literate Luddites, in mindless opposition to all technology.

If the teachers of art, literature, and history could be induced to learn and then teach about the parallel evolution of science and the humanities, then there might develop a new community of scholarship. There would then be an improved basis for reciprocal esteem among the cultures, and students whose primary goals are vocational might be induced to recognize the considerable, albeit nonvocational, value of the humanities.

Slowly the humanities community is beginning to move in this direction. A commission on the humanities, sponsored by the Rockefeller Foundation, urged that "if the aim is to make invention creative and humane, knowledge of the humanities must be coupled with an understanding of the characteristics of scientific inquiry and technological change. Liberal education must define scientific literacy as no less important a characteristic of the educated person than reading and writing."(6) Stating the goal is not the same as achieving it, but it is a start.

If esteem is to be truly reciprocal, however, the science and technology community must also accept the validity of humanists' contributions to joint endeavors. Some progress in this area might be the happy result of an otherwise unhappy situation, namely, the declining number of university-level teaching jobs. A recent study of the job market for Ph.D. students in the humanities and social sciences shows that while nine in ten want a university teaching job, only one in ten succeeds in finding one. Hence, 90 percent of the 11,000 humanities and social science Ph.D.'s produced each year must find employment in "unconventional places," such as industry or government.(7) The University of Michigan, for example, has established a committee on Alternative Careers in the Humanities and several derivative bodies aimed at bringing qualified humanities students into contact with potential industrial employers. A few individuals have been placed. One can hope that as their numbers increase, these people will be a wedge, opening doors wider.

One can also hope that demonstrated ability to master difficult concepts and to write precisely and accurately, coupled with a humanely based awareness of the ambiguities of human relationships, will earn still more places in policy-making bodies of industry and government for humanities-trained individuals. Foreign language skills and appreciation of cultural differences should be highly valued in the practical activities of multinational institutions, public or private. But placement of of humanities Ph.D.'s is hampered by "the prejudice of a number of academics toward nonacademic employment," according to James Krolik, who heads the University of Michigan Office of Nonacademic Career Counseling and Placement for Graduate Students.(8) Many students are unwilling to see themselves in the business world and are overwhelmed by the idea. The problem is exacerbated by faculty who have no contacts outside the academic community and do not reach out to establish new linkages on behalf of their students.

What about those who choose vocational careers after high school? Is there life after vocationalism? The vicissitudes of the economy seem to be driving students to seek relevance and applicability to the world of work when they make choices of field of study. It appears that we will be overrun by engineers and MBA's, mercilessly constructing and trading with scarcely a civilized thought. Meanwhile, the growth of technology has created new jobs in computer-related industries, for example, and this growth has imposed pressure on students to specialize and concentrate their efforts on developing marketable skills. But there are counterpressures building in both the engineering and the business school communities. The very progress that impels schools toward training ultimately robs the training of its value. In the world of computers, technology changes dramatically and a new generation is born about every four years. Naturally, computer-based instruments follow this cycle. The lesson is clear--what is learned in school is useful over a steadily decreasing fraction of a working lifetime. Vocationally useful learning must be undergirded by a basic ability to study and learn anew.

This message, detailing the need for lifelong learning, is applicable to many blue-collar as well as white-collar jobs. In fact, this need is rapidly blurring the distinction between the two categories in many work environments. The basic tool of lifelong learning remains the printed word. Hence, the task of fostering humanities education in colleges and universities naturally falls to the home and the primary and secondary schools, where respect and affection for books must begin. But the secondary schools operate with an undercurrent of class, based on the facts of life as they were decades ago and not as they are today. The assumption on both sides of the teacher's desk is that the humanities are of use only to wearers of white collars. Only they will have the time or money to read and travel. But that has not been true for a long time. Auto workers, admittedly facing hard times now, are trying to maintain average hourly earnings of $17.00, which amounts to about $35,000 a year. Many humanists and other professionals work more for less. Many people who are manual workers by choice have the money and leisure to enjoy the

humanities--to travel and own books. Many of them have the intellect to
do so. Society would not wittingly deny them the chance.   And yet, the
discussions here about vocationalism and the humanities indicate an ei-
ther/or attitude, implying that students who choose vocational programs
in college are lost to the humanities.   There is an assumption of symme-
try: since humanists know little and care less about the "vocations,"
people in the vocations will not care about the humanities. The attitude
is arrogant and the conclusion false.

Fortunately, there are counterpressures building in opposition to
crass vocationalism. A survey of the eight hundred members of one Harvard MBA class showed that the more money they were making, the less happy they were. The factors that accounted for low satisfaction were related to family, way of life, and outside activities, rather than to job or
salary.   In examining these data, Richard Ruch, assistant dean of the
Kansas State University College of Business Administration, proposed that

> it's time to re-examine the nature of our "psychological con-
> tract" with MBA students.   The range of mutual expectations
> that form a bond of understanding between the students and the
> educational machine we run is in need of articulation. Some of
> the unrealistic expectations must be based on bad information--
> information under the control of the faculty members and admin-
> istrators who have direct contact with the MBA students.(9)

Ruch quoted former Senator J. William Fulbright in acknowledging that the
programs and practices of the business schools might be "condemning business organizations and the country to leaders who are hustlers, marketers
of image and plastic personality, individuals with little knowledge or
concern for the needs of a free society, aspirants to personal preroga-
tive but not to real power and its constructive uses."(10)

Perhaps these comments mean that the business schools will learn,
and ultimately teach, that historically some people have moved from scientific, technological, or commercial employment into positions of organ-
izational leadership. In these roles, they have more need for a sense of
history and social equity than for strictly technical ability. This fact
should be central to the design of all curricula; and, in this sense, the
humanities do indeed have vocational value. The challenge for the educational establishment is to convince students that those who have a humane
substructure for their job-oriented education are in fact better equipped
to advance into these leadership positions.

There has been much hand-wringing from critics of vocationalism and
some strategic speculation, but one hears almost no tactical planning.
The humanities faculties should consider sending emissaries to elementary
and secondary schools to talk about the uses of their disciplines. Perhaps it is possible to designate a humanities counselor for every student
to help select an arts sequence to parallel a vocational curriculum.
Perhaps there is room for a combined five-year course in languages and

engineering for those who choose to join one of the multinational corporations.

It is unlikely, however, that the major usefulness of humane studies will be vocational. Art, music, and literature have been and will be useful to us as people rather than employees. They provide the permanent and portable baggage of joy, instantly available to those who choose to carry it. The proper task for those who teach is to muster the confidence truly to profess. Every student, however oriented, will respond to the excitement and passion that are, at the same time, art's reward to us and our debt to it. The teacher's job is to provide the few moments of insight into the emotional and aesthetic "rightness" of classic works to open the door of interest, after which continued involvement follows naturally.

Truth and permanence are not the exclusive provinces of scientific teaching. A high school chemistry teacher once said that the ninety two chemical elements then known comprised a complete and closed set. In fact, at least two additional elements had already been made that year, and ten others have followed. Another high school teacher talked about freedom of the press and pointed to Milton's *Areopagitica* which states, "Though all the winds of doctrine were let loose to play upon the earth, so truth be in the field, we do ingloriously by licensing and prohibiting misdoubt her strength. Let her and falsehood grapple. Who ever knew truth put to the worse in a free and open encounter?" The very perfection of the words lends them truth and endurance, and they have meaning in the context of this discussion. Teachers and professors will do well to accept the freedom of their students to choose vocations, even as they state the case for other learning. Externally imposed distribution requirements are a form of censorship, no likely to produce a lasting positive response. Furthermore, "distribution" smacks of randomness, and what is wanted is an ordered involvement in one or a few humane disciplines.

Perhaps the schools and colleges are trying to do too much. As Marshall McLuhan once put it, "the medium is the message." It seems that the details of content of formal courses are soon lost to the student, while the context in which learning takes place is all that survives. If, indeed, the subject matter of our college courses is fugitive, perhaps we can hope to impart no more than an outlook. If we are willing to accept an eighteenth-century definition of nature or "natural science" as including what we know as the physical sciences, I would propose the briefest of guidelines for all our disciplines: Nature I loved, and next to Nature, Art.

15 Escape from Folly: Academic Standards and the Liberal Arts
RONALD COLMAN

We find ourselves, then, met with the same difference that eternally exists between the fool and the man of sense. The latter is constantly catching himself within an inch of being a fool; hence he makes an effort to escape from the imminent folly, and in that effort lies his intelligence. The fool, on the other hand, does not suspect himself; . . . hence the enviable tranquillity with which the fool settles down, installs himself in his own folly. . . .

There is no question concerning public life, in which he does not intervene, blind and deaf as he is, imposing his "opinions." . . . The "ideas" of the average man are not genuine ideas, nor is their possession culture. . . . Whoever wishes to have ideas must first prepare himself to desire truth and to accept the rules of the game imposed by it. It is no use speaking of ideas when there is no acceptance of a higher authority to regulate them, a series of standards to which it is possible to appeal in a discussion. These standards are the principles on which culture rests."

— Ortega y Gasset

According to the editors of this book, the liberal arts are in crisis largely because of the tendency to infuse practical, vocational courses into the college curriculum, and to train college students with marketable skills rather than to nurture their critical awareness. But the crisis appears to run deeper than that, and to have its origins in the more distant past. For a century and a half, liberals have worried that the mass culture of the industrial era would undermine the process that is at the very core of a liberal education--the development of a critical thinking, rational individual.   Far from producing a greater number of rational individuals, mass education threatened to produce a standardization, a conformity, a complacent acceptance of common (often ignorant) opinion and dogma, and a potentially tyrannous majority. Not without reason, critics have accused liberals like John Stuart Mill, Alexis de Tocqueville, and Ortega y Gasset of a certain elitism that is fundamentally anti-democratic and fearful of mass participation in public affairs. And yet, these writers raised a crucial question which is at the heart of much of the discussion in this volume: Can the concept of a liberal education, which predated the industrial era, be accommodated to the new "mass" society without either a retreat into elitism or a decline in standards? There may be a sense in which "the crisis of the liberal arts" is really a crisis of industrialism and of democracy.

Seen in this way, the issue of standards lies at the very core of the crisis in the liberal arts. Almost by definition, a process that encourages students to think critically and to challenge previously held assumptions requires analytical rigor, accuracy of expression, and the energy and perseverance to test hypotheses by gathering substantive data and by following through the implications of an argument. Yet the prevailing norm in most liberal arts colleges is a tendency to read superficially, to express ideas vaguely, to write poorly, and to accept familiar ideas complacently. It might be argued that such symptoms of sloppy thinking and poor academic standards not only confirm some of the worst fears of Mill and Ortega, but negate the very concept of a "liberal education." If the tools required for critical analysis are in poor repair, then the goal itself will remain elusive.

What follows, however, is not an argument against mass education. While I accept their definition of the problem, I do not share Mill's distrust of public education *per se* nor Ortega's conclusion that ignorant conformity is an inevitable outcome of mass participation in public life. And I strongly believe that one does not need to be a towering genius to be willing and able to challenge a commonly held assumption, to think it through rigorously, and to gather evidence supporting or negating the thesis. Indeed, I will argue that the problem of poor academic standards has far more to do with the *structure* of our educational system than with its "mass-ness"; and that even within the formidable structural constraints that exist, an individual teacher can do much to raise academic standards within the classroom.

THE CONCEPT OF "ACADEMIC STANDARDS"

It is useful to begin with Aristotle's handy distinction between the "necessary conditions" of life and the "integral parts" of life. One could only achieve the "good life" and excellence in one's soul (the "integral parts"), wrote Aristotle, if one first had certain "necessary conditions," such as physical health, material well-being, and leisure time. So, surely, it is with learning.   Correct grammar, sentence structure, and spelling are the necessary conditions for communicating a substantive idea in writing, just as an ability to read is a necessary condition for the comprehension and understanding of the ideas of others. It is no use having brilliant thoughts if the student cannot communicate them.

Many students today reach college with poor reading and writing skills. We cannot undo their past. But we do students a grave disservice if we foster the illusion that they can learn and communicate concepts in philosophy, history, and politics without the necessary basic skills. If the college has no basic commitment to setting high standards in this realm, it is difficult to proceed to the more substantive level of learning.   If we can assume basic reading and vocabulary skills, we can then encourage students to read more carefully and extensively, to think rigorously about what they read, to analyze the assumptions underlying a writer's thesis, and to grapple energetically with a new idea. And if we can assume basic writing skills, we can then proceed to teach greater accuracy and clarity of expression; we can point out the distinction between a vague answer and a specific one; and we can emphasize the importance of supporting a general idea with sufficient concrete evidence.   Finally, if students have basic research skills, including a knowledge of how to use a library, we can then distinguish between the quality of different kinds of evidence.   I do not wish to belabor the point, but it is important to acknowledge that the concept of academic standards applies to both levels--to the necessary conditions of learning as well as to its substance. And it is surely apparent to instructors in all but the very best colleges in the country that many students never grasp the essence and the "integral parts" of a liberal arts education because they do not have the basic skills to do so.   As a caveat here, let me add that Aristotle's distinction might be applied equally to instructors: A teacher's time, effort, and quality of work are necessary conditions for the application of rigorous academic standards to students.

Beyond this distinction, the concept of high standards implies two related goals. The first, and more important, is to expand students' sense of their potential by encouraging them to work to the limits of their capacity, and then gradually to expand those limits during their college careers.   The second, and more controversial goal, is to give students an accurate assessment of where their capacities stand on the hierarchy of academic skills that exist within the classroom, the college, and society at large.   The first goal may strike some as sufficient. But it would only be so if we viewed the individual as an "isolated monad," to borrow Marx's expression, separated from society and others. If we view individual students as fully functioning members of society, then we owe them, also, an evaluation of how their academic capacities fit into the world around them.   Both goals rest on assumptions that are fairly explicitly delineated in Ortega's definition of standards quoted at the beginning of this chapter, and these assumptions are worth examining more closely.

While some of Ortega's conclusions are troubling, he is in fact using the term *standard* according to the strictest dictionary definition of the word. A standard is something set up and established by authority as a model or example. It is a rule for the measure of quantity or quality, and as such, implies the existence of a hierarchy of values that can be measured according to their distance from or proximity to that standard.   In academia we call such measurements "grades," and we compare, for example, succinct and lucid prose against sloppy and muddled writing according to how closely each approximates a generally agreed upon "high" standard of written expression.   It is the existence of such agreed upon standards that makes *culture*, as Ortega calls it, possible. Because they establish common points of reference, these standards are the *sine qua non* of social intercourse and interaction.

This definition raises problems for a society that often propagates a mythology of equality in which all hierarchies are suspect, and a hierarchy of academic quality particularly so.   The general reaction against all forms of grades and authority in the 1960s, and the Californian philosophy of "I'm O.K.—you're O.K.," "I do my thing—you do your thing," have for some, made comparison according to authoritative standards a heretical enterprise. This devaluation of hierarchies and the consequent inability to make distinctions of value and quality are precisely Plato's harshest criticism of democracy. Yet there is a confusion in the egalitarian critique of Plato, Ortega, and others that has unnecessarily clouded the discussion of academic standards. This is a tendency to equate one particular hierarchy with some general amorphous evaluation of the "worth" of an individual human being as a whole. We see students, for example, whose continuous poor academic performance results in a diminished sense of self-worth, a most unfortunate consequence that has no necesesary or logical relationship to the issue of academic standards *per se*. The ancient philosophers, for all their apparent elitism, certainly recognized the existence of a number of different and often crosscutting hierarchies—of birth, wealth, and physical prowess and of various talents, skills, and personal characteristics.   Indeed, most of us would have little difficulty comparing good table manners with poor ones according to certain accepted standards of etiquette, nor even in comparing individuals according to their mechanical skills or physical strength.   Yet Ortega's application of the same logic to "culture," "ideas," and the "pursuit of truth," immediately gives rise to charges of "elitism."

My own position by now should be clear.   There are, I believe, certain definable and identifiable academic skills and capabilities necessary to the critical pursuit of knowledge that is at the core of a liberal arts education. There are also established and authoritative standards by which these skills and capabilities can be judged and measured, and without which it would be impossible to share a meaningful discussion about the quality of "good research" or "lucid writing" or "profound ideas." In each case judgments of value are made about qualities that are no more evenly distributed among the general population than physical prowess, wealth, or political power.

It therefore seems logical to return to one of the two goals of setting high academic standards, to give students as accurate an assessment as possible of where they rank on the hierarchy of academic skill and talent that exists within colleges and society at large. Indeed, given the fact that these skills have an effect in determining a person's professional future, students have a *right* to an accurate evaluation of their place in that hierarchy before they enter the job market, with sufficient time to make the necessary choices to match talents with future vocations. Students are not aided when "C" grade work receives an "A." It is important, however, to make clear to students that we are not judging their total worth as human beings, but only one set of capabilities among many which they undoubtedly possess. At the same time, we academics must maintain the self-discipline to confine our judgments to academic skills alone, while encouraging the academically weak student, if possible, to explore other talents.

The second assumption Ortega makes is of greater importance and gives this chapter its title. The distinction between the fool and the man (or woman) of sense is equally a distinction between tranquillity and turmoil. But while our idioms give ample recognition to the delusions of the fool's paradise and the bliss of ignorance, we are often less willing to acknowledge the restless, troubled life of the man of sense. Yet the pursuit of truth and the process of learning itself is a difficult, turbulent often unenviable activity involving self-doubt, the questioning of previously unquestioned assumptions, and the willingness to step into a void of uncertainty and to recognize seemingly irreconcilable contradictions. Wisdom begins, Plato said, when one realizes that one does not know what one always thought one knew. But while that moment of truth will strike some as an exciting, enlivening experience, others will avoid at all cost that frightening chasm of doubt. To question the prevailing dogmas in which the fool has so comfortably installed himself requires courage, enormous perseverance, and hard work. Ideally, what students should gain from a college education is a growing sense of frustration. As they discover an ever more bewildering array of conflicting ideas and interpretations, and find endless data available to substantiate opinions, they should feel ever more on the brink of folly. And as their own ignorance becomes painfully clear, they should find the need to escape from that folly ever greater.

That process is what Ortega had in mind when he spoke of standards; and that should be our primary goal in setting high academic standards for our students. If we can impart to students a little of that sense of frustration at the abysmal incompleteness of their search for truth, if we can inject an appreciation of the kind of energy and effort that is required in that search, and if we see a willingness on the stu-

dents' part to embrace the turmoil that awaits them, then we have succeeded, in some small way, in establishing high academic standards. Anyone with classroom experience in an American college is familiar with Ortega's fools, who have an opinion on everything albeit unsupported by any
concrete evidence, and who lack both the humility and the energy to escape from their folly. For many students, as a colleague once said, education is ike getting a suntan—they simply expose themselves. To raise
standards means to convert that listless passivity into an active and en-
ergetic pursuit of knowledge. It means encouraging students to read with
a livelier and more curious interest. It means having them write, rewrite, and rewrite again until their words express their thoughts accurately and elegantly. And it means teaching them to be dissatisfied with
the available evidence and reading yet another book to gather more data.
It means, above all, making them aware of the effort and hard work required for quality academic work. In this process, students will find
that they are more willing to learn than they had previously thought, and
that they have expanded the limits of their capabilities and potential.

STRUCTURAL CONSTRAINTS

It is clearly not enough to speak of these goals in the abstract,
however. Despite the sometimes poetic expression of concern by Mill and
Ortega, it requires more than individual willpower and goodwill to attain
critical thinking and creative individuality, which are the goals both of
liberal philosophers and of a liberal arts education. There are practical reasons why the vast majority of students work beneath their potential, approach their studies with a passive, detached, and often resent-
ful attitude, and prefer to conform to conventional dogmas rather than to
question them. As I mentioned earlier, I do not share the view of many
of the early liberal philosophers that mass participation in public life
and mass education *per se* lie at the root of our current crisis. Rather,
I believe, there are serious structural constraints that limit the ability of the individual instructor to work toward the goals outlined above.
Some of these constraints are obvious. First, by the time students enter
college they have already been molded by families and schools that have
often failed either to nurture the spark of curiosity or to apply rigorous academic standards. The students arrive with intellectual and emotional equipment over which we have very limited influence.

Second, an instructor works within a variety of practical limitations, the most important of which is time. No matter how dedicated, a
teacher will clearly not grade a paper as carefully and rigorously if
there are one hundred students in a class rather than only twenty. Nor
will he or she be able to spend as much time during office hours advising
students, identifying their academic problems, and evaluating their progress. In fact, teachers can only be as rigorous toward students as they
are toward themselves. They cannot expect students to write well and ex-

press themselves with precision if they do not painstakingly correct their work and identify fuzzy generalities.   And teachers cannot expect students to be well prepared for a class unless they are well prepared. Only if presentations are planned, questions prepared, and page references kept handy, will teachers be able to keep students on their toes.

Third, we are constrained by the content of the liberal arts curriculum itself, which differs from that of the ancients in several important respects. Our more complex technological era has separated the liberal arts curriculum into distinct disciplines that would have puzzled the ancients. Psychologists, historians, political scientists, and sociologists quickly challenge each other's ability to make informed judgments outside their own fields, and we are generally expected to confine our relationship with our students to our own discipline. Furthermore, unlike Plato and Aristotle, we have separated intellectual capacities from moral character. While the educational systems of Plato and Aristotle would be concerned, for example, with testing and evaluating a person's capacity to control appetites and desires, to resist temptation, or to act for the common interest rather than for individual interests, we would certainly judge such moral training to be beyond the scope of the college classroom. For Plato, the concept of *wisdom* extended far beyond intellectual learning to a knowledge of the transience of material self-interest and of the correct relationship between the carnal, emotional, and intellectual spheres of human activity.

The content of the curriculum constrains us in yet another way, because our liberal arts education has also separated the intellectual realm from the world of work to a greater extent than the ancients did and than many contemporary systems do today. Many students will reach the age of twenty one or more before they ever experience the continuity of a steady job. And most of them will close their college texts upon graduation and never again pick up, voluntarily and to satisfy their own interests, a book of history, philosophy, or social theory. To a certain age we "learn," then we presumably stop learning and begin to "work." Some modern societies have attempted, although usually with imperfect results, to combine work and study more effectively. Many Cuban high school students engage in agricultural work in the morning and study in the afternoon, while a rather short-lived experiment during China's Cultural Revolution sent urban students to the countryside to experience the peasant's lot. The Cuban system also provides adult education classes to many urban workers as part of their regular work day. B. F. Skinner's *Walden Two* utopia recognizes that productive labor can begin much earlier than it does in our own society, that it can form a useful part of the educational system as a whole, and that education itself is a lifelong process which transcends the artificial boundaries imposed by high school and university "graduations." Certainly we would be less concerned about the "vocationalizing" of our liberal arts curriculum if our own system combined study and work more systematically and continuously throughout our lives.

In the meantime, the reality of such distinctions between the academic disciplines, between work and study, and between intellectual and moral activity, engender curricular constraints that severely limit the instructor's ability to assist students to expand their potential. A teacher of medieval history will have insufficient knowledge about the students' other capabilities to advise them in pursuing the studies that best fit their particular talents. The history teacher will have difficulty relating the students' academic skills in that particular field both to other academic skills (such as statistical and quantitative analysis), and to the students' generally limited experiences of work and culture. Given the separation between intellectual and ethical training, the teacher will have even greater difficulty relating the subject matter to the students' personal values, assumptions, and moral characters. Thus, the standards by which the medieval history teacher judges the students 'work and evaluates their performances are so limited to the specific academic and intellectual content of that particular discipline that there will be great difficulty in helping students get a sense of their own capabilities. And clearly our primary goal of setting high academic standards--encouraging students to work to the limits of their capacity-- is dependent first and foremost on an ability to identify the students' academic capabilities as a whole.

I have mentioned some formidable structural constraints on the attempt to maintain standards--constraints imposed by the nature of the liberal arts curriculum itself, by the students' earlier training, and by the instructor's own physical limitations, especially time. I have not analyzed the causes of these problems, let alone discussed how they might be overcome. But I would suggest that the framework within which such discussion might most fruitfully take place is the fourth and most important of the structural constraints that will be considered here. Although it is in many ways the least obvious of the barriers to holding high academic standards, it is at least a contributory cause to some of the problems mentioned above. In sum, *the structure of our education system effectively prevents students from taking responsibility for their learning.*

In a recent article in a campus newspaper, a college vice-president was quoted as arguing that in light of the consumer advocacy movement, students, as consumers of a service, should have the right to evaluate those who teach them. Indeed they should, and as good consumers, students also frequently exercise their right to "shop around" for classes in the first week or two of the semester, dropping and adding classes as they might choose among products on a supermarket shelf. But the students' role as "consumer" also has major structural consequences which are less often analyzed. On the face of it, the student/teacher relationship is defined in educational rather than economic terms as a distinction based on the teacher's greater knowledge and expertise in a particular field of study. Yet the economic division between consumer and producer--between the student who *pays* for his or her education and the teacher who is *paid* to deliver it—skews that educational relationship in certain fundamental ways. Since students come to class to receive a product for which they have paid, they are justifiably enraged if *they* are held responsible for the quality of the product, just as they would be if they were held responsible for the quality of products in the store. Having paid the professors to be responsible for the class, they have, in effect, absolved themselves of that responsibility. Thus, a student who is not "responsible" for the reading will read less actively and less carefully. That student will be less likely to grapple energetically with the ideas if he or she is not responsible for explaining the author's position to the rest of the class. That, after all, is the teacher's job. The student is less likely to come to class with a series of stimulating and thought-provoking questions because the teacher is also held responsible for energizing the class. If the class did not go well, then it is the teacher and not the student who must go home and come up with new ideas and methods to ensure that the class "succeeds" in the future.

This passivity and the unpreparedness of many students in class are really marks of the alienation which exists under conditions of "forced labor." If Marx is correct in assuming that it is the inherent nature of the human species to produce freely, universally, and socially, then presumably a student, in the strict educational sense of the term, would engage voluntarily in all aspects of the learning process. But how many of our students would voluntarily write papers if they were not required? How many would read if they were never tested on the reading?   How many would voluntarily request examinations just to see for themselves whether they had successfully assimilated the material? In fact many of our students produce out of necessity rather than choice because of a basic contradiction in the consumer/producer relationship outlined above.   Unlike most other consumers, the consumer of education—the student—is also required to produce in his or her field of consumption. Since we must expect some resistance and resentment when our startled consumers are suddenly held responsible for the quality of their products, it is inevitable that our tests, papers, and reading assignments will become coercive mechanisms as much as educational tools.   Thus, students very often submit written work at the end of the semester and then fail to pick it up from their professor, so alienated are they from the products that they themselves have produced. The students, in effect, experience their papers, the result of forced labor, as belonging not to themselves but to the professor, the institution, the world separate from themselves. And they are as alienated from the *process* of production as the worker on the assembly line. They write their papers and study for their tests not with a joyful sense of accomplishment, but resentfully, fearfully and nervously, anxiously awaiting the moment of liberation that follows examination day, in the same way that workers begin to "live" when they come home from work. And so Marx would say of our students that they are alienated from their human *essence*, from themselves as human beings, be-

cause they deny the very thing that makes them human--the desire to produce freely and universally. If our aim in setting high academic standards is to convert listless passivity into active energy, to encourage
students to grapple enthusiastically with ideas, and to help them take
responsibility for learning, then we must recognize that the division between consumer and producer on which our educational system rests constitutes the most formidable barrier to this goal.

SOME PRACTICAL SUGGESTIONS

    Given these major constraints, is there anything the individual in-
structor can do to maintain academic standards within the classroom, and
to encourage students to work to the limits of their potential? If we
were to accept completely Plato's dictum that "learning acquired under
compulsion obtains no hold on the mind," then the coercive mechanisms
mentioned above would seem to present an almost insurmountable obstacle.
Indeed, the logical corollary to the previous section and the conclusion
of this paper should perhaps be a prescription to "change the system" so
as to eliminate the coercion, reform the liberal arts curriculum, and
transform the teacher/student relationship in some fundamental way. But
such a conclusion would also be hopelessly abstract and divorced from the
realities in which most of us live. Therefore I will offer instead a few
practical proposals that are rather obvious and not terribly original,
but that are too rarely implemented in practice. It is possible, I believe, to make some fairly significant changes within the existing system, provided we always begin by confronting students with the reality of
their present circumstances.

    If we accept the existence of such structural barriers as those out-
lined above, then we ought not to keep them a secret from our students.
There is no more effective way to reduce the power of these barriers, although we may never eliminate them, than to explain them frankly and directly. We are often so absorbed in the task of explaining the subject
matter of our disciplines that we forget to explain the classroom itself.
If there is coercion in the form of quizzes, grades, and attendance requirements, then let us first frankly acknowledge its existence, and then
help our students understand why this coercion exists in our educational
system. If we notice our students coming to class unprepared and writing
sloppy prose, then we may explain to them why they are not taking responsibility for the quality of their own reading and writing and why this is
a symptom of their alienation from the learning process.

    We can adopt a similar approach in setting standards for the basic
skills. After correcting the students' spelling and grammar, acknowledge
the "structural constraint," by telling them directly that they are not
to blame for the poor training they received in grade school. They
clearly had teachers who allowed them to get away with the most flagrant
abuses of the English language. But while their present illiteracy might

not originally have been their fault, they must at a certain point take reponsibility for their disabilities and overcome them. No one else will take responsibility for their future. Grammar, punctuation, and spelling are, in the end, simple skills like learning to eat with a knife and a fork, which are certainly more easily learned as a child, but which can always be acquired later if need be. To take responsibility for their language means using a dictionary constantly, enrolling in English composition classes, applying for tutorial assistance, reading good literature, and checking their grammar before handing in a written assignment. It requires considerable energy and perseverance to overcome any disability, physical or intellectual, but this is a good concrete place to begin raising academic standards—in an area that can yield tangible, observable results. In the meantime, we ought not to graduate students who cannot write. Future employers will be more concerned that our prospective graduates can write a coherent paragraph in good English than that they remember an esoteric point from a medieval philosophy course. Beyond that, good English has a value in itself, both aesthetically and as a medium for concretizing and extending thought.

What I have described here is, first, an acknowledgment of existing realities and, second, an act of responsibility in correcting past errors. But it also seems possible, in some cases, actually to convert an unsatisfactory structural constraint into an at least partially useful conceptual framework for improving academic standards. We have seen that the relationship between teacher and student mirrors some important aspects of our economic system. It therefore seems that an appropriate framework for that relationship is the concept of the *contract*, which is basic to the economic and social system within which the college community exists. A worker contracting for a job explicitly recognizes certain standards that are appropriate to the performance of that particular work —the quantity of work required, the productivity expected, and the quality of the product.

This framework is particularly useful in delineating basic course requirements, which should be spelled out as specifically as possible at the *beginning* of every course, just as the laborer's work, hours, and salary are made plain at the outset. There are three major components to any liberal arts course—reading, class sessions, and written assignments —and the terms of the contract should cover all three areas. The aim of the course, the specific quantity of reading, the length and due dates of written assignments, attendance requirements, grading criteria, number of tests, and so on, should all be clearly defined in a complete course outline that acts as a binding contract that cannot be changed except by *mutual* agreement. In fact, once the original course outline is handed out and explained on the first day of class, the instructor and students are equally constrained by the terms and conditions of that contract. The instructor cannot, for example, increase the quantity of work required or change the grading system midway through the course.

It will be objected that the relationship is not an equal one, however. The instructor, after all, determines the requirements.   But that is no different from the unequal relationship between employers and employees, in which the former write the contract and the latter can either take it or leave it. The student has a similar freedom either to accept the contract or to reject it and choose another class.   If anything, the student's "freedom of choice" among the manifold offerings of a college catalog is greater than that of the job-seeking employee in the market place. By accepting a particular course outline, the student has entered the contract, in a sense, as a "free" person, with a clear knowledge of the responsibilities and obligations. Such an explicit agreement at the beginning of a course reduces the resentment a student feels about course requirements. There should be no pretense that this device can overcome the student's basic alienation and lack of responsibility that have their roots in the structure of our educational system. Nevertheless, the student's acceptance of an agreement that is scrupulously honored by both parties provides a greater sense of having chosen the work rather than being continuously bombarded by it throughout the semester.

In fact, the contract analogy can be taken one step further.   If a forty-hour work week is the norm in our society, then our students should be required to devote forty hours to a fifteen-credit "full-time load," which is generally five courses. Simple arithmetic indicates that they should spend eight hours per week per three-credit course, and that is all that the instructor is entitled to require of them. Of these eight hours, they spend three hours per week in class, and they should, therefore, spend five hours per week reading. Most students do not challenge the logic of that arrangement. The level of comprehension expected is directly related to the length of time allocated to a particular reading assignment. If a difficult fifty-page passage from Aristotle is assigned one week, they should spend five hours reading those fifty pages (and perhaps rereading them), not one or two hours. Such quantitative measures will not, by themselves, maintain academic standards. But there is at least a partial correlation between productivity and the number of hours worked, and there is no reason why students should expect to spend less time at their books than workers at the assembly line. In fact, our students can be taught to appreciate the considerably greater flexibility that they retain in their work hours.

In the seventeenth century, Thomas Hobbes recognized that a contract is meaningless unless it contains an enforcement apparatus, which represents, of course, the coercive elements of the educational system mentioned above. The most successful method of enforcing the contract that I have yet discovered is the administration of simple weekly ten-minute quiz on the reading assignment for that week. The purpose of these quizzes is not to test the students' analytical abilities (that can be done in papers and exams), but to ensure their compliance with the terms of the contract that specifies that they come to class prepared, having read the specified number of pages assigned for that week. At the beginning of the semester these quizzes are a rather frightening experience, but the students quickly accept them as part of the integral structure of the course. Most important, the level of class discussion improves dramatically when all students have read the assigned material. Their comprehension skills improve as they prepare for the quizzes and they soon find themselves getting more out of their classes and learning at a generally higher level as a result of their own greater preparedness.

If we can encourage more extensive reading, harder work, and greater perseverance on the students' part, then we have already modestly raised academic standards and developed at least a partial appreciation of the difficult path which Ortega described as the "pursuit of truth." Clearly quantity of work is not the only measure of productivity, and it is especially important to recognize that coercive devices like quizzes will not produce qualitative transformations in the students' attitudes toward learning. But there are a number of steps that the instructor might take to improve the quality of the students' work as well. Unfortunately, most students do not have a clear sense of the thought, planning, and effort required by even the brightest of them to produce good written work. Far too many of them simply sit down, write a few pages, and hand them in as a final product. At an early stage in their college careers they must be taught that a first draft is just not acceptable, and that they are capable of producing far better work. It is helpful to require students to bring outlines of their papers to the instructor before they start writing. After going over the outlines in detail with them, they should be asked to revise them and then proceed to write their papers. All papers should be graded and returned with detailed written comments. On the basis of these comments, the students then rewrite the papers and resubmit them. By this time they have usually improved their work substantially, and they are rewarded with higher grades on the final draft. Hopefully, the students will eventually assimilate all these steps into their normal routines as they raise their own expectations of the quality of written work of which they are capable.

Similar qualitative improvements can be encouraged in other areas. If time is available, the instructor can help students improve the quality of their reading by handing out, a week in advance, a fairly detailed series of questions on the following week's readings, directing the students' attention both to important factual information and to the issues that will be raised in the classroom. In grading tests, a premium should be placed on the *accuracy* of answers, with marks deducted for vagueness and fudging. Students should be given examples of precise answers and shown the inadequacy of generalities which fail to answer the specific question being asked. In essays and papers, students should be required to supply substantive evidence to support an argument, and they should be taught to differentiate between a logical and coherently argued case, on the one hand, and the unsubstantiated "opinion" of Ortega's "fool," on the other. These are all skills that can be learned and that are not wholly dependent upon innate ability. There is not space here to explore any of these suggestions in greater detail. Suffice to say that dramatic improvement in the quality of students' work is possible in all these areas provided that the instructor is sufficiently rigorous in his or her approach. Clearly, a flabby class structure will produce flabbiness on the students' part as well.

I have argued that within the constraints imposed by the students' past learning, the instructor's time, the nature of the curriculum, and the coercive structure of the educational system. Individual instructors can still make a modest contribution to the application of the kinds of standards by which Ortega sought to differentiate vulgar opinions from true ideas and learning. In order to make this argument, I have had to take an eclectic approach which may appear to be fraught with internal contradictions, because the structural criticisms draw on different philosophical sources than do the concrete proposals that accept the framework of the existing educational system. In concluding with some fairly straightforward suggestions, however, I do not wish to underestimate the structural barriers, because they are at the very heart of the "crisis" of the liberal arts. Indeed, if analytical rigor, accurate expression, and the perseverance to test hypotheses are central to the learning process required to nurture a critically aware and creative individual, then we might argue that low academic standards negate the very purpose of a liberal arts education. They are, I believe, a more serious danger to our educational system than either the "vocationalizing" of the curriculum so widely feared today or the conformity of mass education feared by writers like Mill, de Tocqueville, and Ortega in the past. If we fail to be rigorous in the quest for high academic standards, we not only legitimize the vulgarity of Ortega's fool, but also fail to encourage "the man [or woma..] of sense" as he or she makes a laborious effort to escape from imminent folly. Indeed, we do a disservice even to the academically weak student if we confirm that tranquil self-justification of a fool's paradise. And what we owe all our students in this process is an honest and accurate evaluation of the station they have reached on that difficult escape route that we call learning.

16 Coda: Confronting the Conservative Crusade for Literacy: Dissenting Voices

LEON BOTSTEIN, JEAN BETHKE ELSHTAIN, MICHAEL ENGEL, ALFRED McCLUNG LEE, HENRY A. GIROUX, and STANLEY ARONOWITZ

Ever since the discovery of the "literacy crisis" at the start of the 1980s, conservative commentators have seized center stage, captured mainstream media attention and, in so doing, have noticeably outmaneuvered the left on what remains a persistent and deepening national scandal. Chief among these conservative academicians has been Allan Bloom, whose 1987 best seller *The Closing of the American Mind* garnered lavish praise from then-secretary of education, William J. Bennett, and set the pace for a rash of denunciations of declining academic standards and recipes for curricular reform.(1)

Conspicuous among the "recipe-writers" from the right was E. D. Hirsch, whose *Cultural Literacy--What Every American Needs to Know* closed with a by-now-famous list, sixty-three pages long, of names, dates, places, titles, and terminology, superficial acquaintance with which was supposed to distinguish the "culturally literate" from the rest of humanity.(2) In the same spirit were jeremiads against the ignorance prevalent in American high schools from, most notably, Diane Ravitch and Chester Finn, Bennett's undersecretary for research, in *What Do Our Seventeen Year Olds Know?* and from Bennett himself in his 1987 Department of Education pamphlet, *James Madison High School--A Curriculum for American Students,* which also detailed a model curriculum and pedagogy bound to tradition and iron discipline and needing only political will to implement.(3) The following year the liberal and lax professoriate became the favored target for Charles Sykes in *Profscam--Professors and the Demise of Higher Education,* whose central claim was that professors "almost singlehandedly . . . have desolated higher education, which no longer is higher or much of an education."(4)

In such a context, it is perhaps understandable and unsurprising if radical academicians seemed hesitant about complaining too loudly about *"illiterate America"*--to borrow the title of Jonathan Kozol's book(5)--or

calling for tougher academic standards, lest they be perceived as jump-
ing on the conservatives' "back-to-basics" bandwagon. Unfortunately,
some of the less principled on the left, explicitly or implicitly, lent
support to the academic *status quo*.(6) Consequently, whether by conscious design or by default, authentic radical voices were seldom heard
in the important debates over the direction of curricular policy and pedagogy.

We thought an appropriate way to conclude this collection of critical essays on literacy and the liberal arts would be to let dissenters
from the left have a chance to be heard—indeed, to have the last word,
for a change.

What follows, then, is a distillation of writings and oral commentary from several of the contributors to this volume: Stanley Aronowitz,
Leon Botstein, Jean Bethke Elshtain, Michael Engel, Henry A. Giroux, and
Alfred McClung Lee.(7) It is presented in dialogue format, with the editor, Barbara Ann Scott, serving as interlocutor and occasional commenta-
tor.

Together, they make a collective rejoinder to the conservative crusade for literacy, by examining its shortcomings (and also some of its
strengths), demystifying its often elitist and anti-democratic underpin-
nings, and offering instead some transcendent visions and transformative
strategies. Responding to these "rumblings from the right," our panel of
dissident academics examines what the quest for literacy can and should
entail: most fundamentally, the quest for democratic empowerment and the
emergence, in Jonathan Kozol's words, of "critical consciousness for
moral action."(8)

*Let us first take on the man who started the present furor: Allan
Bloom. How do you assess his project, his popularity and, perhaps too,
his political agenda?*

MICHAEL ENGEL: Allan Bloom must be right—we live in a period of
academic and intellectual degeneracy. The convincing evidence is the
success of his book. Only in the ideological mire of the Age of Reagan
could such fantastic ideas flourish. Nonetheless, Bloom's prominence and
the popularity of his point of view forces any commentary on higher education to take his critique into account. In actuality, it is not a bad
starting point for designing a left program for the reconstruction of
higher education.

LEON BOTSTEIN: The fact that Allan Bloom's dense polemic about
America's frame of mind was at the top of the nonfiction best seller list
for so long is a heartening sign. Even if Bloom's book remains obscure,
misunderstood, or even unread by many of its owners, its popularity suggests a widespread yearning for a serious description and explanation of
the apparent absence of a center to our cultural life.

What is appealing about Bloom's book is that it is informed by a unifying insight that claims to provide a comprehensive explanation to a host of seemingly unconnected national ills. The reader gets a philosophically laden whirlwind version of the career of thinking and ideas in the West since Socrates.

JEAN BETHKE ELSHTAIN: Bloom recreates a now-gone American academic world in which a few men, those who by *nature* were capable of making the transition from "natural savages" to "knowers," became gentlemen at elite institutions. These students were a charming lot, ripe to be inducted into the great secrets of the Great Books by *bona fide* knowers like Bloom's mentor, Leo Strauss, and later, Bloom himself. This world is nearly lost, or we are in danger of losing it, argues Bloom. Higher mental life in the United States is at stake.

STANLEY ARONOWITZ and HENRY A. GIROUX: Advancing a position that claims schools have contributed to the instrumentalization of knowledge and that the population has fallen victim to a widespread relativism and rampant antiintellectualism, Bloom proposes a series of educational reforms that privileges a fixed idea of Western culture organized around a core curriculum.

ENGEL: Yes, in Bloom's view, to restore the university to its proper function—a refuge for Great Thinkers to think Great Thoughts (or, in Bloom's own words, to provide a place where "society . . . tolerates and supports an eternal childhood for some")—we must return to a classical curriculum grounded in philosophy and Great Books.

What about the central claim posed by the title of Bloom's book? Has there been a "closure" of "the American mind?"

ALFRED McCLUNG LEE: Just what is "*the* American mind?" Apparently, Bloom has spent so much time trying to teach classical philosophy to middle- and upper-class students of relatively similar backgrounds that he thinks of them as only slightly varied clones of the same mind. He gives little evidence of having participantly observed students and other people of diverse ethnic, racial, and class backgrounds. It is also evident that his grasp of social history and of cross-cultural comparisons is limited and warped.

BOTSTEIN: Bloom has, I think, in a dishonest way falsified the intellectual tradition that he relies on to argue that things are coming apart and American minds are closing.

One need not be a fool, a Pangloss, a secret apologist for Stalin, a nutty follower of simplistic relativist notions that fail to help one discern junk from beauty, or a proponent of group sex to reject Bloom's version of the present condition of youth or his account of history. When it comes to America's youth, their minds are less closed and impoverished than Bloom thinks.

ARONOWITZ and GIROUX: Bloom's sweeping agenda intends to eliminate culture as a serious object of knowledge.   According to Bloom, the culturalist perspective is what Plato meant by the allegory of the cave. Thus, we are prevented from seeing the sunlight by culture, which is the enemy of what Bloom calls "openness."   Bloom ends up arguing that the Western tradition is superior to non-Western cultures precisely because its referent is the universal and context-free love of wisdom.   Lower cultures are inevitably tied to "local knowledge"—to family and community values and beliefs, which are overwhelmingly context-specific.

For Bloom, the teachings of Plato and Socrates provide the critical referents with which to denounce contemporary culture.   Bloom systematically devaluates the music, sexuality, and pride of youth and traces what he envisions as the gross excesses of the 1960s to the pernicious influence of German philosophy from Nietzsche to Heidegger as refracted through the mindless relativism of modernizers.   For Bloom, popular culture, especially rock 'n' roll, represents a new form of barbarism.

BOTSTEIN: Despite his disclaimers, his book is a jeremiad, a declaration of how debased the world of the young has become.   The decline of the family, rock music, and a bizarre popularization in American culture of the idea that life contains little else than self-fulfillment, self-interest, and an amalgam of values, each historically and culturally contingent, all, for Bloom, have corrupted life and learning that once stood on a unified, solid ground.

I don't particularly like rock music, and I don't believe that popular culture is on a particularly high level.   But I don't, at the same time, believe rock music is the source of all ills.   I don't believe that young people only have sex without love.   I don't believe in a lot of the idiotic generalizations with which Bloom tries to enhance and legitimize his argument.

Where I agree with Bloom is that undergraduate education is in desperate need of reform.   I believe that popular culture is a mockery of cultural and political life in a democracy.   We are shortchanging ourselves and our children.   But to agree to that is not to agree to the kind of analysis, pessimism, anger, blindness, hostility, and cynicism which Bloom's book reveals.

Are you, then, suggesting that the "closed mind" may very well be Allan Bloom's?

ELSHTAIN: For all his incessant celebration of the elite of knowers and the importance of that elite, Bloom is an ignorant man.   He is unlearned in the ways of the wider world, untutored in subjects on which he makes definitive pronouncements--I have in mind here not Plato but popular culture--untouched by generosity in his response to those who, unlike Bloom himself, whether through necessity or choice, do not date the beginning of their "real lives" from the moment they glimpsed the University of Chicago (or Harvard Yard or the turrets of Oxford).

LEE: Bloom's book is popular because it appeals to those fearful of social change, those who think they can retreat into the mythical absolutes and certainties of the past.

BOTSTEIN: Ironically, Bloom's terms of debate inhibit criticism. Since he operates in a world of absolutes, with definitions of reason, nature, and philosophy anchored in polarities--right and wrong, good and evil, real language and polluted language--beneath the surface of a respect for argument and dialogue lurks a simple calculus: If you're not with us, you're wrong. If you question, you're one of them--a Philistine, a victim of decline and evil, perhaps a nefarious and trendy lefty.

Gray and ambiguity, uncertainty and irony, are absent from Bloom's text. They are signs of either ignorance or corruption.   He has got the truth! The book is so littered with the tone of condemnation and accusation that it deters argument.

ENGEL: Leftists could never get away with such muddled thinking. If they construct paranoid fantasy worlds, revise history as they see fit, and declare their own value system to be a priori truth, they are called Stalinists, usually by people like Bloom.

There have been, both before and after Allan Bloom, a number of oth-er influential harbingers of the literacy crusade who have articulated the conservative agenda for curricular and pedagogical reform: among them, the peripatetic former U.S. secretary of education, William J. Ben-nett, Diane Ravitch and Chester E. Finn, Jr., authors of What Do Our 17 Year Olds Know?, and E. D. Hirsch, author of Cultural Literacy. What do these critics of the crisis of illiteracy have in common with Bloom?

BOTSTEIN: Their views can be characterized as being in a nineteenth century genre--the literature of cultural despair--in which a mythic past is constructed of moral absolutes. Like its nineteenth century predecessors, it is rooted in a profound distrust of modernity. Then, as now, it has cultivated a nostalgic view of tradition that, in turn, shaped an anti-democratic political and social agenda. A century ago, the literature of cultural despair provided, in fact, ideological models for twentieth century fascism.

A sense of the "other" was prevalent: of the enemy within and without.   In the United States and in Germany a century ago, a problematic awareness of a minority population among the majority is and was significant.

Like their German counterparts of a century ago, the writings of these contemporary American academicians are patriotic in the conservative sense that they seek renewal through restoration. The authors identify problems and responses that can result in the overdue regeneration of an American spirit damaged by the traumatic culmination of a putative liberal hegemony during the 1960s. Hirsch, Bloom, Bennett, Ravitch and Finn play upon popular feelings of pessimism and powerlessness and the belief that since the 1960s, the United States has deteriorated as a nation and a culture.

The liberal conceits are declared bankrupt. The United States is viewed as beleaguered externally by economic competition from the Far East and by Soviet power, ideological influence, and expansionism. At the same time, the United States is regarded as internally corrupted by apathy and sloth (e.g., drugs, loss of the work ethic), political factionalism in the name of interest groups (women and minorities, in particular), public and private immorality, divorce and the loss of family values, and a sense of a common heritage and history.

ARONOWITZ and GIROUX: Here we have all the elements of an elitist sensibility: abhorrence of mass culture, a rejection of experience as the arbiter of taste and pedagogy, and a sweeping attack on "cultural relativism," especially on those who want to place popular culture, ethnic and racially-based cultures, and cultures grounded in sexual communities (either feminist or gay and lesbian) on par with classical Western traditions. For conservatives, each of these elements represents a form of anti-intellectualism that threatens the moral authority of the state.

These judgments merely provide a prologue to a much more forceful and unsparing attack on nihilism—a code word to Bloom and others for the glorification of action and power.

How about zeroing in on E. D. Hirsch—next to Bloom, perhaps the most influential of the literacy crusaders. How do you assess his project and its impact?

BOTSTEIN: The problem with Hirsch's seemingly self-evident and common-sense notion of the need for "cultural literacy" among all Americans is that he trivializes the problem. His model of the needed cultural knowledge can be translated into a multiple-choice test of his own design that examines whether the pupil knows a distilled reference or fact associated with a term or phrase. (The terms that make up Hirsch's list range from "literati" to "mafia," "homosexuality" to "Hegelian dialectic," "bite the dust" to "Brooklyn bridge.")

At the heart of Hirsch's program is little else than the reduction of cultural literacy to superficial word and phrase identifications. The

list of items and the test instrument are themselves caricatures of the
very system Hirsch seeks to attack.   All mystery, discovery, ambiguity,
dissent, and drive to extend understanding through inquiry and language
are stifled and rendered superfluous.   All matters of interpretation are
washed away. The maximal power of literacy is replaced by the primitive
packaging of minimalist simplification, which inevitably will reflect
some selective and disputable ideological point of view.

    ARONOWITZ and GIROUX: Hirsch dismisses the notion that culture has
any determinate relation to the practices of power and politics or is
largely defined as a part of an ongoing struggle to name history, experience, knowledge, and the meaning of everyday life in one's own terms.   To
him, culture is a network of information shrouded in innocence and good
will.
    There is a totalitarian unity in Hirsch's view of culture that is at
odds with the concept of democratic pluralism and political difference.
It is silent regarding the ways that tracking, the hidden curriculum, the
denial of student experience as a valid basis for knowledge, and school
practices predicated on class, sexist, and racial interests discriminate
against students.
    Literacy and illiteracy are defined by the information students pos-
sess regarding the canon of knowledge that constitutes, for Hirsch, the
national culture.   It is a canon bequeathed by history as a series of
facts--dates of battles, authors of books, figures from Greek mythology,
and the names of past presidents of the United States.   More important,
his view of history is the narrative of the winners, the discourse of
elites.
    At best, then, Hirsch's analysis serves as a veiled apology for a
highly dogmatic and reactionary view of literacy and schooling.   At
worst, his model of cultural literacy threatens the very democracy he
claims to be preserving.

    *What of the remainder of the "Big 5" spearheading the conservative
crusade for literacy--Diane Ravitch, Chester E. Finn, Jr., and William J.
Bennett? What are the commonalities and, possibly, differences in their
approach to literacy?*

    BOTSTEIN: Bennett's talk is all about heritage, about hammering
into a younger generation that their present and future cannot outstrip
and exceed the past in quality and achievement; that they are in need of
severe restrictive remediation in order to protect the society from deterioration and barbarism of which they are the representatives.   It is
as if the adult generation were exemplars of cultural understanding, and
vulgarity were an exclusive characteristic of the young.   There is no
sense of the utility of education to effect cultural progress, change,
and improvement, except perhaps in the areas of science and technology.

Although Ravitch and Finn are far more sophisticated than Bennett, they also camouflage a desire for restorative renewal through the curriculum under the guise of needing to achieve coverage and commonality over depth.

The call made by all five for simplicity and coverage and the sacrifice of the depth of understanding and the habits of questioning that derive only from a more than superficial grasp of the texts and issues in history and literature must not be accepted!

ARONOWITZ and GIROUX: Given the way they depoliticize the issue of culture and de-contextualize learners, it is not surprising that they espouse a clothesline-of-information approach to literacy that ignores its function as a technology of social control, as a feature of cultural organization that reproduces rather than critically engages the dominant social order.

Pedagogy becomes an afterthought.   It is something one does to implement a preconstituted body of knowledge.   Its profoundly reactionary character can be summed up in the terms "transmission" and "imposition."

More important, the conservatives' literacy crusade is informed by a crippling ethnocentrism and a contempt for the language and social relations fundamental to the ideals of a democratic society.   It is, in the end, a desperate move by thinkers who would rather cling to a tradition forged by myth than work toward a collective future built on democratic possibilities.

How then is the search for excellence and for equity to be reconciled?

BOTSTEIN: Throughout the twentieth century educational progressives understood that individuality and real-life experiences were the best sources of intellectual curiosity about cultural tradition and the motivation to learn.   Therefore, what was taught and how it was taught depended upon the cultivation of the active habits of inquiry and criticism and the linkage of theory to practice. A core curriculum was necessary, but its definition derived from an understanding of the needs and experiences of the learners, not from an artificial construct of a normative tradition. One cannot merely preach an arbitrary canon and impose it in the name of quality.

ARONOWITZ and GIROUX: A more critical understanding of the relationship of culture and schooling would start with a definition of culture as a set of activities by which different groups produce collective memories, knowledge, social relations, and values within historically constituted relations of power.   Literacy, therefore, must be understood dialectically. And that means recognizing that there are different voices, languages, histories, and ways of viewing and experiencing the world.

The recognition and affirmation of these differences is a necessary and important precondition for extending the possibilities of democratic life.

To acknowledge different forms of literacy is not to suggest that they should be given equal weight. On the contrary, it is to argue that their differences are to be weighed against the capacity they have for enabling people to locate themselves in their own histories while simultaneously establishing the conditions for them to function as part of a wider democratic culture. This represents a form of literacy that is not merely epistemological, but also deeply political and eminently pedagogical.

BOTSTEIN: Today, the recognition of the diversity of culture and tradition must be reconciled with common aims of education. These aims include teaching a common culture. But that must be done by cultivating in reflective citizens the capacity for reasoned criticism and encouraging them to recognize and participate in the common cultural tradition. To achieve this, simplified definitions of cultural literacy, reductive tests, narrowly uniform and rigid survey curricula, passive classrooms, and a deep distrust of modernity, pluralism, and dissent, all cast in an anti-democratic context of cultural despair, cannot constitute effective bases for educational reform. Neither can a federal policy that refuses to assist materially.

Can you be more specific? What exactly would a radical agenda for literacy entail—radical, in the sense of being radically different from the conventional (conservative) wisdom, and radical, in the sense of getting at the real roots of the crisis of illiteracy?

ENGEL: A radical program for the renewal of higher education in the United States should be based upon two revolutionary values: *democracy* and *social responsibility*. In a democracy, people make choices for themselves and others and take responsibility for them. The function of democratic colleges and universities (and, indeed, the entire educational system) thus ought to be teaching people how to make those choices—personal, political, moral, and intellectual. This requires more than listening to a professor dish out Great Thoughts. It means that instructors have to create conflict in the classroom by presenting all the choices (including ones the instructor dislikes), discussing the pros and cons and forcing students to take sides. In the social sciences this involves pitting competing theoretical and ideological frameworks against each other. In the humanities, it should mean looking at alternative lists of Great Books, Great Music, or Great Art and challenging the values and standards implicit in each. In the physical sciences, students should become involved with historic conflicts among scientists in the theory and practice of mathematics, biology, physics, and chemistry. In each case, students have to be convinced that choices matter.

ELSHTAIN: Promoting critical literacy in a *"beyond*-the-basics" mode would require, first, careful attunement to the great texts, for one can only challenge the canon with reference to the canon; but, second, assigning texts that open up the canon in new and fruitful ways that are respectful of the enormous importance of, say, Plato and Aristotle.   (I have in mind here Martha Nussbaum's *The Fragility of Goodness*, as one example.)   The quest for literacy would require, third, transgressing hardened disciplinary boundaries and drawing texts from one field to raise questions to and for another; for example, *Antigone* in a course on political theory or a novel such as Don de Lillo's *White Noise*.

ARONOWITZ and GIROUX: We are arguing for the parity of canonical text and popular texts as forms of historical knowledge.   In fact, what counts as high cultural text often originates as popular literature—the works of Dickens, Dostoevsky, and Rabelais are just a few examples. Their narratives were inevitably drawn from the lives of their readers as well as those who had not yet gained their own voice, either in the public sphere or in literature.

But rediscovering the popular is not the only treasure that can be scrounged from the established canon.   We may discover in Gustave Flaubert's *Madame Bovary*, in Mark Twain's *Huckleberry Finn*, and in Theodore Dreiser's *Chronicles of American Plunder*—descriptions of the human sacrifices that were made for the sake of progress at the turn of the century—the modern tragedies and comic narratives of which the dark side of of middle-class and native American culture is made, a revelation that is rarely unearthed by reading traditional narrative history or philosophy. In short, we may take literature as social knowledge, not of an object, but as a part of the truth about ourselves.

The democratic use of literary canons must always remain critical. Above all, the canon must justify itself as representing the elements of our own heritage.   In the final instance, it is to be appropriated rather than revered—and with this appropriation, transformed.

ELSHTAIN: Yes, there should be a commitment to cultural diversity, but without a need to prove one's ideological correctness or doctrinal purity.   Alternative works should be added, not in a mood of affirmative-action-for-texts alone, but in recognition of the strength of their vision, the alternative angle on the world provided, the richness of the language exhibited, and so on. And all of this should be undertaken not in a mood of pompous solemnity but of intellectual playfulness of the most serious sort.

Often talk of democratizing the curriculum is dismissed as another effort by educational radicals to "rally 'round the flag" of relevance,

*which invariably results in a dilution of standards of excellence.   How,
then, is "relevance" to be reconciled with academic rigor?*

LEE: Educational relevance is condemned by Bloom and others because it interferes with dedication to Great Ideas.   Actually, relevance
to students' needs, aspirations, and useful ways of life is precisely
what is lacking in a great many schools at all levels, public and private. Think of the biased and stereotyped history taught to the multi-
ethnic young, so much of it to which they cannot relate.   Think of the
lack of participatory projects in a variety of fields that could grasp
imaginations and motivations. Healthy maturation and intellectual growth
(to the extent that it is accomplished) thus often depends upon fortunate
family and peer-group relations and an occasional inspiring and cooperating teacher.

John Dewey lamented the "isolation of knowledge and practice . . .
the division of aims and dissipation of energy" as too typical of the
"state of education."   It is still too typical. The virtues of their
merger in the learning process through focusing on a series of stimulating and diverse projects is well illustrated by the many thousands of
good teachers who recognize, with Dewey, "the development of intelligence
as a method of action"(9) but who, at the same time, maintain rigorous
expectations of their students' performance.

BOTSTEIN: Let us remember, too, that the lack of motivation to
study and remember course contents can be traced perhaps to a feeling of
powerlessness among many Americans, particularly the young—to the gap
between the promises of democratic participation and the remoteness of
political power. There is a severe problem of generating enthusiasm for
learning and using the humanities in the name of democracy, given the low
percentage of Americans who vote and the poor standard of our advertis-
ing-dominated national political discourse (not to speak of the meager
"cultural literacy" of some of our highest office holders).   Are we ask-
ing of young children habits of curiosity and thinking that are essentially absent from the adult culture?

The low levels of concentration, passion, and memory in school are
not effectively combatted by approaches that cram facts and preach respect for discipline alone. A restorative nostalgia for a lost great age
of teaching and learning (if it ever existed) will not spur on the next
generation. The pleasure and excitement of science and math, of history
and the humanities, must emerge from pedagogical demands on students to
appropriate the material as their own. They way material is selected and
presented is, therefore, crucial.   Setting standards and using great
books alone will not improve the classroom experience.

ENGEL: It should also be noted that educational democracy is not
the same thing as absolute individual freedom of choice.   Indeed, they
may often be mutually exclusive. Thus, a democratic curriculum will have

many required courses in the arts and sciences.   The currently popular
vocational courses would have a much diminished role.

This, of course, raises the thorny issues of who should decide which
courses would be part of a democratic curriculum and how that decision
would be made. At this early point in time, the only answer can be that
if ever a consensus could be reached on actually implementing a democratic curriculum, the matter of course selection would be much less conten-
tious. We should aim for that first big step, which would be the longest
and hardest.

BOTSTEIN: It must also be remembered that no reform of curriculum
of any sort will succeed, nor will academic standards be upheld, unless a
new approach to fair and objective testing is found—one that asks the
student to write and reason and not merely check off answers.

Moreover, if a serious curriculum for the liberal arts and sciences
is put in place, one that motivates and activates the student, then broad
coverage might have a lower priority and become an outgrowth of teaching
in depth.   If one insists on coverage, then one is reduced to teaching an
"official" reductive narrative of American history, for example, whose
purpose is indoctrination, not intellectual enrichment.

ARONOWITZ and GIROUX: What must be accepted in the discourse of
the conservatives' crusade for literacy is that anti-intellectualism in
American education is rampant, influencing even those whose intentions
are actually opposed to closing the doors to genuine learning.   The historical legacy of technicization has been to turn universities into
training institutions, which creates few spaces for intellectuals.   In a
few places, liberal and radical intellectuals are building micro-institu-
tions (centers, institutes, programs) within the universities as outposts
that attempt to resist the larger trends toward instrumentalized curricula.

LEE: Supermarket colleges provide all the different kinds of educational merchandise that will sell and is not too expensive to provide.
This suggests why so many relatively colorless and literarily unproductive teachers are retained and so many colorful and creative ones are encouraged to leave academic life.   The creative are upsetting, might even
get the institution "talked about" and give it a reputation for radicalism. Standard merchandise is desired, colorful only in athletics.   This
also accounts, in part, for the current growth of part-time teachers who
have no claim on continuing tenure and those whose pay and perquisites
are minimal.

The "finishing school" atmosphere is more apparent in private than
in public universities, but it is an academic staple. Athletic teams and
other sports opportunities, fraternities and sororities, and special social events drain off the energy that might be channeled to a greater extent into creative pursuits.   Unfortunately, partying, networking, and

matchmaking are preoccupations that contribute more to the definition of a student's future way of life than do academic routines.

To what degree, then, does the process of educating for literacy depend upon professors and pedagogy? Upon academic administrations?

ARONOWITZ and GIROUX: The challenge is to combine the intellectual work of cultural reclamation with the work of pedagogy. This would entail a deliberate effort to avoid the tendency toward exclusivity on the part of intellectuals; to refuse the temptation to reproduce the "community of scholars" that is the heart of Bloom's program, even if the scholars are democratic intellectuals. The assumption that students are a *tabula rasa*, upon which the teacher—armed with the wisdom of ages—places an imprint, is the basis of the widespread distrust of education among today's students.

LEE: Yes, and the proliferation of passive, non-participant students is encouraged by the format of mass-lecture-type classes in which machine-scored exams are give. To teach chemistry, biology, English composition, or sociology as a joint teacher-student search for knowledge takes a lot of interest and time upon the part of teachers. It requires autonomous, well-trained, well-paid teachers. Experiments with such procedures have almost always brought exciting and useful results in any field. Usually, only a few favored students have such opportunities, however, even in graduate schools.

Teaching, unfortunately, has come to be what faculty members do when they cannot get research grants or contracts. Special interest research in a variety of fields is where the money is for both the aspiring staff member and the institution. It is also a dependable way to advance in academic hierarchies. It places a premium on selling and on a sales-type personality, rather than on intellectual creativity and concern for student growth.

ARONOWITZ and GIROUX: Nonetheless, there are on the front lines, some teachers, buffeted and bewildered, who continue to maintain a fresh, creative, and critical approach to their tasks. In doing so, however, they receive little or no sustenance from the "intellectuals" (of the sort favored by Bloom and his cohorts.)

ENGEL: Earlier I argued for *social responsibility* being one of two essential values of a renewed higher education. This has two ramifications: first, that education is what economists call a"public good" and, therefore, ought to be paid for by the society as a whole and provided to anyone who wants or needs it; and second, that those involved in higher education have to recognize their accountability to those footing the bill—i.e., everyone.

Students, faculty, and administrators should function within a system that guarantees mutual accountability, responsible decision-making, and collective accountability to the taxpayers. If students receive education as a right--and they ought to--then they have a responsibility to repay society, at least in the form of progressive taxes or at most in the form of nonmilitary public service. If faculty have the right to unionization, tenure, and academic freedom--as they must have--they also have the responsibility to accept and respond to intellectual and professional challenges from those whom they teach and from those who pay their salaries. Administrators, of course, will have a whole new set of lessons to learn: how to exert leadership in such an environment. Both faculty and administrators are going to have to lose some of their arrogance.

BOTSTEIN: The task of real schooling for all Americans is more daunting and more expensive than we would like to admit. Without federal assistance, the number of teachers and their quality will not be assured. Neither will the required individual attention for all students.   Enormous resources will be needed to bring educational excellence to all citizens on an equitable basis.

ENGEL: I would have to add that a democratic higher education system, devoid of sexual, racial, ethnic, class, or financial discrimination, must be publicly owned and controlled.   Higher education must, therefore, be tuition-free, open to all high school graduates, financed by progressive taxation, and administered by federal, state, and local governments.   What is more, there can be no justification--including claims to "independence," "diversity," or "freedom of choice"--for diverting any public funds to private colleges and universities.   The distinction between private and public must be made crystal clear, with the former left entirely on their own to survive in a free market.
     I should add that society's responsibility to educate should go beyond the present focus on young people and should break the lockstep toward the four-year baccalaureate. Lifelong continuing education should be the norm. An educational system of this kind would de-emphasize the residential aspect of higher education and focus on the community or regional college as its mainstay. The major public research universities might assume a more national role, taking up many of the functions of their private counterparts.
     To be sure, a program for higher education based upon values of democracy and social responsibility poses a clear and direct challenge to the *anti*-democratic and socially *ir*responsible values held by Bloom and his cohorts and exposes their dishonesty in concealing their actual beliefs: that education is only for the chosen few and the search for truth ends at their lecterns. The Platonic ideas they pose as a solution are, in fact, the problem. The higher education system is a disaster because knowledge is still considered the property of a privileged minority

to be dispensed in small doses to those considered worthy.   Our struggles
to change the system must be based upon a commitment to a vision of higher learning as something for which everyone has equal responsibility and
to which everyone has an equal right.

Notes

INTRODUCTION

1. Ernest Becker, *Beyond Alienation* [New York: George Braziller & Company, 1967], p. 286.

2. Committee for Economic Development, *The Management and Financing of Colleges* [New York: Committee for Economic Development, 1973], pp. 51-52. And Carnegie Commission on Higher Education, *Priorities for Action: The Final Report of the Carnegie Commission* [New York: McGraw-Hill Book Company, 1973], p. 47.

3. Committee for Economic Development, *Management and Financing*, p. 17.

4. Academy for Educational Development, *Higher Education with Fewer Teachers* [New York: Academy for Educational Development, 1972], p. 4.

5. It was C. Wright Mills who first coined the phrase, the *"new [illiberal] practicality"*--an orientation which he found detrimental to the pursuit of liberal learning and, with that, "intellectual craftsmanship." See Chapter 4, "Types of Practicality," in *The Sociological Imagination* [New York: Oxford University Press, 1959].

PROMOTING THE "NEW PRACTICALITY"

1. Peter McClure, "Grubstake: A Radical Proposal," *Change* 8:5 [June 1976]: 38. Thorstein Veblen, *The Higher Learning in America* [New York: Hill and Wang, Inc., 1957, 1918]. Robert Maynard Hutchins, *The Higher Learning in America* [New Haven, Conn.: Yale University Press, 1936].

2. Gene I. Maeroff, "The Liberal Arts Degree and Its Real Value," *The New York Times* [June 12, 1977]: C-6.

3. *Ibid.*, p. C-6.

4. Some 58 percent of undergraduates major in professional studies: 11 percent in the natural sciences, another 11 percent in the social sciences, and only 5 percent in the humanities. See The Carnegie Council on Policy Studies in Higher Education, *A Summary of Reports* [San Francisco, Calif.: Jossey-Bass, 1980], p. 132.

5. Gene I. Maeroff, "Students Flock to Job-Related Courses," *The New York Times* [November 3, 1975]: C-10.

6. *Ibid.*, p. C-10.

7. Data from an editorial, "The Future Forsaken," *Change* 10:9 [October 1978]: 3.

8. Carl Kaysen, *The Higher Learning, the Universities, and the*

Public [Princeton, N.J.:   Princeton University Press, 1969], p. 7.

9. "The Great American Dream Freeze," *Dollars and Sense*   no. 5 [March 1975]: 5.

10. Cited in James O'Toole, "The Reserve Army of the Underemployed" [Part II], *Change* 7:6 [June 1975]: 30.

11. Carnegie Commission on Higher Education, *A Digest of Reports* [New York: McGraw-Hill Book Company, 1973], p. 43.

12. *Ibid.*, p. 44.

13. Committee for Economic Development, *Management and Financing*, pp. 51-52.

14. The term *career education* is little more than a euphemism for vocational training that, many educators feel, has suffered a somewhat tarnished image in recent times. To image-makers in educational planning circles, "career" is, apparently, a cut above "job" or even "vocation," and "education" has a nobler and more sophisticated ring than "training." The term thus serves to legitimate the growing movement toward vocationalizing the educational curriculum.

15. Data from *The Chronicle of Higher Education* 29:22 [February 18, 1985]: 32.

16. Data extrapolated from studies of the federal education budget in various issues of *The Chronicle of Higher Education* [1985 and 1986].

17. The Newt Davidson Collective, *Crisis at C.U.N.Y,* [New York: Newt Davidson Collective, 1973], p. 83.

18. "High Tech and the Schools," *Dollars and Sense* [May/June 1983]: 7.

19. Colman McCarthy, "Big Man on Campus," *The Nation* [February 28, 1987]: 253; and National Public Radio, "Morning Edition" newsbroadcast [July 25, 1989].

20. Ann Crittenden, "Industry's Role in Academia," *The New York Times* [July 22, 1981]: D-1; and Katherine Bouton, "Academic Research and Big Business—A Delicate Balance," *The New York Times Magazine* [September 11, 1983]: 63.

21. MIT Alternative News Collective and Science Action Coordinating Committee, *How to Fathomit—MIT Disorientation Manual 1988-89*, second edition [Cambridge, Mass.: MIT Alternative News Collective, November 1988] p. 59.

22. Arthur M. Cohen, "Stretching Pre-College Education," *Social Policy* 2:1 [May/June 1977]: 6.

23. "Vocational Schools Get Respect," *Newsweek* [March 7, 1983]: 79.

24. "The Great Training Robbery: Does Career Education Do Any Good?" *Dollars and Sense* no. 41 [November 1978]: 12.

25. Edward B. Fiske, "Booming Corporate Education Efforts Rival College Programs, Study Says," *The New York Times* [January 28, 1985]: A-10.

26. William D. Marbach and Jacob Young, "GM's Own College," *Newsweek* [May 11, 1981]: 62.

27. Fiske, "Booming Corporate Education," p. A-10.

28. *Ibid.*, p. A-10.

29. *Ibid.*, p. A-10.

30. "The Great Training Robbery," p. 12.

31. *Crisis at CUNY*, p. 81.

32. Carnegie Commission on Higher Education, *Less Time, More Options* [New York: McGraw-Hill, 1971], p. 13.

33. New York State Board of Regents, *Master Plan* [Albany: New York State Education Department, 1972], p. 12.

34. "SUNY, NY Tel. in Major Accord," *The News* (newspaper of the State University of New York), 4:5 [March 1975]: 1.

35. Clifton R. Wharton, Jr., "SUNY's Third Mission: Public Service" *Universitas.* 1:1 [September 1978]: 13.

36. Beverly T. Watkins, "Contracts to Provide Courses for Workers Can Be a 'Win/Win Deal,' Universities Are Learning," *The Chronicle of Higher Education* 28:18 [June 27, 1984]: 1.

37. *Ibid.*, p. 10.

38. "Vocational Schools Get Respect," *Newsweek* [March 7, 1983]: 80.

39. Richard B. Freeman, *The Over-Educated American* [New York: Aca-Academic Press, 1976]. Also Caroline Bird, *The Case Against College* [New York: David McKay Company, 1975.

40. Jerome Karabel, "Protecting the Portals: Class and the Community College," *Social Policy* 5:1 [May/June 1974]: 16.

41. *Ibid.*, p. 16.

42. *Ibid.*, p. 17.

43. Cited in Fred M. Hechinger, "Federal Aid and the Colleges," *The New York Times* [February 21, 1985]: C-1.

44. Maeroff, "The Liberal Arts Degree" [June 12, 1977]: C-6.

45. Maeroff, "Students Flock" [November 2, 1975]: C-10.

46. Mary Beth Bruno, "The Liberal Arts and the World of Work," *The New York Times Winter Survey of Education*, section 12 [January 6, 1985]: 18.

47. E. Patrick McQuaid, "New Morrill Actought to Generate $1 Billion for High Technology Education," *The Chronicle of Higher Education* 25:3 [September 15, 1982]: 8.

48. Robert Maynard Hutchins coined this vivid and appropriate metaphor. See *The Higher Learning in America* [New Haven, Conn.: Yale University Press, 1936].

49. Carnegie Commission on Higher Education, *The Open Door Colleges: Policies for Community Colleges* [New York: McGraw-Hill, 1970], p. 21.

50. Carnegie Commission on Higher Education, *A Digest of Reports of the Carnegie Commission* [New York: McGraw-Hill, 1970], pp. 23 and 25.

51. Fred L. Pincus, "Tracking in Community Colleges," *The Insurgent Sociologist* 4:3 [Spring 1974]: 28.

52. *Ibid.*, p. 29.

53. Janet Winn and O. Howard Winn, "Pre-Packaging Authoritarianism: Mix Business Values and Community Colleges and You Don't Get Democracy" [Poughkeepsie, N.Y.: Dutchess Community College (unpublished manuscript)

1977], p. 10.

54. Steven L. Zwerdling, *Second Best: The Crisis of the Community College* [New York: McGraw-Hill, 1976], pp. 60–61.

55. *Ibid.*, p. 60.

56. *Ibid.,* p. 61.

57. Robert Reinhold, "At Brown, Trend is Back to Grades and Tradition," *The New York Times* [February 24, 1976]: C-5.

58. Cited in *The Brown Alumni Monthly* [Providence, R.I.: Brown University, May 1974], p. 34.

59. *Ibid.*, p. 34.

60. Malcolm Scully, "Tightening the Curriculum: Enthusiasm, Dissent, and 'So What Else Is New?'" *The Chronicle of Higher Education* 16:2 [May 8, 1978]: 1.

61. It should be noted that neither (former) Secretary Bennett's nor the CFAT's widely publicized endorsements of the revival of general education [See *The New York Times* April 7, 1981, and November 26, 1984] should be construed as contradictory in either spirit or substance to the curricular policies advocated, respectively, by the U.S. Department of Education or by the Carnegie Commission on Higher Education and its successor, the Carnegie Council on Policy Studies in Higher Education, which the CFAT sponsored and funded. In fact, the Carnegie Council had, as early as 1977, given its blessing to the "boomlet" in favor of general education; as had previous federal education officials, including Secretary of Education Terrel H. Bell and Commissioner of Education Ernest L. Boyer. [See *Missions of the College Curriculum* (New York: McGraw-Hill)].

Overall, however, the record of foundation- and government-sponsored research has been more oriented to promoting the vocationalizing of higher education. In tandem with "selective philanthropy," selective curricular reform—targeted, that is, to different sectors of the academic system and with different outcomes—has been a constant feature of administrative policy.

Advocacy of the practical and the theoretical, the specialized and the generalized, can readily coexist and be generated by the same policy research organization or by the same individual. For example, Ernest L. Boyer, well known for his advocacy of career education, is also, as the current president of the CFAT, articulating the case for general education.

In a time of crisis, paradoxically, the call for general education may serve to facilitate and legitimize all the more the implementation of plans for practical education.

62. Carnegie Commission on Higher Education, *College Graduates and Jobs* [New York: McGraw-Hill, 1973], p. 160.

63. Academy for Educational Development, *319 Ways Colleges and Universities Are Meeting the Financial Pinch* [New York: Academy for Educational Development, 1973], pp. 7–8.

IDEOLOGY AND THE POLITICS OF PUBLIC HIGHER EDUCATION

1. James E. Anderson, *Public Policy Making* [New York: Holt, Rinehart & Winston, 1979], p. 157.

2. Daniel C. Rogers and Hirsch C. Ruchlin, *Economics and Education*
[New York: Free Press, 1971], p. 46.

3. Irving J. Goffman, J. Ronnie Davis, and John F. Morall, III, *The
Concept of Education as an Investment: Report to the President's Commission on School Finance* [Washington, D.C.: ERIC, 1971], p. 2.

4. *Ibid.*, p. 4.

5. Charles S. Benson, Jo Ritzen, and Irene Blumenthal, "Recent Perspectives on the Economics of Education," *Social Science Quarterly* [Sep-
tember 1974], p. 245.

6. Theodore Schultz, "Higher Education as an Investment in People,"
in Selma J. Mushkin, ed., *Economics of Education* [Washington, D.C.: Department of Health, Education and Welfare, 1962], p. 101.

7. Edward Denison, "Education and Growth," in Rogers and Ruchlin,
Economics and Education p. 249.

8. W. Lee Hansen and David Witmer, "Economic Benefits of Higher Education," in American Council on Education, ed., *Universal Higher Education: Costs and Benefits* [Washington: D.C.: American Council on Educa-
Education, 1971], p. 25.

9. Benson, et al., "Recent Perspectives," p. 248.

10. W. Lee Hansen, "Total and Private Rates of Return to Investment
in Schooling," in Rogers and Ruchlin, *Economics and Education* p. 186.

11. Hansen and Witmer, "Economic Benefits," p. 36.

12. Richard Eckaus, "Education and Economic Growth," in Mushkin,
Economics of Education, p. 112.

13. Benson, et al., "Recent Perspectives," p. 261.

14. Richard B. Freeman, "On the Mythical Effects of Public Subsidi-
zation of Higher Education," in Lewis Solmon and Paul J. Taubman, eds.,
Does College Matter? [New York: Academic Press, 1973], p. 324.

15. Burton A. Weisbrod, *External Effects of Public Education*
[Princeton, N.J.: Industrial Relations Section, 1964], p. 99.

16. Milton Friedman, *Capitalism and Freedom* [Chicago: University of
Chicago Press, 1962], p. 98.

17. Robert W. Hartman, "The Rationale for Federal Support for Higher
Education," in Solmon and Taubman, *Does College Matter?* p. 285.

18. Neil Singer and Paul Feldman, "Criteria for Public Investment in
Higher Education," in U.S. Congress Joint Economic Committee, *Economics
and Finance of Higher Education in the United States* [Washington, D.C.:
91st U.S. Congress, 1st Session, 1969], p. 125.

19. D. Kent Halstead, *Statewide Planning in Higher Education* [Wash-
ington, D.C.: Department of Health, Education, and Welfare, 1974],
p. 571.

20. Hansen and Witmer, "A New Approach to Financing Higher Education," in M.D. Orwig, ed., *Financing Higher Education: Alternatives for*

the Federal Government   [Iowa City, Iowa: American College Testing Program, 1974], p. 119.

21. See Carnegie Commission on Higher Education, *Higher Education: Who Pays? Who Benefits? Who Should Pay?* [New York: McGraw-Hill, 1973]; Committee for Economic Development, *The Management and Financing of Colleges* [New York: Committee for Economic Development, 1973]; David W. Breneman and Chester E. Finn, Jr., eds., *Public Policy and Private Higher Education* [Washington, D.C.: Brookings Institution, 1978]; Sloan Commission on Government and Higher Education, *A Program for Renewed Partnership* [Cambridge, Mass.: Ballinger, 1980].

22. See U.S. Department of Health, Education, and Welfare, Special Task Force to the Secretary, *The Second Newman Report* [Cambridge: Massachusetts Institute of Technology Press, 1973]; National Commission on the Financing of Post-Secondary Education, *Financing Post-Secondary Education in the United States* [Washington, D.C.: U.S. Government Printing Office, 1973].

23. New Jersey State Commission on Financing Post-Secondary Education, *Post-Secondary Education Vouchers: The Case for a Demonstration* [Trenton: New Jersey State Commission, 1977], p. 112.

24. *The Morning Union*, Springfield, Mass. [December 24, 1979].

25. Kenneth E. Young, ed., *Exploring the Case for Low Tuition in Public Higher Education* [Iowa City, Iowa, A.C.T. Program, 1974], pp. 182-183.

26. Larry L. Leslie and Gary P. Johnson, "The Market Model and Higher Education," *Journal of Higher Education* 45 [January 1974]: 10 and 15.

27. Robert Paul Wolff, "Appearance and Reality in Higher Education," Chancellor's Lecture, University of Massachusetts at Amherst [Amherst: University of Massachusetts, 1974], p. 53.

28. Russell I. Thackrey, *The Future of the State University* [Urbana: University of Illinois Press, 1971], p. 85.

29. Louis T. Benezet, "Private Higher Education: What Price Diversity?" *Educational Record* [Spring 1977]: 205.

30. Association of American Colleges, *A National Policy for Private Higher Education* [Washington, D.C.: AAC, 1974], p. 10.

31. Thackrey, *Future of the State University*, pp. 63-65.

32. Samuel Bowles and Herbert Gintis, *Schooling in Capitalist America* [New York: Basic Books, 1976], p. 234.

33. John S. Brubaker and Willis Rudy, *Higher Education in Transition* [New York: Harper & Row, 1976], p. 64.

34. Wolff, "Appearance and Reality," p. 58.

35. Ira Shor, *Critical Teaching and Everyday Life* [Boston: South End Press, 1980], p. xvii.

36. Carnegie Commission on Higher Education, *The Purposes and Performance of Higher Education in the United States* [New York: McGraw-Hill 1973], p. 29.

THE THERAPEUTIC CLASSROOM

1. Jean Bethke Elshtain, "The Social Relations of the Classroom: A Moral and Political Perspective," *Telos* 27 [Spring 1976]: 97-110. A revised version appears in Theodore Mills Norton and Bertell Ollman, eds., *Studies in Socialist Pedagogy* [New York: Monthly Review Press, 1978], pp. 291-313. See also my defense of the essay in "Reviews and Notes," *New Political Science* nos. 5 and 6 [Winter/Spring 1981]: 126-28.

2. See Bruce Rappaport, "On Radical Teaching," Part Two: "Marxist Teaching Practice," *Bulletin of the Union of Marxist Social Scientists* [April 1974], *passim*. A version of this essay also appears in Norton and Ollman, *Studies*, pp. 275-90 under the title, "Toward a Marxist Theory and Practice of Teaching."

3. Sherry M. Weber and Bernard J. Somers, "Humanistic Education at the College Level: A New Strategy and Some Techniques" [unpublished manuscript; copyright November 20, 1973]: 18.

4. *Ibid.*, p. 4.

5. Antonio Gramsci, *Selections from the Prison Notebooks*, edited and translated by Quintin Hoare and Geoffrey Nowell Smith [New York: International Publishers, 1971], p. 101.

6. Paolo Freire, *Pedagogy of the Oppressed* [New York: Seabury Press, 1968], p. 23.

7. I do not presume some entirely separate "feminist pedagogy." It is simply that the demands for warmth and community in the classroom bear most heavily on teachers of feminism and require the most cogently developed response. A fuller explication of my philosophic presumptions and conceptual method can be found in my book, *Public Man, Private Women: Women in Social and Political Thought* [Princeton, N.J.: Princeton University Press, 1981].

8. Susan Sontag, "Notes on Art, Sex and Politics," *The New York Times* [February 8, 1976]: D-36.

9. Madeleine Grumet, "Autobiography and Reconceptualization" [unpublished manuscript]: 1.

THE DREAD OF INNOVATION IN UNIVERSITIES

1. Alfred McClung Lee, *Sociology for Whom?* second edition [Syracuse, N.Y.: Syracuse University Press, 1986], chapter 8, and *Sociology for People* [Syracuse, N.Y.: Syracuse University Press, 1988], chapter 6.

2. Francis Bacon, "Advancement of Learning: Divine and Humane," in R. F. Jones, ed., *Advancement of Learning, New Atlantis and Other Pieces* [New York: Odyssey Press, 1937 (1605)], p. 229.

3. Ralph Waldo Emreson, "Self-Reliance" in *The Complete Writings of Ralph Waldo Emerson* [New York: William H. Wise & Company, 1929 (1841)], p. 139.

4. Bertrand Russell, *Principles of Social Reconstruction* [London:

Allen & Unwin, 1916], pp. 178-79.

5. Ted G. Goertzel, "The Role of Marxism in American Sociology," *The Insurgent Sociologist* 8:1 [Winter 1978]: 68.

6. Editorial, *Science* [December 8, 1978].

ACADEMIC FREEDOM, LITERACY, AND THE LIBERAL ARTS

1. Randall Collins, *The Credentialed Society* [Berkeley, Calif.: University of California Press, 1978].

2. Pierre Bourdieu and Jean-Claude Passeron, *Reproduction in Education, Society, and Culture* [Los Angeles, Calif.:   Sage Publications, 1979].

3. A possible objection to this assertion might be that even in large universities, especially graduate programs, students are subject to the tutelage and ultimate judgment of a single advisor. However, the advisor is also certified by the academic system; his/her right to certify others is a privilege conferred impersonally. The degree is not signed by the advisor alone, but also by the administration of the university that reserves, at least putatively, the ultimate authority over the process.

4. I am not claiming that the diploma is entirely superceded by a bachelor's degree. The diploma is still a prerequisite for many public sector jobs and clerical positions in the private sector, but is no longer a sufficient credential for technical and administrative occupations. Post-secondary education of some kind has become the *sine qua non* of these jobs.

5. Talcott Parsons, *Essays in Social Theory* [New York: Free Press, 1958].

6. Herbert Marcuse, *One Dimensional Man* [Boston: Beacon Press, 1964].

7. Wilhelm Reich, *The Imposition of Compulsory Sexual Morality* [New York: Farrar, Straus & Giroux, 1971].

8. See Jurgen Habermas, *Communication and the Evolution of Society* [Boston: Beacon Press, 1980], pp. 130-77.

9. Pierre Bourdieu, *Outline of a Theory of Practice* [Cambridge and New York: Cambridge University Press, 1980].

10. Here, "social contract" theory refers to those perspectives in which the subjects of social domination accept their situation as part of a larger agreement with those in power. Bourdieu, the Frankfort School, and Reich, among others, argue that the process by which authority establishes itself entails a transformation of the largely unconscious, habitual processes of everyday life.

11. Bourdieu and Passeron, *Reproduction*, pp. 141-76.

12. Paul Willis, *Learning to Labor* [New York: Columbia University Press, 1981].

13. Alain Touraine, *The Academic System in American Society* [New

York: McGraw-Hill, 1971].

14. As a result of the June 1983 election, neither union received final certification because there were more than 500 challenged ballots, enough to swing the election to the AAUP. However, the stunning victory for faculty unionism is unmistakable: of 14,000 votes, only 2,500 were nonunion. Similar victories were won by the AAUP at Rutgers and Wayne State University. The AFT represents faculty and some staff at the City University of New York and the faculty in the State University of New York system.

15. *National Labor Relations Board v. Yeshiva University*, 444 U.S. 672 [1980].

16. The recruitment of administrators from faculty ranks is rapidly receding in importance as the academic system increasingly adopts the corporate-managerial practice of recruiting professional managers for high university positions. In many cases, even when administrators hold formal academic credentials, these serve as legitimating "fig-leaves" for a professionalized management.

THE DECLINE OF LITERACY AND LIBERAL LEARNING

1. Karl Marx was, to my knowledge, the first to make such an analogy—remarkably, a full century before the rise of the "multiversity." In a famous passage from volume I of *Capital* [New York: International Publishers, 1967 (1887)], p. 509, elaborating the relation between wage labor and capital, Marx with wry humor remarked:

> If we may take an example from outside the sphere of production of material objects, a schoolmaster is a productive laborer when, in addition to belaboring the heads of his scholars, he works like a horse to enrich the school proprietor. That the latter has laid out his capital in a *knowledge factory*, instead of in a sausage factory, does not alter the relation.

2. Clark Kerr, *The Uses of the University* [Cambridge, Mass.: Harvard University Press, 1963], p. 20.

3. Thorstein Veblen, *The Higher Learning in America* [New York: Hill and Wang, 1957 (1918)], p. 163.

4. The acronym "FTE" stands for "full-time equivalent." It is sidely used as a measure of the "drawing power" or productivity of college faculty—expressed as a ratio of actual enrollments to the mean standard enrollment for full-time teaching (usually around 80 students per semester). For example, Professor "X" with 160 students in a given semester would be said to be "producing two FTEs," or the equivalent of two full-time faculty members.

5. The term "professional entrepreneurs" is Robert A. Nisbet's. See *The Degradation of the Academic Dogma* [New York: Basic Books, 1970],

p. 75.

6. Veblen, *The Higher Learning*, pp. 136-38.

7. Ernest Becker, *Beyond Alienation* [New York: George Braziller, 1967], p. 286.

8. Both terms ("methodological inhibitions" and "pretensions") are C. Wright Mills's. See "Abstracted Empiricism," chapter 3, in *The Sociological Imagination* [New York: Oxford University Press, 1959].

9. Edward B. Fiske, "Commission on Education Warns 'Tide of Mediocrity' Imperils U.S.," *The New York Times* [April 27, 1983]: B-6.

10. Associated Press, "Scores on College Entrance Tests Climb, Reversing 19-Year Decline," *The Poughkeepsie Journal* [September 20, 1982]: 1; and Lee Mitgang, "SAT Scores Remain 'Too Low'," *The Poughkeepsie Journal* [September 23, 1987]: 1.

11. Fiske, "Commission on Education," p. B-6.

12. Christopher Lasch, "The New Illiteracy," *New Times* [January 8, 1979]: 36. See also "Schooling and the New Illiteracy," chapter 6 in *The Culture of Narcissism* [New York: W. W. Norton, 1979].

13. *Ibid.*, p. 36.

14. Joseph F. Sullivan, "Jersey Finds Lack of Student Skills," *The New York Times* [December 23, 1987], B-3.

15. C. Wright Mills, *The Sociological Imagination*, p. 105.

16. The term is Stephen Muller's. See "Higher Education or Higher Skilling?" *Daedalus* 102:4 [Fall 1974]: 149.

17. Nisbet, *The Degradation*, p. 109.

18. William J. Bennett, *To Reclaim a Legacy*—Report of the National of the National Endowment for the Humanities' Study Group on the State of Learning in the Humanities in Higher Education [Washington, D.C.: National Endowment for the Humanities, November 1984]. Reprinted in *The Chronicle of Higher Education* 29:11 [November 28, 1984]: 16.

19. Stanley Aronowitz, "Mass Culture and the Eclipse of Reason," chapter 11 in *The Crisis in Historical Materialism: Class Politics and Culture in Marxist Theory* [New York: Praeger Publishers, 1982], p. 282.

20. Lasch, "The New Illiteracy," p. 36.

21. *Ibid.*, p. 36.

22. Aronowitz, "Mass Culture," p. 282.

23. *Ibid.*, p. 284.

24. Lasch, "The New Illiteracy," p. 36.

25. Robert A. Nisbet, appropriating the radical Marx for the conservative purposes of his argument, describes his "academic bourgeousie" in terms familiar to readers of *The Communist Manifesto*: "The bourgeoisie, wherever it has got the upper hand, has left remaining no other nexus between man and man than naked self-interest, than callous 'cash payment.'"

These words come close, Nisbet argues, to describing the changes that have been taking place in the American university since the early 1950s. "The new wealth from government bureaus and the foundations, the new structures for this wealth provided by dazzled trustees, administrators and faculty in the forms of institutes, centers, and bureaus and the whole entrepreneurial atmosphere that began to envelope the university could not help but produce a new class on the American campus: a new bourgeoisie." [*The Degradation of the Academic Dogma* (New York: Basic Books, 1971), p. 101.]

26. The term, "hired heads," was coined by Herman and Julia R. Schwendinger in *The Sociologists of the Chair* [New York: Basic Books, 1974], p. 518.

27. The term is part of the subtitle of Edgar Litt's book, *The Public Vocational University: Captive Knowledge and Public Power* [New York: Holt, Rinehart, Winston, 1969].

28. Irwin Sperber, "The Decline in Academic Standards and the Conservative Mood," *Hudson Valley Chronicle* 1 [Summer 1977]: 9.

29. Stanley Aronowitz, "The New Literacy Movement and the New Right" Remarks delivered at a conference on *The Liberal Arts in a Time of Crisis*, State University of New York College at New Paltz, January 31, 1981.

30. Edward B. Fiske, "Three Year Survey Finds College Curriculums in U.S. in 'Disarray,'" *The New York Times* [February 11, 1985]: A-1. See also Association of American Colleges, *Integrity in the College Curriculum: A Report to the Academic Community* [Washington, D.C.: Association of American Colleges, 1985].

31. Jean Evangelauf, "Academe, States Urged to Pursue New 'Covenant,'" *The Chronicle of Higher Education* 30:18 [July 3, 1985]: 1 and 9.

32. Malcolm G. Scully, "Nation is Urged to Link College with Civic Goals," *The Chronicle of Higher Education* 31:3 [September 18, 1985]: 1 and 17.

33. Edward B. Fiske, "Colleges in U.S. Need Overhaul, Study Contends," *The New York Times* [November 2, 1986]: A-1 and A-38.

34. See Allan Bloom, *The Closing of the American Mind—How Higher Education Has Failed Democracy and Impoverished the Souls of Today's Students* [New York: Simon & Schuster, 1987]. See also E. D. Hirsch, Jr., *Cultural Literacy—What Every American Needs to Know* [Boston: Houghton Mifflin, 1987].

35. Alfred McClung Lee, review-essay of Allan Bloom, *The Closing of the American Mind* (prepared for this volume, unpublished 1988); and Leon Botstein, "Education Reform in the Reagan Era—False Paths, Broken Promises," *Social Policy* 16:4 [Spring 1988]: 8.

36. See Charles Sykes, *Profscam—Professors and the Demise of Higher Education* [Washington, D.C.: Regnery, Gateway, 1988].

37. Cited in Fiske, "Commission on Education Warns," p. B-6.

38. Edward B. Fiske, "Study Asks Tighter Curriculums," *The New York Times* [September 16, 1983]: A-13.

39. Commission on International Education of the American Council on Education, *What We Don't Know Can Hurt Us: The Shortfall in International Competence* [Washington, D.C.: American Council on Education, 1984], p. 5.

40. Fiske, "Study Asks," p. A-13. See also *From the Newman Report to the Carnegie Foundation for the Advancement of Teaching* [September

1985]; cited in Scully, "Nation is Urged," p. 17.

41. The two main exceptions to this among policy studies are those of the National Institute of Education (NIE) Study Group on the Conditions of Academic Excellence in Higher Education and the Association of American Colleges (AAC). The NIE Study Group, to its credit, recognized that the "college has become excessively vocational" and even recommended that all bachelor's degree recipients have "at least two full years of liberal education," even if that means extending the length of undergraduate education in such professional fields as agriculture, business administration, engineering, pharmacy, and teacher education. [See *Involvement in Learning: Realizing the Potential of American Higher Education* (Washington, D.C.: National Institute of Education, October 1984). Reprinted in: *The Chronical of Higher Education* 29:9 (October 24, 1984): 1.]

In a similar vein, the AAC Report condemned a "misguided marketplace philosophy" that had engulfed collegiate culture, making today's students "more vocationally oriented and apparently more materialistic than their immediate predecessors." [See *Integrity in the College Curriculum*, reprinted in *The Chronicle of Higher Education* 29:22 (February 13, 1985): 12.]

42. See chapter 2 in this book, "Promoting the 'New Practicality:' Curricular Policies for the 1990s." See also chapters 6, 8, and 9 in my book, *Crisis Management in American Higher Education* [New York: Praeger, 1983].

43. Most of the policy reports typically exaggerate the need for highly skilled workers in the supposedly "high technology" U.S. economy. According to data from the Bureau of Labor Statistics, high-tech industries accounted for only 3.2 percent of all employment in 1982 and are expected to account for no more than 6 percent of all new jobs that will be created by 1995. The data also show that "most workers in high-tech industries have extremely modest levels of skill. Only one quarter of these employees have professional and technical jobs that require sophisticated theoretical and technical skills. Most . . . hold blue collar and clerical jobs. . . . Only 10 of the top 40 occupations that will provide the most new jobs by 1995 require a college degree." See Fred L. Pincus, "Conservative Reports on Educational Problems Are Becoming Part of the Problem," *The Review of Education* 9:4 [Fall 1983]: 352-353.

44. Fiske, "Commission on Education Warns," p. B-6.

45. A staple of educational conservatism has always been to limit access to the ivory tower to an elite few. Bennett's brand of conservative ideology is quite conspicuous, not only in the NEH report on the Humanities in Higher Education he authored, but also in his widely-publicized statements to the press after succeeding Terrel H. Bell as Reagan's secretary of education.

Defending the administration's cutbacks in financial aid to students in the fiscal 1986 budget, Bennett insinuated that many of the beneficiaries were freeloaders who would do well to "divest" themselves of their stereos, automobiles, and "three-weeks-at-the-beach." When asked about low-income students who would be financially forced to drop out, Bennett further suggested that there were perhaps too many students in college anyway. To underscore his point, he noted that while more than half of all U.S. high school graduates attend college, only about 15 percent do so in such industrial countries as Great Britain, Japan, and West Germany. [See *The Chronicle of Higher Education* 29:23 (February 20, 1985): 21 and 24.]

It is clear, moreover, that Bennett's ringing defenses of humanities education (especially contained in the NEH report) represent a "trickle down" ideology primarily intended to buttress and benefit an educational elite.

46. Aronowitz, *The Crisis in Historical Materialism*, p. 283.

INTRODUCTION TO PART II: TOWARD RECOVERY OF THE HIGHER LEARNING

1. John Stuart Mill, cited in Richard Lichtman, "The University: Mask for Privilege," in Immanuel Wallerstein and Paul Starr, eds., *The University Crisis Reader* vol. 1 [New York: Random House, 1971], p. 101.

2. C. Wright Mills, *The Sociological Imagination* [New York: Oxford University Press, 1959], p. 105. See also Lichtman, "The University," p. 101.

3. Lichtman, "The University," p. 117.

4. Bernard Murchland, "The Eclipse of the Liberal Arts," *Change* 8 [November 1976]: 23.

5. Lichtman, "The University," p. 118.

CRITICAL LITERACY AND THE LEGACY OF MARXIST DISCOURSE

1. Some representative examples include: Michael Apple, *Ideology and Curriculum* [Boston: Routledge and Kegan, Paul, 1979]; Samuel Bowles and Herbert Gintis, *Schooling in Capitalist America* [New York: Basic Books, 1976]; Martin Carnoy, ed., *Schooling in Corporate Society* [New York: David McKay, Inc., 1975]; Madan Sarup, *Marxism and Education* [London: Routledge and Kegan, Paul, 1978]; Paul Willis, *Learning to Labor* [Lexington, Mass.: D. C. Heath, 1977]; Michael Young and Geoff Whitty, eds., *Society, State and Schooling* [Lewes, England: Falmer Press, 1977]; Theodore Mills Norton and Bertell Ollman, eds., *Studies in Socialist Pedagogy* [New York: Monthly Review Press, 1978]; Pierre Bourdieu and Jean-Claude Passeron, *Reproduction in Education, Society and Culture* [Beverly Hills, Calif.: Sage Publications, 1977]; Stephen Castles and Wiebke Wiestenberg, *The Education of the Future* [London: Pluto Press, 1979]; Rachel Sharp, *Knowledge, Ideology and the Politics of Schooling: Toward a Marxist Analysis of Education* [London: Routledge and Kegan, Paul, 1980]; Henry A. Giroux, *Ideology, Culture, and the Politics of Schooling*

[Philadelphia, Penn.: Temple University Press, 1981]; Michael Apple, *Education and Power* [Boston: Routledge and Kegan, Paul, 1982].

2. Bowles and Gintis, *Schooling in Capitalist America;* Henry A. Giroux and Anthony Penna, "Social Education in the Classroom: The Dynamics of the Hidden Curriculum," *Theory and Research in Social Education* 7:1 [1979]: 21-42.

3. Jean Anyon, "Social Class and School Knowledge," *Curriculum Inquiry* 11:1 [1981]: 3-41; Bourdieu and Passeron, *Reproduction in Education.*

4. The most celebrated example is Willis, *Learning to Labor.* See also Henry A. Giroux, *Theory and Resistance in Education: A Pedagogy for the Opposition* [South Hadley, Mass.: Bergin and Garvey, 1983].

5. See the various articles in Paul Olson, ed., "Rethinking Social Reproduction," *Interchange* 12:1/3 [1981]. See also George Wood, "Beyond Radical Cynicism," *Educational Theory* 32:2 [1982]: 55-71; Henry A. Giroux, "Theories of Reproduction and Resistance in the New Sociology of Education: A Critical Analysis," *Harvard Educational Review* [forthcoming].

6. Gilbert G. Gonzalez, *Progressive Education: A Marxist Interpretation* [Minneapolis, Minn.: Marxist Educational Press, 1982].

7. Bowles and Gintis, *Schooling in Capitalist America;* Roslyn Arlin Mickelson, "The Secondary School's Role in Social Stratification: A Comparison of Beverly Hills High School and Morningside High School," *Journal of Education* 162:4 [1980].

8. Louis Althusser, "Ideology and the Ideological State Apparatuses," in *Lenin and Philosophy and Other Essays,* trans. Ben Brewster [New York: Monthly Review Press, 1977], pp. 127-86.

9. William A. Proefiedt, "Socialist Criticism of Education in the United States: Problems and Possibilities," *Harvard Educational Review* 50:4 [1980]: 467-80.

10. Jean Anyon, "Ideology and U.S. History Textbooks," *Harvard Educational Review* 49:3 [1979]; Apple, *Ideology and Curriculum* [1979]; Giroux, *Ideology, Culture* [1981].

11. Philip Wexler, "Movement, Class, and Education," in Len Barton and Stephen Walker, eds., *Race, Class and Education* [London: Croom-Helm, 1983], pp. 17-39. This is an important essay because of its focus on the relationship between education and social movements. Unfortunately, Wexler's attack on other leftist educators does not represent a scholarly attempt to deal with their work. In the place of such an attempt, the reader is treated to a series of strawmen that Wexler conveniently creates and dismisses.

12. Giroux, *Theory and Resistance.*

13. Two excellent examples are: George Rude, *Ideology and Popular Protest* [New York: Pantheon, 1980]; and Alain Touraine, *The Voice and the Eye: Analyses of Social Movements* [Cambridge, England: Cambridge University Press, 1981]; see also the special issue on social movements in *Telos* 52 [Summer 1982].

14. Richard Johnson, "Socialism and Popular Education," *Socialism*

and Education 8:1 [1981]: 12.

15. Two useful examples are: Richard Lichtman, *The Production of Desire* [New York: Free Press, 1982]; Philip Wexler, *Critical Social Psychology* [Boston: Routledge and Kegan, Paul, 1983].

16. See especially Stanley Aronowitz, *The Crisis of Historical Materialism* [South Hadley, Mass.: J. F. Bergin Publishers, 1981].

17. *Ibid.*, pp. 297-98.

18. Stanley Aronowitz, "Socialism and Beyond: Remaking the American Left [Part Two]," *Socialist Review* 13:3 [May/June 1983]: 7-42.

19. Antonio Gramsci, *Prison Notebooks*, trans. Quintin Hoare and Geoffrey Nowell Smith [New York: International Publishers, 1971].

20. Aronowitz, "Socialism and Beyond," pp. 16-17.

HUMANITIES IN THE EDUCATION OF MINORITIES

1. Editorial, *Change* [Summer 1975]: 41.

2. Editorial, "Graduates Without Jobs," *The Washington Star* [April 5, 1979].

3. Cited in Malcolm G. Scully, "Reinvigorating the Humanities," *The Chronicle of Higher Education* 11:2 [September 22, 1975]: 32.

4. From the enabling legislation establishing the National Endowment for the Humanities: The National Foundation for the Arts and the Humanities Act of 1965 [Washington, D.C.:   U.S. Government Printing Office, 1977].

5. See James A. Davis, *Undergraduate Career Decisions* [Chicago: Aldine Publishing Company, 1965], p. 95.

6. Frank Newman, et al., *Report on Higher Education* [Washington, D.C.: U.S. Department of Health, Education, and Welfare; Office of Education, 1972], p. 47.

7. Frederick Douglas, *My Bondage and My Freedom* [New York: Dover Publications, 1969], p. 445.

8. W. E. B. DuBois, *The Souls of Black Folk* [Grenwich, Conn.: Fawcett Primer Book, 1963], p. 156.

9. Jacob Neusner, "To Weep With Achilles," *The Chronicle of Higher Education* [January 29, 1979]: 40.

10. Alex Haley, letter to Huel D. Perkins [March 24, 1979].

11. Data from Alice Dunbar-Nelson, "Negro Literature for Negro Pupils," *The Southern Workman* 51:2 [February 1922]: 59.

12. A. Bartlett Giamatti, testimony before the Congress of the United States, State Governmental Affairs Committee; reported in *The Washington Star* [March 18, 1989]: B-1.

13. W. E. B. DuBois, *The Souls of Black Folk*, p. 164.

14. Sophocles, *Antigone* [Baltimore, Md.: Penguin Books, 1955], p. 135.

REFLECTIONS ON THE EDUCATION OF WOMEN

1. Dumas Malone, et al., eds., *Dictionary of American Biography*, 26 volumes [New York: Scribner, 1980 (1927)].

2. Roscoe C. Hinkle, *Founding Theory of American Sociology: 1881–1915* [Boston: Routledge and Kegan, Paul, 1980], chapters 1 and 2.

3. Thomas Woody, *A History of Women's Education in the United States* volumes 1 and 2 [New York: Science Press, 1929].

4. *Dictionary of American Biography*, volume 17, pp. 635–36.

5. J. M. Cattell and Jacques Cattell, eds., *American Men of Science* fourth edition [Lancaster, Penn.: Science Press, 1927].

6. Carl Murchison, ed., *A History of Psychology in Autobiography*, volume 1 [Worcester, Mass.: Clark University Press, 1930]; obituary, *The Boston Transcript* [February 27, 1930].

7. W. W. Atwood, memorial in *Journal of Geography* [September 1932]; and *The New York Times* [May 9, 1932].

8. From the very extensive literature now available, recommended references include: Harold H. Anderson, ed., *Creativity and Its Cultivation* New York: Harper, 1959]; Helene Deutsch, *The Psychology of Women* [New York: Grune & Stratton, 1944–45]; Matina S. Horner, "Toward an Understanding of Achievement-Related Conflicts in Women," *Journal of Social Issues* volume 28, [1972]: 157–76; Karen Horney, *Feminine Psychology* [New York: Norton, 1967]; Mirra Komarovsky, *Women in the Modern World* [Boston: Little, Brown, 1953]; Abraham H. Maslow, *Motivation and Personality* [New York: Harper, 1959]; and Martha T. S. Mednick, Sandra S. Tangri, and Lois W. Hoffman, eds., *Women and Achievement* [New York: Wiley, 1975].

9. *Who Was Who in America*, volume I [1942].

10. Harry L. Hollingworth, *Leta Stetter Hollingworth* [1943]; and A. T. Poffenberger in *American Journal of Psychology* [April 1940].

11. The Harriet Boyd Hawes Papers in the Smith College Archives; obituary, *Wellesley Magazine* [June 1945].

12. Doris Wilkinson, "Percentages of Women Doctorates in Sociology Increases," American Sociological Association, *Footnotes* 5:9 [December 1977]: 8.

13. Ravenna Helson, "The Changing Image of the Career Woman," in Martha T. S. Mednick, et al., *Women and Achievement*. Further discussion is available in Pamela Roby, "Structural and Internalized Barriers to Women in Higher Education," in Constantina Safilios-Rothschild, ed., *Sociology of Women* [Boston: Ginn-Blaisdell, 1971]; and in John W. Atkinson and Joel A. Raynor, eds., *Motivation and Achievement* [New York: Wiley, 1974].

FOREIGN LANGUAGES AND HUMANISTIC LEARNING

1. From the report of the Committee on Foreign Language and Inter-

national Studies.   [Washington, D. C.:   U.S. Government Printing Office, November 1979].

2. The analysis of Noam Chomsky's theories is derived from two of his books: *Language and Mind* [New York: Harcourt Brace, 1972] and *Reflections on Language* [New York: Pantheon, 1976].

3. Mark Van Doren, "Education by Books," *The Nation* [December 6, 1933].

REVITALIZING THE MODERN HUMANITIES

1. Lewis Mumford, *Art and Technics* [New York: Columbia University Press, 1952], p. 3.

2. T. S. Eliot, "Tradition and the Individual Talent" [1917] in *Selected Essays* [New York: Harcourt Brace, 1932], p. 11.

3. George Berkeley, as cited in Ernest Lee Tuveson, *Redeemer Nation: The Idea of America* [Chicago: University of Chicago Press, 1968], p. 93.

4. Gene Lyons, "The Higher Illiteracy: On the Prejudice Against Teaching College Students to Write," *Harper's* 253 [September 1976]: 33-40.

5. Kingman Brewster, as cited in Lyons, *ibid.*, p. 36.

6. Jeffrey Record, "The Fortunes of War," *Harper's* 260 [April 1980].

7. Robert M. Nisbet, *Sociology as an Art Form* [New York: Oxford University Press, 1976], p. 17. See also *The Degradation of the Academic Dogma* [New York: Basic Books, 1971].

8. Julian Huxley, "A Redefinition of Progress," *New Bottles for New Wine* [New York: Harper & Row, 1957], p. 31.

9. Stephen Muller, "Higher Education or Higher Skilling?" *Daedalus*, Special Issue on American Higher Education, 1 [Fall 1974] 148-58. See also *The New York Times Magazine* [January 7, 1979].

10. Christopher Lasch, *The Culture of Narcissism: American Life in an Age of Diminishing Expectations* [New York: W. W. Norton, 1978].

11. Jerry Rubin, *Growing Up at Thirty-Seven* [New York: M. Evans Co., 1976].

12. Alfred North Whitehead, "The Aims of Education," [1917] in *The Aims of Education and Other Essays* [New York: Free Press, 1929], p. 2.

13. Clifton Fadiman, "The Decline of Attention," in *Party of One* [Cleveland, Ohio: World Publishing, 1955], pp. 354-68.

14. Eugene Kinkhead, *In Every War But One* [New York: W. W. Norton, 1959].

15. Dennis Gabor, "Can We Survive Our Future?" *Encounter* 37 [February 1972]: 54-58.

16. Cyrus Vance, speech to the American Association of Community and Junior Colleges [Washington, D.C.: May 4, 1979].

THE UNITY AND UTILITY OF LEARNING

1. C. P. Snow, *The Two Cultures—A Second Look* [Cambridge: Cambridge University Press, 1964].

2. Glenn Seaborg, cited in George E. Brown, "The Bond Between Chemistry and Society," *Chemical and Engineering News* [September 8, 1980]: 5.

3. A. Bartlett Giamatti, cited by Marvin N. Olasky, "Business and the Universities: A New Season," *Du Pont Context* 8:1 [January 1979]: 16-19.

4. Subranmanyan Chandrasekhar, "Beauty and the Quest for Beauty in Science," *Physics Today* [July 1979]: 25-30.

5. Jacob Rabinow, "Inventing is an Art Form," *Industrial Research and Development* [November 1980]: 108-112.

6. The Rockefeller Foundation Commission on the Humanities, *The Humanities in American Life* [Berkeley, Calif.: University of California Press, 1980].

7. Data from U.S. Department of Commerce, Bureau of the Census, in *Statistical Abstract of the United States* [Washington, D.C.: U.S. Government Printing Office, 1989], p. 157.

8. *Rackman Reports*, quarterly publication of the H. H. Rackham School of Graduate Studies, University of Michigan [Spring 1980].

9. Richard Ruch in *The Chronicle of Higher Education* [May 27, 1980]: 56.

10. *Ibid.*, p. 56.

CODA: CONFRONTING THE CONSERVATIVE CRUSADE FOR LITERACY

1. See Allan Bloom, *The Closing of the American Mind: How Higher Education Has Failed Democracy and Impoverished the Souls of Today's Students* [New York: Simon & Schuster, 1987].

2. See E. D. Hirsch, *Cultural Literacy: What Every American Needs to Know* [Boston: Houghton Mifflin, 1987].

3. See Diane Ravitch and Chester E. Finn, Jr., *What Do Our Seventeen-Year-Olds Know?* [New York: Harper & Row, 1987]; and William J. Bennett, *James Madison High School: A Curriculum for American Students* [Washington, D.C.: U.S. Department of Education, 1987]. See also William J. Bennett, *To Reclaim a Legacy: The Report of the National Endowment for the Humanities' Study Group on the State of Learning in the Humanities in Higher Education* [Washington, D.C.: National Endowment for the Humanities, 1984].

4. Charles Sykes, *Profscam: Professors and the Demise of Higher Education* [Washington, D.C.: Regnery Gateway, 1988].

5. Jonathan Kozol, *Illiterate America* [Garden City, N.Y.: Anchor Press/Doubleday, 1985].

6. For a discussion of this issue, see pages 81-90 of chapter 7 in this book: "The Decline of Literacy and Liberal Learning" by Barbara Ann

Scott.

7. Commentaries contained in this coda were excerpted from the following sources:

Stanley Aronowitz and Henry A. Giroux, "Schooling, Culture, and Literacy in the Age of Broken Dreams: A Review of Bloom and Hirsch," *Harvard Educational Review* 58:2 [May 1988]: 172-94.

Leon Botstein, "Education Reform in the Reagan Era: False Paths, Broken Promises," *Social Policy* [Spring 1988]: 1-11.

Leon Botstein, "Review of *The Closing of the American Mind* by Allan Bloom," *The Boston Globe* [August 9, 1987]: A-12.

Jean Bethke Elshtain, "Allan in Wonderland," [Review of *The Closing of the American Mind* by Allan Bloom], *Cross Currents* [Winter 1987-88]: 476-79.

Jean Bethke Elshtain, unpublished commentary on critical literacy [1988].

Michael Engel, unpublished essay on an alternative approach to literacy and the academic curriculum [prepared for this book, 1988].

Alfred McClung Lee, "Comments on Allan Bloom's *The Closing of the American Mind*," [review essay prepared for this book, 1988].

8. Kozol, *Illiterate America*, p. 160.

9. John Dewey, *The Quest for Certainty* [New York: G. P. Putnam's Sons, 1929], p. 252.

Selected Bibliography

Academy for Educational Development. *Higher Education with Fewer Teachers*. New York: Academy for Educational Development, 1972.

American Council on Education. *Universal Higher Education: Costs and Benefits*. Washington, D.C.: American Council on Education, 1971.

------. *What We Don't Know Can Hurt Us: The Shortfall in International Competence*. Washington, D.C.: American Council on Education, 1984.

Apple, Michael. *Education and Power*. Boston, Routledge and Kegan, Paul, 1982.

------. *Ideology and Curriculum*. Boston: Routledge and Kegan, Paul,

Aronowitz, Stanley. *The Crisis in Historical Materialism: Class Politics and Culture in Marxist Theory*. New York: Praeger, 1982.

------, and Henry A. Giroux. *Education Under Siege: The Conservative, Liberal, and Radical Debate Over Schooling*. South Hadley, Mass.: Bergin & Garvey, 1985.

Association of American Colleges (AAC). *A National Policy for Private Higher Education*. Washington, D.C.: AAC, 1974.

------. *Integrity in the College Curriculum: A Report to the Academic Community*. Washington, D.C.: AAC, 1985.

Becker, Ernest. *Beyond Alienation*. New York: George Braziller and Company, 1967.

Bennett, William J. *James Madison High School: A Curriculum for American Students*. Washington, D.C.: U.S. Department of Education, 1987.

------. *To Reclaim a Legacy: The Report of the National Endowment for the Humanities' Study Group on the State of Learning in the Humanities in Higher Education*. Washington, D.C.: National Endowment for the Humanities, November 1984.

Bird, Caroline. *The Case Against College*. New York: David McKay Company, 1975.

Bloom, Allan. *The Closing of the American Mind: How Higher Education Has Failed Democracy and Impoverished the Souls of Today's Students*. New York: Simon & Schuster, 1987.

Bourdieu, Pierre, and Jean-Claude Passeron. *Reproduction in Education, Society and Culture*. Los Angeles, Calif.: Sage Publications, 1979.

Bowles, Samuel, and Herbert Gintis. *Schooling in Capitalist America*. New York: Basic Books, 1976.

Breneman, David W., and Chester E. Finn, Jr. *Public Policy and Private Higher Education*. Washington, D.C.: Brookings Institution, 1978.

Brubaker, John S., and Willis Rudy. *Higher Education in Transition*. New York: Harper & Row, 1976.

Carnegie Commission on Higher Education (CCHE). *College Graduates and*

Jobs. New York: McGraw Hill, 1973.

Carnegie Commission on Higher Education (CCHE). *Higher Education: Who Pays? Who Benefits? Who Should Pay?* New York: McGraw Hill, 1973.

------. *Less Time, More Options.* New York: McGraw Hill, 1971.

------. *The Open Door Colleges: Policies for Community Colleges.* New York: McGraw Hill, 1970.

------. *Priorities for Action: The Final Report of the Carnegie Commission.* New York: McGraw Hill 1973.

------. *The Purposes and Performance of Higher Education in the United States.* New York: McGraw Hill, 1973.

Carnegie Council on Policy Studies in Higher Education. *A Summary of Reports.* San Francisco, Calif.: Jossey Bass, 1980.

Carnoy, Martin, ed. *Schooling in Corporate Society.* New York: David McKay Company, 1975.

Collins, Randall. *The Credentialed Society.* Berkeley: University of California Press, 1978.

Committee for Economic Development. *The Management and Financing of Colleges.* New York: Committee for Economic Development, 1973.

Elshtain, Jean Bethke. *Public Man, Private Woman: Women in Social and Political Thought.* Princeton, N.J.: Princeton University Press, 1981.

Freeman, Richard B. *The Overeducated American.* New York: Academic Press, 1976.

Freire, Paolo. *Pedagogy of the Oppressed.* New York: Seabury Press, 1968.

------. *The Politics of Education: Culture, Power, and Liberation.* South Hadley, Mass.: Bergin & Garvey, 1987.

------, and Donaldo Macedo. *Literacy: Reading the Word and the World.* South Hadley, Mass.: Bergin & Garvey, 1987.

Giroux, Henry A. *Ideology, Culture, and the Process of Schooling.* Philadelphia, Penn.: Temple University Press, 1981.

------. *Teachers as Intellectuals: Toward a Critical Pedagogy of Learning.* South Hadley, Mass.: Bergin & Garvey, 1988.

------. *Theory and Resistance in Education: A Pedagogy for the Opposition.* South Hadley, Mass.: Bergin & Garvey, 1983.

Goffman, Irving J., J. Ronnie Davis, and John F. Morall, III. *The Concept of Education as an Investment: Report to the President's Commission on School Finance.* Washington, D.C.: ERIC, 1971.

Gonzales, Gilbert G. *Progressive Education: A Marxist Interpretation.* Minneapolis, Minn.: Marxist Educational Press, 1982.

Goodman, Paul. *Compulsory Miseducation and the Community of Scholars.* New York: Alfred A. Knopf, 1962.

Habermas, Jurgen. *Communication and the Evolution of Society.* Boston: Beacon Press, 1980.

Hirsch, E. D., Jr. *Cultural Literacy: What Every American Needs to Know.* Boston: Houghton, Mifflin, 1987.

Holtz, Harvey, *et al.* *Education and the American Dream: Conservatives,*

Liberals, and Radicals   Debate the Future of Education.   South Hadley, Mass.: Bergin & Garvey, 1989.

Hutchins, Robert Maynard.   *The Higher Learning in America.*   New Haven, Yale University Press, 1936.

Illich, Ivan.   *Deschooling Society.*   New York: Harper & Row,   1970.

Karabel, Jerome, and A. H. Halsey, eds. *Power and Ideology in Education.* New York: Oxford University Press, 1977.

Kaysen, Carl.   *The Higher Learning, the Universities, and the Public.* Princeton, N.J.: Princeton University Press, 1969.

Kerr, Clark.   *The Uses of the University.*   Cambridge, Mass.:   Harvard University Press, 1963.

Kozol, Jonathan. *Illiterate America.* New York: Anchor Press/Doubleday, 1985.

Lasch, Christopher. *The Culture of Narcissism: American Life in an Age of Diminishing Expectations.* New York: W. W. Norton, 1978.

Lee, Alfred McClung Lee.   *Sociology for People.*   Syracuse, N.Y.: Syracuse University Press, 1988.

------.   *Sociology for Whom?*   Second Edition. Syracuse N.Y.: Syracuse University Press, 1986.

Litt, Edgar. *The Public Vocational University: Captive Knowledge and Public Power.* New York: Holt, Rinehart, Winston, 1969.

Mills, C. Wright. *The Sociological Imagination.*   New York: Oxford University Press, 1959.

National Commission on Financing Post-Secondary Education. *Financing Post-Secondary Education in the United States.* Washington, D.C.: U.S. Government Printing Office, 1973.

National Institute of Education Study Group on the Conditions of Academic Excellence in Higher Education. *Involvement in Learning: Realizing the Potential of American Higher Education.*   Washington, D.C.: National Institute of Education, October 1984.

Newman, Fred, *et al.*   *Report on Higher Education.*   Washington, D.C.: U.S. Department of Health, Education, and Welfare, 1972.

Newson, Janice, and Howard Buchbinder. *The University Means Business: Universities, Corporations and Academic Work.*   Toronto: Garamond Press, 1988.

Nisbet, Robert A. *The Degradation of the Academic Dogma.* New York: Basic Books, 1970.

Norton, Theodore Mills, and Bertell Ollman, eds.   *Studies in Socialist Pedagogy.* New York: Monthly Review Press, 1978.

Orwig, M.D., ed. *Financing Higher Education: Alternatives for the Federal Government.* Iowa City, Iowa: American College Testing Program 1974.

Ravitch, Diane, and Chester E. Finn, Jr. *What Do Our Seventeen-Year-Olds Know? A Report on the First National Assessment of History and Literature.* New York: Harper & Row, 1988.

Rogers, Daniel C., and Hirsch C. Ruchlin.   *Economics and Education.* New York: Free Press, 1971.

Russell, Bertrand.   *Education and the Good Life*. New York: Avon Books,
    1926.

------.   *Principles of Social Reconstruction*.   London: Allen & Unwin,
    1916.

Scott, Barbara Ann.   *Crisis Management in American Higher Education*. New
    York: Praeger, 1983.

Sharp, Rachel.   *Knowledge, Ideology, and the Politics of Schooling:
    Toward a Marxist Analysis of Education*. London: Routledge and Keg-
    an, Paul, 1980.

Shor, Ira.   *Critical Teaching and Everyday Life*.   Boston: South End
    Press, 1980.

Sloan Commission on Government and Higher Education.   *A Program for Re-
    newed Partnership*. Cambridge, Mass.: Ballinger, 1980.

Solmon, Lewis, and Paul J. Taubman, eds. *Does College Matter?* New York:
    Academic Press, 1973.

Spring, Joel.   *The Sorting Machine: National Educational Policy Since
    1945*. New York: David McKay Company, 1976.

Sykes, Charles.   *Profscam: Professors and the Demise of Higher Educa-
    tion*. Washington, D.C.: Regnery, Gateway, 1988.

Thackrey, Russell I.   *The Future of the State University*. Urbana, Ill.:
    University of Illinois Press, 1971.

Toffler, Alvin, ed. *Learning for Tomorrow: The Role of the Future in
    Education*. New York: Vintage, 1974.

Touraine, Alain.   *The Academic System in American Society*.   New York:
    McGraw Hill, 1971.

Veblen, Thorstein.   *The Higher Learning in America*. New York: Hill &
    Wang, 1957 (1918).

Weisbrod, Burton A.   *External Effects of Public Education*.   Princeton,
    N.J.: Industrial Relations Section, 1964.

Whitehead, Alfred North.   *The Aims of Education and Other Essays*. New
    York: Free Press, 1929.

Willis, Paul.   *Learning to Labor*.   Lexington, Mass.: D.C. Heath, 1977.

Young, Kenneth E., ed.   *Exploring the Case for Low Tuition in Public
    Higher Education*. Iowa City, Iowa: American College Testing Pro-
    gram, 1974.

Young, Michael, and Geoff Whitly, eds.   *Society, State, and Schooling*.
    Lewes, England: Falmer Press, 1977.

Zwerdling, Stephen L.   *Second Best: The Crisis of the Community College*.
    New York: McGraw Hill, 1976.

About the Contributors

BARBARA ANN SCOTT, editor of this volume, was also the co-chair, along with Richard P. Sloan, of the 1981 Conference on *The Liberal Arts in a Time of Crisis* at the State University of New York College at New Paltz. Now an associate professor, she first joined the Sociology Department at the College at New Paltz in 1972. Her doctoral dissertation, *Crisis Management in American Higher Education*, received the Albert Salomon Memorial Award from the New School for Social Research and in 1983 was published by Praeger Publishers.

She has received research grants from the American Association of University Women, the American Council of Learned Societies and the State University of New York and in 1988 won second prize in the national Quest for Peace Writing Contest sponsored by the Citizen Education for Peace Project of the University of California at Irvine.

Dr. Scott served as a visiting scholar at the Center for Defense Information in Washington, D.C., was a founder and coordinator for the Mid-Hudson Chapter of Educators for Social Responsibility, and has lectured and written widely on the topics of international security and disarmament, women's studies, and education. Currently, she is working on two books about women's peace activism.

RICHARD P. SLOAN, assistant to the editor of this volume, was also the co-chair, along with Barbara Ann Scott, of the 1981 Conference on *The Liberal Arts in a Time of Crisis* at the State University of New York College at New Paltz. For ten years he was on the faculty of the Psychology Department at the College at New Paltz and was director of the Graduate Program in Psychology.

Currently, Dr. Sloan is on the faculty of the Department of Psychiatry at Columbia University's College of Physicians and Surgeons, coordinator of the Behavioral Medicine Program at Columbia-Presbyterian Medical Center and associate director of the Biological Sciences Unit, New York State Psychiatric Institute. He is the author of numerous papers on health promotion and cardiovascular psychophysiology.

STANLEY ARONOWITZ boasts an extremely varied career: steelworker, trade union organizer, manpower training program director and, finally, college professor. He is currently a member of the faculty of the Graduate Center of the City University of New York. Previously, he was on the faculty of the University of California at Irvine. He has also held visiting professorships at Columbia University, the University of Wisconsin, the University of California at San Diego, and the University of Paris at Vincennes.

Dr. Aronowitz is the author of more than one hundred journal articles, book reviews, and papers given at academic conferences.   His books include: *False Promises: The Shaping of Working Class Consciousness* [1973], *Food, Shelter and the American Dream* [1974], *The Crisis of Historical Materialism* [1981], *Working Class Hero* [1983], *Education Under Siege* with Henry A. Giroux [1985], and *Science as Power: Discourse and Ideology in Modern Society* [1988].

LEON BOTSTEIN is a professor of history at and president of Bard College, Annandale-on-Hudson, New York, and also president of Simon's Rock, an affiliate of Bard College, in Great Barrington, Massachusetts. He formerly served as president of Franconia College and was special assistant to the president of the New York City Board of Education.

He is chairman of the *Harper's* Magazine Foundation and past chairman of the Association of Episcopal Colleges and of the New York Council for the Humanities; consultant to the National Endowment for the Humanities, and co-conductor of the Hudson Valley Philharmonic Chamber Orchestra. He served as chairman of the summer 1987 session of the Salzburg Seminar, and has been a visiting professor at the Manhattan School of Music, as well as at the *Lehrkanzel fur Kultur und Geistesgesschichte* in Vienna.

The author of over eighty articles and book reviews in leading journals on such diverse topics as higher education, history, philosophy, and culture, Professor Botstein recently completed two books on music criticism and is at work on a third, tentatively titled *Diploma Madness: Higher Education and the American Intellectual in Crisis*.

RONALD COLMAN recently served on the faculty of the Department of Political Science and International Relations at the University of Colorado at Boulder. Previously, he taught political science at the State University of New York College at New Paltz and was director there of the United Nations Semester program.

Dr. Colman holds a Ph. D. degree in political science from Columbia University and has a continuing research interest in the politics of the Middle East and the Arab/Israeli conflict—topics about which he has written and lectured frequently. A native of Australia, he was a former education correspondent for *The Canberra Times*.

JEAN BETHKE ELSHTAIN was named Centennial Professor of Political Science at Vanderbilt University in 1988, after having served for fifteen years on the faculty of the University of Massachusetts at Amherst. Her research interests are in political theory, moral philosophy, and women's studies.

Dr. Elshtain has been a Woodrow Wilson fellow, an NEH fellow at the Institute for Advanced Study in Princeton, a writer-in-residence at the MacDowell Colony, and a scholar-in-residence at the Rockefeller Foundation's Bellagio Conference and Study Center.

In great demand as a speaker at academic forums, she was invited both to deliver the 1980 Phi Beta Kappa address and the 1984 Chancellor's Lectures at the University of Massachusetts. Widely published in professional journals and news magazines, Dr. Elshtain is the author of *Public Man, Private Woman: Women in Social and Political Thought* [1981], *Meditations on Modern Political Thought* [1986], and *Women and War* [1987], and is the editor of *The Family in Political Thought* [1982].

MICHAEL ENGEL is an associate professor in the Political Science Department at Westfield State College, Massachusetts, and has previously taught at Brooklyn College. He holds a Ph.D. degree from the City University of New York.

Dr. Engel's research interests lie in the fields of public policy and the politics of education. He is the author of the recently published *State and Local Politics: Fundamentals and Perspectives*.

HENRY A. GIROUX is a professor and "renowned scholar-in-residence" in the School of Education and Allied Professions at Miami University, Ohio, where he also serves as the director of the Center for Education and Cultural Studies. Three of his books have been named by the American Educational Studies Association as "among the most significant books in education:" *Ideology, Culture, and the Process of Schooling* [1982], *Theory and Resistance in Education* [1984], *Education Under Siege* [with Stanley Aronowitz; 1986]. His two most recent books, both published in 1988, are: *Schooling and the Struggle for Public Life*, and *Teachers as Intellectuals*. Over one hundred of his articles and book reviews have appeared in professional journals on topics in the areas of education, literacy, critical pedagogy, and cultural studies. Dr. Giroux serves as an editor to the journals, *Curriculum Inquiry* and *Curriculum and Teaching* [Australia], and is on the Advisory Board to the *Journal of Education* and the *Journal of Curriculum Theorizing*.

ALFRED McCLUNG LEE was president of the American Sociological Association and co-founder and first president of the Association for Humanist Sociology. Together with his wife, Elizabeth Briant Lee, he organized the Society for the Study of Social Problems, subsequently becoming its second president. He has also been president of the Michigan and the Eastern Sociological Societies and United States delegate to the International Sociological Association.

Currently, he is professor emeritus of sociology at Brooklyn College and a visiting scholar at Drew University in New Jersey. Dr. Lee has been on the faculties of Yale, New York University, Wayne State University, the University of Kansas, the University of Michigan, and the City University of New York's Graduate Center. He was UNESCO Professor at Milan where he organized an Institute for Sociological Research, and was a senior Fulbright lecturer at the University of Rome.

A prolific writer, Dr. Lee is the author or co-author of nineteen books, among them: *The Daily Newspaper in America* [1937, 1973], *Multi-Valent Man* [1966], *Sociology for Whom?* [1978, 1986], *Terrorism in Northern Ireland* [1983], and *Sociology for People* [1988].

ELIZABETH BRIANT LEE was a co-founder, with her husband, Alfred McClung Lee, of the Association for Humanist Sociology and served as its president in 1978. She was also a vice-president and co-founder (again, with Alfred McClung Lee) of the Society for the Study of Social Problems and secretary-treasurer of the Eastern Sociological Society.

Dr. Lee received a Ph.D. degree from Yale University in 1937. She has taught sociology and anthropology on the faculties of Wayne State University, Brooklyn College, Hartford Seminary Foundation, Fairleigh Dickinson University, and Connecticut College, as well as at universities and research institutes in Europe and the Middle East. At present, she is a visiting scholar in anthropology at Drew University.

In addition to having written numerous journal articles, Dr. Lee is the author or co-author of six books, including *Eminent Women: A Cultural Study* [1937], and *The Fine Art of Propaganda* [with Alfred McClung Lee, 1939, 1979].

ROSETTE LIBERMAN was, until recently, the assistant director of disability services at Yale University. Previously, she served as principal of the New Haven Hebrew Day School and the Beth Hannah Academy in Orange, Connecticut. She has also taught foreign languages, English, and history in elementary and secondary schools in the states of Connecticut and New York, and is presently teaching English in Connecticut's Amity Regional School District.

Fluent in Russian, French, Iranian, and Spanish, she holds a master's degree in French literature from Vassar College and a doctorate in educational administration from the University of Bridgeport's College of Business and Public Management.

Dr. Liberman was the recipient in 1987 of a dissertation award from the National Organization on Legal Problems in Education and is the founder and executive director of the Shoreline Foundation for Folk Literature and Art, Inc., publisher of *Tall Tales* magazine.

In 1989, she was appointed by the Connecticut Commissioner of Education to the state's Permanent Advisory Council on the Teaching Profession.

EMIL OESTEREICHER was, until his death in October 1983, an associate professor and chairman of the Department of Sociology at the College of Staten Island and also taught at the Graduate Center of the City University of New York and at the Graduate Faculty of the New School for Social Research. Previously, he was on the faculties of the State University of New York at Stony Brook and Oakland University in Michigan.

Dr. Oestereicher twice was a recipient of a summer stipend from the National Endowment for the Humanities and published numerous journal articles in the areas of sociological theory and the sociology of knowledge.

HUEL D. PERKINS is the executive assistant to the chancellor of Louisiana State University in Baton Rouge, where he also held the posts of assistant vice-chancellor for academic affairs and professor of humanities in the Division of Honors and Interdisciplinary Studies until his official retirement in 1988. He was appointed to the State Board of Elementary and Secondary Education by the governor upon retiring.

Prior to joining the faculty of LSU in 1979, he served as deputy director of the Division of Education Programs for the National Endowment for the Humanities in Washington, D.C. Dr. Perkins has served as chairman of the Louisiana Endowment for the Humanities and was named Humanist of the Year for 1988 in the state of Louisiana.

He is completing a book titled, *The Harlem Renaissance: Biography of a Movement.*

HENRI PEYRE was distinguished professor and chairman of the Department of French at the Graduate Center of the City University of New York, until his retirement in 1981. Previously, he had been chairman of the Department of French at Yale University and at the University of Cairo, and is the author of over forty books and hundreds of journal articles.

GILBERT J. SLOAN is a senior research fellow in the Polymer Products Department of E. I. Dupont de Nemours & Company. He has been an associate editor of *The Journal of Crystal Growth*, is co-author of *Techniques of Melt Crystallization* and a member of the Solid State Sciences Panel of the National Academy of Sciences. He was chairman of a Gordon Conference on Separation and Purification and has published numerous articles on zone refining and crystal growth.

Index